Posttraumatic Stress Disorder in Childhood and Adolescence

Posttraumatic Stress Disorder in Childhood and Adolescence

A Developmental Psychopathology Perspective

Patricia K. Kerig

MOMENTUM PRESS HEALTH

MOMENTUM PRESS, LLC, NEW YORK

Posttraumatic Stress Disorder in Childhood and Adolescence: A Developmental Psychopathology Perspective

First published in 2017 by
Momentum Press, LLC
222 East 46th Street, New York, NY 10017
www.momentumpress.net

ISBN-13: 978-1-60650-929-6 (paperback)
ISBN-13: 978-1-60650-930-2 (e-book)

Momentum Press Child Clinical Psychology "Nuts and Bolts" Collection

Cover and interior design by Exeter Premedia Services Private Ltd., Chennai, India

First edition: 2017

10 9 8 7 6 5 4 3 2 1

Printed in the United States of America.

This book is dedicated to the memory of my mother, Dorothy Pierson Kerig. I found my voice as an author through writing to her and in my heart she is still listening, with all her patience, grace, and intelligence.

Abstract

With the publication of the new *Diagnostic and Statistical Manual of Mental Disorders* (*DSM-5*), and the recent release of the draft diagnostic criteria to be used in the forthcoming *International Classification of Diseases* (*ICD-11*), students, researchers, and clinicians are in need of an authoritative and practical guide to understanding the diagnosis of posttraumatic stress disorder (PTSD) in childhood and adolescence. This is particularly the case given that, other than designating a separate diagnosis with a smaller number of symptoms for preschoolers, these new diagnostic compendia provide little information regarding developmental differences in the onset, expression, and course of the disorder. Child and adolescent mental health professionals—whether they are students in training, practitioners, or scientists—will benefit from this book's summaries of the available research on PTSD in young persons, descriptions of how the expression and consequences of PTSD might change across developmental periods, and suggested strategies for differential diagnosis between PTSD and other disruptive behavioral and emotional disorders that present with overlapping symptoms across childhood and adolescence. The chapters also discuss cutting-edge issues, such as the constructs of posttraumatic growth and resilience, and summarize the evidence base for treatments focused on alleviating PTSD in young persons through interventions targeting the individual youth, the family, and their larger ecological contexts.

Keywords

adverse childhood experiences, child abuse, complex PTSD, developmental psychopathology, developmental trauma disorder, disaster, injury, maltreatment, medical trauma, posttraumatic growth, posttraumatic stress disorder, PTSD, trauma, traumatic stress

Contents

CHAPTER 1

Description and Diagnosis

A Brief History of the Posttraumatic Stress Disorder (PTSD) Diagnosis

The PTSD diagnosis first entered the psychiatric diagnostic lexicon in the 3rd edition of the *Diagnostic and Statistical Manual of Mental Disorders* (*DSM-III*; American Psychiatric Association, 1980), and it may be fair to say that it is the only diagnosis that has found its way there through political activism. In the 1970s, pressure for the psychiatric and psychological fields to recognize and respond to traumatic stress came through the actions of three groups: the battered/sexually assaulted women's support community, military veterans, and—although the original conceptualization of the disorder erroneously precluded its application to children—child abuse specialists. As Friedman, Resick, and Keane (2014) state: "Unlike … other … disorders, PTSD emerged from converging social movements rather than academic, clinical, or scientific initiatives" (p. 4). van der Kolk (2007) echoes this point: "The DSM-III PTSD diagnosis was not a result of careful factor-analytic studies … but a compilation of symptoms arrived at on the basis of literature searches, scrutiny of clinical records of veterans, and a thoughtful political process" (p. 31).

Despite the thoughtfulness of the process, as van der Kolk describes it, it has not been without conflict nor controversy. For example, from the outset, one of the conundrums that has plagued the field has to do with the definition of what might at first blush seem to be the most straightforward aspect of the diagnosis: What defines a "traumatic" experience? In the *DSM-III*, this was defined as an event "generally beyond the realm of normal human experience" (American Psychiatric Association, 1980, p. 236). However, this definition came to be understood as problematic given the unfortunate prevalence of traumatic events in the lives of ordinary adults, adolescents, and children. In the *DSM-IV* (American Psychiatric Association, 1994), greater specificity was introduced, limiting such events to those that involve "actual or threatened death or serious injury, or a threat to the physical integrity of oneself or others" and adding a requirement of a traumatized response in the form of "fear, helplessness, or horror." However, in response to concerns about "criterion creep," in that the diagnosis of PTSD was being applied to a wide range of stressful or distressing experiences not intended to be encompassed within the definition of "trauma," the *DSM-5* (American Psychiatric Association, 2013) developers restricted the definition even more, removing the subjective elements of the individual's reaction. Perhaps the most notable feature of the *DSM-5* revision is that PTSD is no longer considered to be one of the anxiety disorders but is now placed in a new category comprising "trauma and stressor-related disorders." These changing definitions of trauma, as well as the changes in the types and numbers of symptoms required for the diagnosis, have had implications across the spectrum but particularly for children and adolescents. We will review these in this chapter, with special attention to the most recent wave of changes brought by the publication of the 5th edition of the *DSM* in 2013 and the forthcoming release of the new edition of the *International Classification of Diseases* (*ICD-11*).

Diagnostic Criteria for PTSD Applied to Children and Adolescents

PTSD in the DSM-5

The *DSM-5* includes two versions of the PTSD diagnosis: one for children older than 6 years as well as adults and adolescents (see Table 1.1), and the other for children between 1 and 6 years of age (see Table 1.2). For all individuals, the manual requires a number of clusters of symptoms to be present, which are detailed in Table 1.1.

Trauma Exposure (Criterion A). First, the DSM-5 specifies that the individual must have experienced a traumatic event, which is defined as "exposure to actual or threatened death, serious, injury, or sexual violence" (p. 271). For older children, adolescents, and adults, "exposure" is further

Table 1.1 Summary of DSM-5 criteria for the PTSD diagnosis in school-age children, adolescents, and adults

1. Criterion A: Traumatic event Exposure to an event involving actual or threatened death, injury, or sexual violence through directly experiencing or witnessing the event, learning about an accidental or violent event occurring to a family member or close friend, or exposure to aversive details of an event (not via media such as television, Internet, or movies)
2. Criterion B: Intrusions (one or more symptoms required) Distressing memories Distressing dreams (in children, these may be frightening dreams not directly related to the traumatic event) Flashbacks Psychological distress upon exposure to internal or external reminders (in children, these may involve reenactments in the context of play) Physiological distress upon exposure to internal or external reminders
3. Criterion C: Avoidance (one or more symptoms required) Efforts to avoid memories, thoughts, or feelings about the event Efforts to avoid people, places, things, etc. that arouse memories about the event
4. Criterion D: Alterations in cognitions and mood (two or more symptoms required) Amnesia about the event Negative beliefs about the self, others, or the world Distorted cognitions about the cause or consequences of the event Persistent negative emotional state Loss of interest in previously enjoyed activities Feelings of detachment or estrangement Lack of positive emotions
5. Criterion E: Alterations in arousal and reactivity (two or more symptoms required) Irritability and anger Reckless or self-destructive behavior Hypervigilance Exaggerated startle response Concentration problems Sleep disturbance
6. Duration of symptoms is more than 1 month
7. Symptoms cause significant distress or functional impairment
8. Specify whether dissociative symptoms are present

defined as occurring in four possible ways: the event directly happening to the person, the person witnessing the event, the person learning about something violent or accidental happening to a loved one or close friend, or the person being exposed to horrific details of a traumatic event in an extreme or repeated way (e.g., a caseworker continually being exposed to the details of children's abuse). The manual further specifies that exposure

Table 1.2 Summary of DSM-5 criteria for the PTSD diagnosis in children 6 years and younger

1. **Criterion A: Traumatic event** Exposure to an event involving actual or threatened death, injury, or sexual violence through directly experiencing or witnessing the event (not being exposed via electronic media or pictures), or learning about an accidental or violent event occurring to a parent or caregiver
2. **Criterion B: Intrusions (one or more symptoms required)** Distressing memories (may be expressed as play enactments) Distressing dreams (may be frightening dreams not directly related to the traumatic event) Flashbacks Psychological distress upon exposure to internal or external reminders (in children, these may involve reenactments in the context of play) Physiological distress upon exposure to internal or external reminders
3. **Criterion C: Avoidance/alterations in cognitions and mood (one or more symptoms required)** Avoidance Efforts to avoid memories, thoughts, or feelings about the event Efforts to avoid people, places, things, etc. that arouse memories about the event Negative alterations in cognitions or mood Substantial increase in negative emotional states Diminished interest or participation in previous activities; constricted play Social withdrawal Reduced positive emotions
4. **Criterion D: Alterations in arousal and reactivity (two or more symptoms required)** Irritable behavior and angry outbursts Hypervigilance Exaggerated startle response Concentration problems Sleep disturbance
5. Duration of symptoms is more than 1 month
6. Symptoms cause significant distress or functional impairment
7. Specify whether dissociative symptoms are present

cannot occur only through electronic media, such as television or the Internet, unless it is related to the individual's work (e.g., a Federal Bureau of Investigation agent tasked with trolling online sites for images of child pornography). For children younger than 6 years, exposure to trauma must involve directly experiencing the event, witnessing it, or learning about an event that occurred to a parent or caregiving figure, specifically.

In the explanatory text regarding diagnostic features of PTSD in the *DSM-5*, the only notation about developmental differences is that, for children, "sexually violent" experiences may not necessarily involve violence but rather may be developmentally inappropriate, such as children who are shown pornography or confronted by a "flasher." However, for all ages, events that are interpersonal and intentional in nature—such as physical or sexual abuse—are those most likely to result in severe and prolonged symptoms.

Intrusions (Criterion B). Intrusions involve one or more ways in which the traumatic event intrudes upon the person's daily functioning. Intrusions may take various forms, the first of which involves distressing memories of the event that are "recurrent, involuntary and intrusive" (p. 271). In youth, these may take the form of preoccupations about the trauma and sometimes their focus is on intervention fantasies. In young children especially, intrusions may be demonstrated by traumatic play in which the themes of the event are played out, either directly or symbolically. For example, a 3½-year-old girl, after being severely scalded by a careless babysitter who ran a too-hot bath, repeatedly and grimly played out the scene of the ambulance coming to take her to the hospital. To take another example, in the aftermath of his father's death, a 6-year-old boy repetitively played a game in which an action figure was falling from a great height and others were trying to rescue him. As noted in the section of the manual describing the development and course of the disorder, this kind of play is not necessarily accompanied by overtly fearful or distressed reactions. However, characteristic of posttraumatic play, in contrast to the kind of healing play that allows children to work through and master difficult experiences, is its driven and repetitive quality and the fact that it is not associated with emotional relief (Erikson, 1964).

A second form of intrusions is represented by *distressing dreams* related to the traumatic experience; in children, these may be generic nightmares that are not directly related to the specific event. A third form of intrusions are *dissociative reactions*, more commonly termed flashbacks, during which individuals feel like they are back in the event; in children, these too may be expressed through intense and immersive play. The fourth and fifth forms of intrusions are seen in *psychological distress reactions* (e.g., crying, fearfulness, lashing out) or *physiological distress reactions* (e.g., rapid heartbeat, dizziness, sweating, loss of bowel control) when the individual is exposed to internal stimuli (e.g., thoughts) or external stimuli (e.g., people, places or things) that are reminiscent of or trigger memories of the trauma. For example, a 4-year-old who had undergone a life-saving but painful emergency medical procedure performed by doctors wearing latex gloves began screaming when confronted with the glove-wearing server replenishing the salad bar at a buffet.

Avoidance (Criterion C). Avoidance of trauma reminders may take the form of either effortfully avoiding thoughts, feelings, or memories about the trauma, or actively avoiding people, places, or things associated with the traumatic event. For example, a 10-year-old boy who witnessed a friend's accidental death began walking home from school via a long and circuitous route in order to avoid passing by the street corner where the accident had occurred. Perhaps because of their developmentally limited capacities for mental compartmentalization, avoidance in children often paradoxically is accompanied by preoccupation with the trauma reminders they are trying to avoid. As noted in the manual's section on development and course of the disorder, avoidance may be expressed in developmentally specific ways: loss of interest in play in young children, withdrawal from typical activities in school-agers, and reticence to engage in age-appropriate new activities (e.g., dating, driving) in adolescence.

Negative Alterations in Cognitions and Mood (Criterion D). This new symptom cluster is a complex combination of symptoms, all of which involve ways in which the occurrence of the event is followed by changes in an individual's thoughts, feelings, or view of the world. For older children, adolescents, and adults, two or more of these symptoms must be seen. The first is amnesia, or inability to remember key aspects of the event, which must not be associated with a head injury or intoxication. The second is "persistent and exaggerated negative beliefs about oneself, others, or the world" (p. 272). For example, a teenage girl who had been sexually assaulted believed that she was now "ruined" and would never find a romantic partner. To take another example, experiences involving betrayal, such as when a youth is harmed by a family member he or she should have been able to trust and rely on for protection and care, may be followed by a pervasive sense of distrust of authority figures. As noted in the section on the development and course of the disorder, older children and adolescents are prone to making harsh judgments of themselves, such as labeling themselves as "cowardly" for not having intervened to stop the event.

The third symptom relates to *distorted cognitions* about the event, which might include exaggerated self-blame or blame of others; for example, an 8-year-old boy who was in a car accident blamed himself for causing it because he was quarreling with his brother in the back seat and this might have distracted his mother while she was driving. The fourth symptom is a *"persistent negative emotional state"* such as fearfulness, anger, or shame. The fifth symptom involves a *withdrawal of interest* in previously enjoyed activities, such as play, socializing, or sports. The sixth symptom is characterized by feelings of *alienation or detachment* from others. According to the section on the development and course of the disorder, this sense of alienation may be particularly characteristic of adolescents, whose penchant for social comparison may lead them to be concerned that they are now "different" from their peers and no longer socially desirable; teenagers also may lose faith in their aspirations and develop a sense of "futurelessness." Finally, the seventh symptom in this cluster is the *inability to experience positive emotions* such as happiness, pleasure, or intimate closeness to others.

For children younger than 6 years, many of these symptoms represent cognitively complex processes that are not developmentally appropriate. In particular, because their capacities for identifying emotions and expressing thoughts are limited, evidence for symptoms in this cluster are mostly seen in the form of changes in behavior and mood. Therefore, the most significant adaptation of the diagnosis for preschoolers is that Criteria C and D are collapsed into one cluster, of which one or more of the following must be seen: avoidance of activities, places, or physical reminders; avoidance of people, conversations, or interpersonal reminders; increased negative emotional states; diminished interest in activities; social withdrawal; and reduced expression of positive emotions.

Arousal and Reactivity (Criterion E). Two or more symptoms must be present in this cluster. These include irritability and angry outbursts (e.g., temper tantrums or aggression in the absence of provocation) that may interfere with a youth's peer relationships and performance in school. Other symptoms in this cluster include hypervigilance (e.g., hypersensitivity to perceived threats, being continually on the lookout for danger), exaggerated startle response (e.g., jumping at unexpected sounds or movements), problems with concentration (e.g., being unable to focus on tasks such as schoolwork), and sleep disturbances (e.g., restlessness or inability to fall asleep or stay asleep). For older children, adolescents, and adults, also included here is recklessness or self-destructive behavior (e.g., being heedless of danger, putting oneself at risk, self-harming), which can lead to accidental injuries and engagement in high-risk behaviors such as driving too fast, experimenting with drugs, or having unprotected sex.

Additional Criteria. In addition to the symptoms just listed, the duration (Criterion F) of the symptoms must be more than 1 month after the event and there must be evidence of distress or functional impairment (Criterion G) in that the symptoms interfere with the individual's ability to function in social, academic, or other important contexts. Rule-outs of other causes (Criterion H) require the clinician to determine that the symptoms are not due to intoxication via alcohol, drugs, or medications, or a medical condition (e.g., a brain injury).

Dissociative Subtype. Finally, the DSM-5 requires a specification whether the diagnosis of PTSD occurs together with persistent or recurrent symptoms of dissociation. These can take two forms, only one of which must be present. The first is depersonalization, defined as feeling as if the self is unreal, detached from reality, or an external observer of one's own body or mental processes. The second form of dissociation is derealization, the sense that the environment is unreal, dreamlike, or distorted. For example, a 14-year-old boy who witnessed a school shooting reported that he felt like he was "watching himself in a movie" in which the events unfolded in slow motion.

Empirical Validations of the DSM-5 Diagnosis in Children and Adolescents. Because the DSM-5 diagnostic criteria are so new, few empirical investigations to date have been published including children and adolescents. In one such test, Hafstad and colleagues (2014) applied the new

DSM-5 criteria to a sample of adolescents who had experienced a horrific mass shooting in Norway. A confirmatory factor analyses supported the four-factor structure of the DSM-5 criteria. However, other investigations, which we will review in a separate section describing alternative models of PTSD, have identified different symptom structures from those in the DSM-5 manual.

Some attention has been paid to validating the dissociative typology in young people. For example, Bennett, Modrowski, Kerig, and Chaplo (2015) studied a sample of traumatized adolescents involved in the justice system and their analyses confirmed two groups of youth based on their levels of self-reported dissociation. In addition, youth with high levels of dissociation reported the highest levels of posttraumatic stress symptoms overall, as well as the specific symptoms of intrusions and emotional numbing. Consistent with theoretical conceptualizations of the origins of posttraumatic dissociation, youth in the high-dissociation group were those most likely to report having dissociated during the traumatic event, and this phenomenon, termed *peritraumatic dissociation*, accounted for the relationship between trauma exposure and persistent dissociation months or years later.

PTSD in the ICD-11

Post-traumatic Stress Disorder. At the time of this writing, the ICD-11 is still "under construction" and only the draft criteria are available. However, they have gone through multiple iterations and validation studies and appear to be close to their final version (Keeley et al., 2016; Maercker et al., 2013); accessed online at https://gcp.network/en/private/icd-11-guidelines/categories/trastornos-asociados-especificamente-con-el-estres, December 22, 2016. The draft description that has been released to date (see Table 1.3) lists four criteria: "exposure to an extremely threatening or horrific" event or situation followed by symptoms of reexperiencing the event as though it is occurring in the present (e.g., through intrusive images or memories, flashbacks, or nightmares accompanied by "strong or overwhelming emotions" or physical sensations); avoidance of thoughts or reminders of the event; and current perceptions of threat, including hypervigilance or an exaggerated startle response. The symptoms cause

Table 1.3 Draft criteria for the diagnosis of PTSD in ICD-11

1. Exposure to an "extremely threatening or horrific" event or situation, following which the following symptoms arise
2. Reexperiencing the event as though it is in the present, including flashbacks, intrusive images or memories, or nightmares, accompanied by strong emotions or physical reactions
3. Avoidance, either of internal thoughts and memories, or external avoidance of people, activities, or situations that are reminiscent of the event
4. Perceptions of current threat, indicated by hypervigilance, startle reaction, or changes in behavior designed to ensure safety
5. Impairment in personal, social, occupational, or other areas of functioning

impairment in the individual's ability to function in important areas of life. As the brevity of these criteria suggest, the goal of the ICD-11 committee was to simplify the diagnosis by focusing on those symptoms that comprise "core elements" of PTSD and are clearly distinguished from the symptoms of other disorders.

The descriptive information goes on to state that those with PTSD often also demonstrated accompanying features of dysphoria, dissociation, somatic complaints, suicidality, and social withdrawal, and symptoms of anxiety, particularly in regard to trauma reminders; they may also engage in substance abuse as a method for managing emotional distress. In addition, common emotions experienced by those with the disorder include anger, shame, sadness, guilt, and humiliation. However, the "core features" of the disorder in the criteria are those most central to the diagnosis.

Complex Posttraumatic Stress Disorder. Although the ICD-11 definition is more streamlined than the DSM-5 definition, the criteria for the diagnosis of PTSD in both diagnostic manuals are not widely discrepant. The ICD-11 diverges in the inclusion of a separate set of criteria for the diagnosis of complex PTSD (C-PTSD). Originally proposed by Judith Herman (1994) and previously termed Disorders of Extreme Stress, Not Otherwise Specified (DESNOS), this is a type of PTSD conceptualized to follow from long-term, repeated traumas, in which "the symptom picture in survivors of prolonged trauma often appears to be more complex, diffuse, and tenacious than in simple PTSD" (Herman, 1992, p. 379). The ICD-11 version defines C-PTSD

Table 1.4 Draft criteria for the diagnosis of complex PTSD in ICD-11

1. Exposure to extremely threatening or horrific event(s) that are prolonged and repeated and from which escape is not possible
2. All three core symptoms of PTSD in the *ICD-11* (re-experiencing, avoidance, and threat) are present at some point during the course of the disorder
3. Severe and persistent problems in affect regulation (e.g., heightened emotional reactivity, reckless or self-destructive behavior, dissociation in response to stress, emotional numbing)
4. Persistent negative belief about the self (e.g., as believing the self to be worthless, guilty, shameful)
5. Persistent interpersonal difficulties (e.g., trouble sustaining relationships or feeling close to others)
6. Significant impairment in functioning

as a disorder that occurs following exposure to threatening or horrific events that are "extreme and prolonged or repetitive" and from which "escape is difficult or impossible" (e.g., children forced into commercial sexual activity, exposure to intimate partner violence, child abuse). C-PTSD requires that all the diagnostic criteria for PTSD be met along with the following: (1) pervasive problems in affect regulation; (2) persistent negative beliefs about the self, such as shame, worthlessness, or guilt; and (3) difficulties in sustaining relationships and feeling close to others. As with all disorders, the symptoms must be severe enough to cause impairments in the individual's ability to function in important life contexts (see Table 1.4).

To date, most of the research confirming the validity of the C-PTSD diagnosis has been conducted with adults (Cloitre et al., 2013; Keeley et al., 2016). However, a recent study also confirmed that the C-PTSD diagnosis could be applied to children and adolescents. Using the *ICD-11*-proposed criteria, Sachser, Keller, and Goldbeck (2016) assessed a sample of 155 children and adolescents seeking treatment for posttraumatic stress. The investigators found that two distinctive groups could be reliably distinguished: those youth with elevated scores on the core symptoms of PTSD only, and those with elevated PTSD symptoms plus disturbances in self-organization as described by the C-PTSD diagnosis. Furthermore, although both groups responded well to an evidence-based treatment for PTSD, children and adolescents in the C-PTSD group ended treatment with higher levels of residual symptoms.

Prevalence of PTSD Among Children and Adolescents

Prevalence of Trauma Exposure

Regarding trauma exposure, several large-scale epidemiological studies find that, by the time they reach the end of their teens, between 60% and 87% of young people in the United States report exposure to a potentially traumatic event (see Fairbank, Putnam, & Harris, 2014, for a review). For example, in their nationally representative sample, Finkelhor and colleagues (2009) found that 61% of children and adolescents had witnessed or experienced violence in the past year. A nationally representative study of 6,789 ninth-grade students in Switzerland found similar results, with 56% of youth reporting at least one potentially traumatic event (Landolt et al., 2013). In another recent study of the prevalence of trauma exposure, based on a nationally representative sample of 6,483 Swedish adolescents aged 13 to 17 years, 61.8% of these teens reported experiencing a potentially traumatic event (McLaughlin, Koenen, et al., 2013). However, it is notable that these studies were not constrained to those meeting the *DSM* Criterion A definition but included other adversities, such as divorce, economic hardship, and parental substance abuse or mental illness. Other sources also confirm the high prevalence of violence in the lives of young people. For example, the Centers for Disease Control and Prevention (2010) report that, in a given year, more than 740,000 youth in the United States are treated in hospital emergency rooms for injuries resulting from violence and more than 3 million cases of suspected child abuse are filed.

Studies adhering more strictly to the DSM definition of trauma exposure, not surprisingly, find lower rates. For example, Perkonigg and colleagues (2000) followed a sample of urban adolescents and emerging adults in Germany and found that 21.4% reported lifetime exposure to a *DSM-IV* Criterion A1 event; 17% also met criteria for the A2 requirement. These investigators also looked at changes in vulnerability related to age and found a dramatic increase in trauma exposure beginning at age 11 years, particularly related to a rising risk of sexual abuse and sexual assault for girls from ages 11 to 15 years. From age 15 years on, the most prevalent forms of trauma exposure were witnessing violence and experiencing physical violence.

Risk Factors for Trauma Exposure. In Landolt and colleagues's (2013) Swiss sample, risk factors for trauma exposure included low parent education, immigrant status, and living in a single-parent family; whereas in McLaughlin, Rith-Najarian and colleagues' (2013) Swiss sample, the likelihood was higher for youth living in single-parent families as well as those with preexisting behavioral problems. Rates of exposure to traumatic stressors also are more prevalent in communities beset by violence, such as inner city environments. For example, in a study of middle school children in central Los Angeles, Jaycox and colleagues (2002) found that 63% reported witnessing and 40% reported being direct victims of gun or knife violence in the past year; in a study of detained youth in Utah, Kerig, Chaplo, Bennett, and Modrowski (2016) found that those involved in gangs were disproportionately exposed to traumatic events, and this was particularly true for girls.

Another risk factor for youth is sexual or gender atypicality. Numerous studies have replicated the finding that sexual minority status youth report disproportionately high rates of physical, sexual, and psychological abuse by their parents (Belknap, Holsinger, & Little, 2012; Corliss, Cochran, & Mays, 2002; Saewyc, 2011) as well as by peers (D'Augelli, Pilkington, & Hershberger, 2002). Furthermore, in a study of 9,864 youth followed longitudinally in the United States, Roberts and colleagues (2012) found that childhood gender nonconformity was associated with higher rates of physical, psychological, and sexual abuse, as well as elevated levels of PTSD, above and beyond the effects of sexual orientation.

Prevalence of PTSD

Because both the *ICD-11* and the *DSM-5* are so new, most available research on prevalence rates among children and adolescents comes from data utilizing the *DSM-IV* and *ICD-10* criteria. Regarding *DSM-IV* PTSD in the aftermath of trauma exposure, the lifetime prevalence of PTSD in McLaughlin and colleagues's (2013) Swedish sample was 4.7% overall, with rates higher for girls than boys (7.3% versus 2.2%). These rates are comparable to those found in another nationally representative survey of U.S. adolescents aged 12 to 17 years, in which the prevalence rate of PTSD was 6.3% for girls and 3.7% for boys (Kilpatrick et al.,

2013) and Landolt and colleagues's (2013) Swiss sample, in which 4.2% (6.2% of girls and 2.4% of boys) met *DSM-IV* criteria for the PTSD diagnosis. Strikingly, large-scale studies also show that as many as 75% of adolescents with PTSD also meet criteria for a comorbid diagnosis, mostly major depression or substance abuse (Kilpatrick et al., 2003).

Risks Increasing the Likelihood of PTSD. Regarding factors that increase the likelihood of PTSD following trauma exposure, McLaughlin and colleagues (2013) found that, among Swiss youth, female gender, prior trauma exposure, and prior internalizing disorders were implicated. In turn, recovery from PTSD was impeded by poverty, bipolar disorder, experiencing a subsequent additional traumatic event, and being born in the United States. Consistent with a large body of previous research, McLaughlin and colleagues's (2013) Swedish study found that rates of PTSD were highest among trauma-exposed adolescents who had experienced interpersonal (e.g., assault, maltreatment) versus noninterpersonal (e.g., accidents, disasters) events. Rates of PTSD also are disproportionately high in clinical or at-risk samples, such as psychiatrically hospitalized youth (Lipschitz et al., 1999), victims of childhood sexual abuse (Paolucci, Genuis, & Violato, 2001), and youth involved in the juvenile justice system (Kerig & Becker, 2012). Among justice-involved youth, those in gangs report the highest levels of posttraumatic symptoms, especially among girls, and this posttraumatic stress is associated with both victimization and perpetration of violence (Kerig, Chaplo, et al., 2016). It is of further concern that youth who have experienced one traumatic event are highly likely to experience subsequent traumatic events, a phenomenon known as revictimization (Trickett et al., 2011). For example, in a national prevalence study, Walsh and colleagues (2012) found that, among 1,763 sexually assaulted adolescent girls, 53% reported revictimization and their odds of meeting criteria for PTSD were between 4.3 and 8.2 times higher than that of their non-revictimized peers.

Other factors that increase youth vulnerability to developing PTSD in the aftermath of trauma exposure also have emerged from the literature. Children who experience maltreatment "close to home" in the form of parental abuse are at increased risk of PTSD (Fairbank, Putnam, & Harris, 2014). In addition, research studies are consistent in showing a dose–response relationship implying that children and adolescents who experience higher levels of accumulated trauma, as well as those who experience multiple forms of trauma, termed polyvictimization (Finkelhor, Ormrod, & Turner, 2007; Ford et al., 2010), are at increased risk of developing PTSD.

More broadly, a recent meta-analysis on the prevalence of PTSD among trauma-exposed children and adolescents uncovered 72 peer-reviewed articles representing 43 independent samples involving a total of 3,563 youth (Alisic et al., 2014). The authors excluded from their review samples youth who were undergoing mental health treatment, which almost certainly reduced their estimates substantially. Overall, 15.9% of trauma-exposed youth were found to meet criteria for PTSD using well-validated diagnostic instruments. Female gender and interpersonal trauma were both risk factors, with the highest rates of PTSD found among girls exposed to interpersonal traumas (32.9%) and the lowest rates among boys exposed to noninterpersonal traumas (8.4%).

Gender Differences. The disproportionate vulnerability of girls to PTSD has emerged in many of the studies we have reviewed and is worth consideration in its own right. This gender difference is one that emerges across developmental periods (Kessler et al., 2012; Tolin & Foa, 2006) and is one for which a number of explanatory hypotheses have been offered (Kimmerling et al., 2014). In part, the gender disparity may be accounted for by the fact that girls and women are disproportionately victims of sexual abuse and rape, which, particularly because of the social stigma involved (Andrews, Brewin, & Rose, 2003), are among the traumatic experiences most predictive of PTSD—boys and men who undergo these traumas are equally likely to develop PTSD (Tolin & Foa, 2006). However, concerns remain about the potential for reporting biases, in that adolescent boys may be less inclined to endorse PTSD symptom items related to distress, fear, or anxiety, given their discrepancy with the masculine gender role (Saxe & Wolfe, 1999). For example, in a sample of Japanese detained youth, Yoshinaga and colleagues (2004) found that girls and boys reported having undergone traumatic experiences at equal rates although girls were three times more likely than boys to admit to posttraumatic symptoms. In a second sample of more than 600 U.S. detained youth, adolescent girls and boys also were equally likely to endorse having experienced a DSM-IV Criterion A1 event, but girls were significantly more likely to endorse the A2 criteria of "fear, helplessness, or horror" necessary to qualify for a DSM-IV diagnosis of PTSD (Kerig & Becker, 2012). Thus, reporting biases and gender-related response styles may lead males to underreport feeling traumatized after a traumatic event.

Changes in Prevalence Rates Associated with the Changing Diagnostic Criteria

Of course, one of the complications in describing the prevalence of PTSD in child and adolescent samples is that it currently is a moving target given the changing and competing criteria for the diagnosis. This is a very new question but one that is beginning to be investigated. A few studies have emerged examining this critical issue.

In a recent study including a sample of 710 seven- to 11-year-old children who had been exposed to hurricanes in the Southern United States, Danzi and La Greca (2016) compared diagnostic rates using the criteria in *DSM-IV*, *DSM-5*, and *ICD-11*. Overall rates of PTSD were similar across the systems, although they were slightly lower when the *DSM-5* criteria were used. More strikingly, there was low agreement across the different diagnostic manuals, resulting in different children being placed in the "PTSD probable" category. In fact, only one third of cases were identified simultaneously by all three systems. Children who met the *DSM-5* criteria were highly likely to also be identified by the other two systems, but 19% of those who met criteria under *DSM-IV* no longer met criteria for the diagnosis under *DSM-5*. Furthermore, a surprisingly large proportion (24%) met criteria only according to *ICD-11*. These children tended to have more severe "core" PTSD symptoms (i.e., those shared by three diagnostic manuals) but also tended to have lower levels of functional impairment and "non-core" symptoms (i.e., those unique to the *DSM* systems) in comparison to the children identified only by the *DSM-IV* and *DSM-5*. The authors also noted the specific symptom clusters with low endorsement, which prevented children from meeting full diagnostic criteria, which were re-experiencing in *ICD-11*, avoidance in *DSM-IV*, and changes in cognition and mood in *DSM-5*. This latter finding corroborated concerns that this symptom cluster involves "cognitively sophisticated and highly internalized symptoms" (Scheeringa, Zeanah, & Cohen, 2011, p. 6) that are not developmentally appropriate for children. Moreover, the findings were concerning in that many children no longer met criteria for the diagnosis in the move from *DSM-IV* to *DSM-5*; despite displaying significant levels of symptoms, these children might be no longer be considered eligible for clinical services and could be excluded from research on childhood PTSD.

In contrast, another study investigated the implications of the changes from *DSM-IV* to the *DSM-5* for uncovering PTSD in a sample of detained adolescents aged 12 to 17 years, most of whom had experienced chronic or multiple traumas (Modrowski et al., 2016). Comparisons were made to determine how many youth met criteria for the diagnosis when administered screening measures following the *DSM-IV* versus the *DSM-5* criteria for PTSD. Overall, a *higher* percentage of youth met criteria for PTSD according to the *DSM-5* (19.60% versus 17.70%), with the removal of the A2 criterion being one of the principal factors accounting for the different prevalence rates. Another study of a sample of 512 Italian adolescents who survived an earthquake also found higher prevalence rates of PTSD using *DSM-5* than using *DSM-IV* criteria overall, with 87.1% correspondence between the two diagnostic systems (Carmassi et al., 2013). The discrepancies were attributed to differences in the two systems related to avoidance and numbing symptoms; however, the investigators did not include the A2 criterion and so could not assess the impact of its absence. Overall, the higher prevalence rates reported for *DSM-5* among adolescents are surprising because, with the addition of new symptoms, such as those in the new Criterion D, the total number of symptoms required for the diagnosis increased from 17 in the *DSM-IV* to 20 in the *DSM-5* and thus the newer manual would seem to set a higher bar.

Yet another study compared the *ICD-11* criteria to those of the *DSM-IV* and *ICD-10* and found a striking decrease in prevalence in a sample of 159 traumatized children and adolescents in Germany (Sachser & Goldbeck, 2016). The prevalence rates dropped from 88.1% using *ICD-10*, to 76.1% using *DSM-IV*, and to 61.0% using *ICD-11*. The key reasons for the difference were the more restrictive definitions of re-experiencing and hyperarousal in *ICD-11*, which led children and adolescents to be less likely to meet criteria for the diagnosis.

Comparing the Diagnostic Systems and Their Implications for Youth

What Is a Traumatic Event to a Child?

The Child's Eye View. It is intriguing that the most recent versions of the DSM and ICD diagnostic systems were revised during the same time period, sometimes involving overlapping panels of experts, and yet the two manuals arrived at rather different destinations. One of these concerns the definition of what constitutes a traumatic event. DSM-5's definition is intentionally more restrictive than that of DSM-IV, limiting the qualifying events to those involving actual or threatened death or serious injury or sexual violence. The DSM-5 also now explicitly includes acknowledgment of the possibility of secondary traumatic stress, the idea that one can develop PTSD in the aftermath of exposure to another person's trauma, such as by being told about the gruesome details of that event. In contrast, the ICD-11's definition casts a wider net in that it does not specify the exact events that qualify as traumatic but refers only to their qualities, such as that they are "horrific" or "threatening." This definition also seems to retain a subjective element in that what is perceived as "horrific" or "threatening" may depend on the eye of the beholder.

However, it is notable that—other than *DSM-5*'s noting that sexual traumas need not involve actual violence for youth—neither diagnostic manual explicitly addresses how the definition of trauma might need to be informed by developmental considerations. A developmentally informed perspective on trauma suggests that events that might not be experienced as traumatic by an adult could be experienced as such by a youth:

> Events that do not meet the A1 criterion for trauma among adults—for example, abandonment by a caregiver—may loom large when viewed from a child's point of view and when processed through a child's perceptual framework, and thus be interpreted as terrifying and even life-threatening (Bowlby, 1973/1998b) (Kerig & Bennett, 2013, p. 432).

To take another example, research has confirmed that the forcible arrest or deportation of a parent—while not an event that, viewed objectively, would constitute an literal threat to the parent's life—is associated with significant posttraumatic stress reactions in children (Rojas-Flores et al., 2016). In fact, developmentally oriented scholars long sought to influence the *DSM-5* committee to expand the definition of Criterion A for children by including attention to attachment-related traumas, such as separation and loss of loved ones—or threats of harm to, or from, a caregiver—given the unfortunate prevalence and significance of such events for young people (Pynoos et al., 2009). Moreover, there are normative developmental changes in what children tend to find fearful; for example, for infants, physical insecurity, looming objects, and loud noises are the prime sources of fear, while separation anxiety peaks after the first year of life; toddlers' prominent fears are of storms, animals, and darkness; for preschoolers, imaginal threats, such as ghost as monsters, loom largest; whereas for school-age children and adolescents, reality-based threats such as of burglars, social embarrassment, and coming to physical hard are paramount (Pappagallo, Silva, & Rojas, 2004). However, in revising the *DSM-5*, the committee did not include developmental considerations in defining what constitutes a Criterion A event.

The idea that there is a "child's eye" view of Criterion A was confirmed in a study by Taylor and Weems (2009), in which they asked a sample of community youth between the ages of 6 and 17 years to identify the events they had experienced that they considered to be most "upsetting or frightening." Many of the events reported met the Criterion A definition (e.g., exposure to community violence) but others were expressly disallowed by the *DSM-5* (e.g., exposure to media violence). Yet other events did not fall within the purview of the *DSM* definitions of trauma at all (e.g., separations from family members, nightmares, drug use, depression) but were highly endorsed among these youth. Developmental differences were apparent in that younger children were more likely to report as traumatic nightmares or fears (e.g., of going to the dentist, swimming pools), whereas adolescents were more likely to report experiences related to substance use and emotional distress (e.g., eating disorders, suicide attempts). Similarly, a study of a community sample of adolescents by Costello and colleagues (2002) found that youth reported non–Criterion

A events such as teen pregnancy, changing schools, and parent job loss to represent sources of traumas in their lives.

It is possible, of course, that the experiences listed by the youth in the aforementioned studies were not truly "traumatic" but were termed that way in a loose use of the word by children and adolescents who have not undergone truly Criterion A–worthy events. The proof in the pudding, so to speak, is whether these experiences were indeed associated with symptoms of posttraumatic stress. In fact, Copeland, Keeler, Angold, and Costello (2010) found that, in a representative community sample of 1,420 children and adolescents followed from ages 9 to 16 years, more youth reported exposure to low-magnitude stressors (e.g., interpersonal losses such as nonviolent death of a loved one, parental separation, breakup of a romantic relationship) than to Criterion A stressors. Most importantly, those low-level stressors were associated with significant levels of PTSD symptoms. Yet another study utilized data from a national survey of 963 children in eighth and ninth grades to test the hypothesis that the experience of being bullied—a non–Criterion A event yet one well known to cause distress among youth—would be associated with PTSD symptoms (Idsoe, Dyregrov, & Idsoe, 2012). Among schoolchildren who reported being bullied, 40.5% of the girls and 27.6% of the boys had scores in the clinical range on a measure of PTSD. Similar findings were reported by Lansing and colleagues (2016), who found that, among a sample of 118 justice-involved girls, non–Criterion A events (e.g., death of a loved one by natural causes, incarceration, being "jumped into" a gang, being involved in or coerced into perpetrating violence that was upsetting to the youth) were associated with symptoms that were equally severe and functional impairments that were even greater than those associated with Criterion A stressors. The construct of perpetration-induced trauma (PIT) (McNair, 2002)—the idea that perpetrating violence may be a source of traumatic stress for youth—was confirmed in another study of gang-involved adolescents, in which, among more than one third of the youth who reported that one of the most distressing events they had experienced involved their being compelled to do harm to another person, PIT was associated with the highest levels of posttraumatic symptoms (Kerig et al., 2016). Each of these developmentally salient sources of posttraumatic stress is overlooked by the current *DSM* criteria.

Can Childhood Trauma Exposure Occur in the Absence
of Being "Traumatized"?

Another controversial change the *DSM-5* made to the definition of
trauma exposure was to remove the previous stipulation in the *DSM-IV*
that the experience of the event had to be accompanied by *peritraumatic
reactions* of fear, helplessness, or horror (or, in young children, uncon-
trolled behavior). The *ICD-11* does not require these specific reactions
but retains the notion that the event must be "horrific" or "frightening";
in other words, that the event has to be accompanied by a subjective
reaction that suggests that the individual has been "traumatized" by it
(Weathers & Keane, 2007). This expectation is in keeping with cognitive
models of psychology that posit that it is not the event itself that affects
us, but it is the meaning that we make of it (Bovin & Marx, 2010).
And children, who are at different cognitive levels at different ages, will
construe different meanings of the same event (Cowan, 1978). Thus,
considering event appraisals may be especially important for understanding PTSD among children and adolescents (Cohen & Scheeringa, 2009;
Trickey et al., 2012).

The *DSM-5* committee's decision to eliminate the peritraumatic
requirement (Criterion A2) was informed by research showing that it was
not helpful in differentiating adults who did and did not meet criteria
for the diagnosis (Brewin et al., 2009). However, other research suggests
that subjective appraisals during an event are even more strongly related
to posttraumatic stress reactions than are the event's objective features
(Trickey et al., 2012), and this may be especially true for youth. Studies of
traumatic events ranging from earthquakes (Giannopoulou et al., 2006)
to road accidents (Stallard, Velleman, & Baldwin, 1998) are consistent in
showing that, among children and adolescents, PTSD is predicted not by
the objective features or severity of the event but by the youth's subjective
appraisal of the experience. For example, in a study of 588 Dutch school
children, Verlinden and colleagues (2013) found that Criterion A2 was
a stronger predictor of posttraumatic stress reactions than was Criterion
A1, the event itself. Children who met Criterion A2 were nine times more
likely to develop PTSD than their peers; in contrast, children who met
Criterion A1 only were only two times more likely to develop PTSD than

other children. The authors concluded that "an event must be subjectively experienced as traumatic before a child is likely to develop PTSD"; in fact, "The remarkably high negative value of Criterion A2 indicates that if a child does not have a subjective reaction during an event that it is unlikely he or she will develop PTSD" (no page specified). Moreover, other studies have found that when A2 criteria are expressed in a child-friendly language (e.g., "feeling you couldn't stop what has happening and needed someone to help," or as intense physical reactions such as "sick to my stomach") they are highly related to PTSD in schoolchildren (Pynoos et al., 2009).

The weak findings for the *DSM-IV*'s A2 criterion also may have arisen from the fact that it was limited to the specific reactions of fear, helplessness, and horror, which may not be most characteristic or discriminating of the adults, adolescents, or children who go on to develop PTSD (Lancaster, Melka, & Rodriguez, 2011; Resick & Miller, 2009). In samples of youth, other reactions accompanying a traumatic event, such as disgust, shame, and anger, in addition to peritraumatic dissociation and confusion, appear to be even more strongly related to PTSD than those listed in *DSM-IV* (Bui et al., 2011; Deblinger & Runyon, 2005; Dyb et al., 2008; Kerig & Bennett, 2013; Kletter, Weems, & Carrion, 2009).

Other Restrictions to the Definition of Trauma in DSM-5. The DSM-5 definition of trauma also precludes two other types of experiences that have been linked to posttraumatic reactions in studies of children. The first of these is the restriction that exposure to a traumatic event cannot be based on media exposure alone. However, in the wake of 9/11, studies found that, among children and adolescents whose only exposure to the event was watching images on television, more than 62% felt directly threatened (Gil-Rivas et al., 2007) and many evidenced posttraumatic symptoms both in the immediate aftermath (Lengua et al., 2005) and 7 months later (Gil-Rivas et al., 2007). Although unfortunately only including adults in their sample, Holman, Garfin, and Silver (2014) studied individuals' reactions in the wake of the Boston Marathon bombings and made the important discovery that posttraumatic stress symptoms increased as a function of the amount of time individuals spent watching media coverage of the atrocity and, most strikingly, that those exposed only via the media evidenced higher levels of symptoms than those who were directly exposed to the event. Thus, media such as television can be potent "diffusers" of traumatic stress across a wide swath of the population. The implications for children in the United States, who spend an average of 28 hours a week viewing television, 71% of them on a TV set in their own bedrooms (http://kff.org/other/poll-finding/report-generation-m2-media-in-the-lives), are important to consider.

The second change in the Criterion A definition that has unfortunate implications for children is the qualification that trauma only pertains when a loved one's death is accidental, unexpected, or violent. However, recent research calls into question the developmental appropriateness of this assumption that only an unexpected or violent death should be considered traumatic for a child. In fact, quite the opposite appears to be true: counterintuitively, children are most likely to demonstrate posttraumatic stress reactions in the aftermath of a loved one's *anticipated* death, as in the case of a lingering medical illness (Kaplow, Howell, & Layne, 2014). Explanations for this finding might include that, in contrast to when a death occurs suddenly, in the case of an anticipated death, children are more likely to be exposed to upsetting or graphic information (e.g., overhearing details about the disease process, seeing an intravenous needle in the patient's arm, or glimpsing a pained expression) as well as to family members' distress and anticipatory mourning over a long period.

How Do Children and Adolescents Express Posttraumatic Stress?

The *DSM-5* criteria provide only a few modifications of the diagnosis related to children's developmental status. We have noted the different set of criteria for children younger than 6 years, which are characterized by a lower number of symptoms being required and the removal of symptoms involving higher-order cognitions that are not developmentally appropriate. Other than that, the developmental modifications consist of notations that children's bad dreams may include content that is not overtly trauma related and that children might evidence intrusions through traumatic play. The fact that traumatized children often display developmental regressions and the loss of previously acquired skills, such as toilet training, is noted as an "associated feature" but not a symptom of the diagnosis. Other developmental considerations we have described are included in the text of the "development and course" (p. 277) section of the *DSM-5*.

However, despite these descriptive nuances, adults, school-age children, and adolescents are expected to meet the criteria for the diagnosis in the same way and with the same number of symptoms in each cluster. Whether the research on developmental differences in reactions to trauma supports this assumption is an important question that we will turn to in Chapter 2, when we review this research and clinical work in detail. But it is notable that some of the new symptoms included in the *DSM-5* definition of trauma arose from observations of the unique posttraumatic reactions displayed by young people. For example, Nader (2011) noted the importance of recognizing aggression as a common reaction to trauma exposure in children—once relegated to the background of the "associated features" text, irritability and aggression are now included as symptoms in *DSM-5* Cluster E. Risky behaviors, now also included as a symptom of PTSD in Cluster E, also have a developmental origin. In a seminal developmental critique of the *DSM-IV*, Pynoos and colleagues (2009) noted that, due to the stage-salient issues of adolescence, interpersonally traumatized teenagers are particularly vulnerable to coping through throwing themselves heedlessly into dangerous or self-harming activities. In agreement with this view, risky behaviors have been viewed by other scholars in the field as not relevant for younger children and only being seen in adolescent samples (Danzi & La Greca, 2016; Friedman et al., 2011). However, despite the possible developmental salience of this symptom, this risk-seeking dimension is now included in the *DSM-5* criteria as they are applied equivalently across all developmental periods. Nonetheless, developmentally oriented clinicians have long been pointing toward ways in which each of the diagnostic criteria could have been made more developmentally friendly in *DSM-5*.

Developmental Expressions of Criterion B. For example, regarding Criterion B, clinical observations of young children suggest that play reenactments and recollections of the traumatic event are not necessarily accompanied by overt indications of distress, which could mislead observers (Scheeringa et al., 1995). In addition to reenacting events through play, children also may enact them behaviorally in ways that can be mistaken for disruptive or disobedient behaviors (Pappagallo, Silva, & Rojas. 2004). In turn, intrusions among school-age children commonly take the form of preoccupation with "rescue fantasies" and intense wishful thinking that they had intervened and protected themselves and others from the traumatic event (Pynoos et al., 2009). Alternatively, for adolescents, age-related body consciousness increases the likelihood of experiencing distressing reactions to physical reminders of the event (e.g., scars, disfigurement, etc.) (Pynoos et al., 2009).

Developmental Expressions of Criteria C and D. Regarding Criterion C, Pynoos and colleagues (2009) point out that the avoidance symptoms listed in DSM are under-endorsed by children in part because children often have little choice about whether or not they will actively avoid a situation. Instead, avoidance may take more general forms, such as the emergence of new nonspecific fears and anxieties not specifically related to the traumatic event, as well as age-inappropriate anxiety about being separated from a caregiver (Pappagallo, Silva, & Rojas. 2004). In addition, avoidance in children may take the form of isolative behavior and refusal to go to places not obviously connected to the trauma, such as school, which, especially when accompanied by irritability, can be mistaken for oppositionality (Pappagallo, Silva, & Rojas, 2004). Other observations of avoidance-related symptoms in young children suggest that social withdrawal, muted affect, the emergence of new fears, and loss of previous developmental attainments (e.g., toileting, language skills) are important indicators (Scheeringa et al., 1995). In turn, regarding Criterion D, the symptoms of numbness and alienation now associated with this cluster do not tend to be labeled by youth using those terms, and younger children especially may not have sufficient self-awareness of those states so as to identify them (Pynoos et al., 2009).

Developmental Expressions of Criterion E. Criterion E symptoms of arousal also may take different forms in children and adolescents. While disrupted sleep is seen in PTSD across developmental periods, nightmares may be particularly relevant for young children (Pappagallo, Silva, & Rojas, 2004). Nonspecific sleep difficulties and night terrors (awakenings in a state of fear without a recollection of any specific night-mare content) also are evident among younger children (Scheeringa et al., 1995). Aggression and irritability are particularly apparent as symptoms of arousal among children (Scheeringa et al., 1995) and sleep deprivation also can contribute to increasing children's irritability (Pappagallo, Silva, & Rojas, 2004). Difficulty concentrating is another salient consequence of arousal for children (Scheeringa et al., 1995) and thus arousal symptoms might first become apparent when they negatively affect the youth's academic performance (Pappagallo, Silva, & Rojas, 2004).

Developmental Expressions of Functional Impairment. Finally, observations of functional impairment in youth point to the importance of attending less to overt problem behavior and assessing more subtle failures to master stage-salient tasks, such as the school-age youth who behaves well in school and at home but reacts to the death of his friend by avoiding developing a "chumship" with any other boys (Pynoos et al., 2009).

Developmental Concerns Regarding Dissociation

The inclusion of a dissociative subtype in *DSM-5* moves dissociation from *DSM-IV*'s back burner of "associated features" to a potentially salient feature of the diagnosis. Dissociation in youth is differentially associated with the most severe forms of trauma exposure, such as chronic and repeated physical and sexual abuse (Bernier, Hébert, & Collin-Vézina, 2013; Brunner et al., 2000; Kisiel & Lyons, 2001; Modrowski & Kerig, under review), and is associated with the most severe levels of PTSD (Bennett et al., 2015), as well as related symptoms such as aggression and self-harming (Chaplo et al., 2015; Kisiel et al., 2014; Zoroglu et al., 2003). However, concerns have been expressed that *DSM-5* does not consider developmental differences in the prevalence, phenomenology, and significance of dissociation among children and adolescents. Some kinds of dissociative experiences, such as shifts in identity and loss of conscious control, may be common and even normative earlier in development (Carlson, Yates, & Sroufe, 2009). The *DSM-5* definition, which requires the endorsement of only one symptom consistent with depersonalization or derealization, may capture too many young people in its net. Indeed, in a sample of 784 mostly interpersonally traumatized youth in a detention setting, our lab found that an astonishing 83% of youth met *DSM-5* criteria for the dissociative subtype on a screening measure (Kerig et al., 2016), whereas samples of adults typically find the dissociative subtype represents only a small minority. Thus, the *DSM-5* definition of trauma may be overly inclusive and not developmentally sensitive.

Can Youth Have Posttraumatic Stress Without a Diagnosis of PTSD?

Earlier versions of the *DSM* allowed for a diagnosis of partial PTSD when youth or adults met criteria for only two of the three required symptom clusters. This was seen by developmentally oriented researchers and clinicians as particularly valuable given that children frequently display symptoms in some clusters but not in others (Cohen & Scheeringa, 2009). For example, results of a study of 7,688 foster children in Illinois, the majority of whom had experienced documented abuse, found that 63% evidenced posttraumatic symptoms but only 5.5% of them did so in all the symptom clusters required for the PTSD diagnosis (van der Kolk et al., 2009). Similarly, analyses of data from a national study of 9,336 children receiving treatment in the aftermath of trauma exposure found that, despite high levels of posttraumatic symptoms, only 25% met full diagnostic criteria for PTSD (Pynoos et al., 2008).

Despite this research, in an attempt to be more stringent and discriminating between PTSD and other disorders, the *DSM-5* now eliminates the option of a partial PTSD diagnosis for either children or adults. This is the case in *ICD-11* as well, in that the diagnostic criteria require that all symptoms be displayed even though some of them appear to be quite discrepant from one another (e.g., it is difficult to avoid a thought or image while simultaneously re-experiencing it). Although the *DSM-5* does acknowledge that certain symptoms are more salient or distressing for some individuals than others, all nonetheless must be present concurrently.

Alternative Empirically and Theoretically Derived Models of PTSD

Seven-Cluster Model

Just as was true with the previous version of the *DSM* (Bennett et al., 2014), an emerging literature suggests that, among youth as well as adults, the dimensions underlying the diagnosis do not fit the *DSM-5's* four-cluster model as well as they fit alternative configurations. One that has emerged as a leading alternative is a seven-factor "hybrid" model (Armour, Müllerová, & Elhai, 2016) that includes the following factors: *intrusions, avoidance, negative affect* (e.g., negative beliefs, blame of self or others), *anhedonia* (e.g., loss of interest, restricted affect), *externalizing* (e.g., irritability, reckless behavior), *anxious arousal* (e.g., hypervigilance), and *dysphoric arousal* (e.g., difficulty concentrating, sleep problems). For example, in two large-scale samples of Chinese adolescents exposed to a devastating earthquake, Cao , Wang, Cao, Zhang, & Elhai (2016) and Wang and colleagues (2015) confirmed that the seven-factor model best fit the data for both genders and that specific symptom clusters were helpful in understanding youth outcomes in the aftermath of trauma. Specifically, PTSD symptoms of anhedonia were associated with social withdrawal, whereas PTSD symptoms of externalizing were associated with delinquent behaviors and aggression. Similarly, in a community sample of traumatized 12- to 18-year-old youth recruited from schools in China, Liu and colleagues (2016) found the seven-factor model to provide the best fit to the data; further, the validity of the factors was supported by their differential associations with symptoms of depression, anxiety, and aggression.

Overmodulation Versus Undermodulation

Another alternative model typologizes PTSD symptoms according to whether they represent the tendency to *overmodulate* emotions (i.e., to restrict or clamp down on emotional experiences, as indicated by post-traumatic symptoms of avoidance, numbing, and dissociation) or to undermodulate emotions (i.e., to experience heightened emotional reactivity, as indicated by posttraumatic symptoms of intrusions and arousal).

As reviewed by Lanius and colleagues (2012), a strong body of research is emerging confirming this model, including research showing through functional magnetic resonance imaging (fMRI) scans that PTSD patients high in overmodulation demonstrate distinctive brain patterns consistent with emotional repression. However, until recently, validations of this model have not been conducted on child or adolescent participants. As an exception to this, in a study of traumatized adolescents involved in the juvenile justice system, Modrowski, Chaplo, Mozley, and Kerig (2016) found that youth who demonstrated posttraumatic overmodulation were those most likely to engage in maladaptive strategies to avoid experiencing their emotions, such as nonsuicidal self-injury; further, overmodulation uniquely served to account for the association between exposure to interpersonal traumas (i.e., assault, abuse, violence) and self-harming behavior.

Phasic Dysregulation Model

Horowitz (1993, 2011) has long posited that PTSD can best be understood as a syndrome of dysregulated affective responding. However, instead of typologizing individuals as over- versus undermodulators, Horowitz proposes that these represent two phases in the affect modulation cycle. Symptoms of undermodulation, such as intrusions and arousal, are inherently aversive and difficult to tolerate. In an attempt to cope, individuals engage emotion repression strategies, such as avoidance and numbing, to quell these symptoms. However, the effort to suppress these experiences is difficult to sustain, and when the individual's reserves are depleted, symptoms of undermodulation once again emerge.

Sequential Defensive Reaction Model

A common way of referring to the stress response system is one of "fight or flight." In the face of a perceived stressor, any organism becomes psychologically and physiologically aroused and prepares to take action in order to overcome the threat, if possible, or to escape it, if necessary. However, this is oversimplified in that we have a wider range of potential responses. Moreover, Gray (1988, 2003) has proposed that these potential responses can be viewed on a continuum of continuing escalation as we attempt to regulate our emotions and behavior in response to a traumatic event. As with the overmodulation/undermodulation model and cyclical models just described, PTSD can be considered to be a disorder of emotion dysregulation, the symptoms of which represent an overreliance on a limited set of affect regulation strategies. What is particularly useful about Gray's typology, moreover, is that, rather than placing all the diverse symptoms of PTSD into one undifferentiated "pot," it helps to organize them into a hierarchical sequence that might help to explain why an individual would display one set of symptoms rather than another.

Prototypically, there are a series of four escalating responses for regulating affect and behavior in response to threat. Initially, as we encounter a threat, we may "freeze" as we seek to limit harm to ourselves and appraise our options; this may be seen in symptoms such as hypervigilance, behavioral inhibition, and emotional constriction. (For example, imagine a 9-year-old child in a violent home who hears his abusive father come home in the evening, slamming the door angrily. He makes himself very still and quiet and listens carefully for his step in the hallway.) If the threat does not pass, the next escalation in the stress response system is to engage in "flight," as seen in symptoms of avoidance, isolative behavior, and attempts to escape. (Hearing raised voices and his father threatening to "give you all something to cry about," the boy goes to his window and tries to decide if he is strong enough to climb down the fire escape.) Should flight be thwarted or ineffective, the next stage of escalation is to "fight," which may be seen in increased arousal, reactivity, and irritability. (As the sounds next door become more frightening, the boy runs into the room and lashes out at his father, yelling at him to stop.) Should flight be impossible or ineffective, the next available option is termed "freeze" (or sometimes "fright") and is evidenced by tonic immobility as well as dissociative strategies that allow for psychological escape when physical escape is not possible, that is, "playing dead" or evidencing dissociative derealization or depersonalization. (As his father turns his wrath on the boy, he gazes up at the ceiling and has the sensation that he is looking down on the scene from afar.) Further, recent theorists have added an additional response to the sequence, that of "faint," in which, when escape is impossible and the trauma too horrific to bear, the defensive posture of last resort is assumed when the individual's system shuts down entirely and consciousness is abandoned (Schauer & Elbert, 2010). These different patterns can be understood as reflections of the particular fear circuitry involved, which is governed either by sympathetic nervous system activation in the initial stages or by parasympathetic responding in the latter stages (Schauer & Elbert, 2010). Moreover, some research is emerging that shows neuropsychological and psychophysiological differences among individuals whose PTSD symptoms are dominated by one or the other type of defensive reaction (Gray, 2003; Koutsikou et al., 2014; Lanius et al., 2012).

Unlike the *DSM-5* or *ICD* criteria, this conceptual model views the differences between the various PTSD symptoms as meaningful in that they represent discrete attempts at achieving affective and behavioral regulation via engaging in defensive responses that are specific to particular kinds of stressors and particular phases of the threat response system. Not all individuals would be expected to display all symptoms simultaneously. Moreover, this model suggests that, given the different underlying neurological, physiological, and psychological processes involved, these manifestations of PTSD would call for different therapeutic interventions and management strategies (Schauer & Elbert, 2010).

Developmental Trauma Disorder

As we have noted, the inclusion of the C-PTSD diagnosis is an important discriminator between the *ICD-11* and *DSM-5* diagnostic systems. In the description of associated features of the diagnosis, the *DSM-5* does acknowledge that individuals who undergo "prolonged, repeated, and severe traumatic events" (p. 276), such as chronic child abuse, may also demonstrate dissociative symptoms and problems in regulating emotions or maintaining close relationships, but these are not seen as requiring a separate subtype. The decision to not include this alternate type in *DSM-5* was made after extensive reviews and critiques of the literature (Resick et al., 2012) and was not without significant controversy (Goodman, 2012; Herman, 2012; Lindauer, 2012). In fact, one of the strongest voices of dissent came from developmental psychopathologists who for years had been lobbying for recognition of a second subtype of posttraumatic response that followed from chronic, pervasive, inescapable traumas such as childhood maltreatment (Cook et al., 2005; D'Andrea et al., 2012; van der Kolk et al., 2005), termed developmental trauma disorder (DTD).

The proposal to create this diagnosis came to the *DSM-5* committee in the form of a 34-page, single-spaced monograph coauthored by 12 of the leading developmental scholars in the field, dense with rationale and cited research findings (van der Kolk et al., 2009). The authors argued for the parsimony of gathering together diverse symptoms, all stemming from the same cause, into one heading rather than the current practice of diagnosing complexly traumatized youth with myriad disorders, each requiring its own set of criteria and calling for its own set of interventions. Recognition of the shared developmental origins of children's symptoms, the authors argued, also would help to facilitate developing, and directing youth in need to, appropriate treatments.

The consensus-proposed criteria for DTD are summarized in Table 1.5. Unlike the C-PTSD criteria in *ICD-11*, which emphasize the repetitive and inescapable nature of the traumatic experience, the DTD diagnosis is specifically developmental in focus. First, the DTD proposal specifies that the origins of trauma must occur early in life and, second, that the traumatic experiences must involve not only interpersonal violence but also attachment disruptions. Examples of such attachment-related traumas include repeated changes in caregivers (e.g., a foster child transferred from home to home), repeated separations from parenting figures (e.g., parental incarceration or abandonment of the child), and exposure to severe and persistent emotional abuse (e.g., rejection) at the hands of caregivers. The DTD criteria then go on to describe ways in which there is evidence that these experiences have interfered with the developing child's capacity to engage in adaptive regulation in three areas of functioning: affective and physiological, attentional and behavioral, and self and relational.

A preliminary evaluation of the utility of these criteria was performed in a study using archival data drawn from a sample of 214 children who received treatment after exposure to a traumatic event an urban clinic in the United States (Stolbach et al., 2013). The investigators found that 32% of the youth had histories that met both of the DTD trauma exposure criteria; further, these children were more likely than the other youth in the sample to meet the criteria for the other DTD symptom clusters,

Table 1.5 Consensus draft criteria for Developmental Trauma Disorder (DTD)

A. Exposure to multiple or prolonged adversities for at least 1 year beginning in childhood or early adolescence, involving both:
   A1. Direct experiencing or witnessing of interpersonal violence
   A2. Significant disruptions in caregiving (e.g., repeated changes in caregiver, separations from caregiver, emotional abuse)
B. Affective and physiological dysregulation (two or more of the following):
   B1. Inability to modulate, recovery from, or tolerate strong affective states (e.g., extreme tantrums, immobilization)
   B2. Disturbances in regulations of body functions (e.g., disturbed sleeping, eating, elimination; over- or under-reactivity to touch and sounds)
   B3. Diminished awareness of sensations, emotions, or bodily states
   B4. Impaired capacity to describe emotions or bodily states
C. Attentional and behavioral dysregulation (three or more of the following):
   C1. Preoccupation with threat or impaired capacity to perceive threat
   C2. Impaired capacity for self-protection, including extreme risk taking
   C3. Maladaptive attempts at self-soothing
   C4. Intentional self-harm
   C5. Inability to initiate or sustain goal-directed behavior
D. Self and relational dysfunction
   D1. Preoccupation with safety of the caregiver or difficulty tolerating reunion after separation
   D2. Persistent negative sense of self
   D3. Extreme and persistent distrust, defiance, or lack of reciprocity in close relationships
   D4. Reactive physical or verbal aggression
   D5. Inappropriate attempts to achieve intimate contact or excessive reliance on others
   D6. Impaired capacity to regulate empathic responding (e.g., lack of empathy, intolerance for others' distress, or excessive responsiveness to others' distress)
E. Posttraumatic spectrum symptoms: The child exhibits at least one symptom in at least two of the three *DSM* symptom clusters.
F. The duration of the disturbance is at least 6 months.
G. Functional impairment in at least two areas: scholastic, familial, peer, legal, health, or vocational

including expressing such symptoms as inability to tolerate strong affect states and use of maladaptive self-soothing strategies. Similarly, Wamser-Nanney and Bandenberg (2013) found that children and adolescents in treatment who met criteria for complex PTSD exposure—by virtue of enduring chronic interpersonal traumas beginning early in life—demonstrated higher levels of trauma symptoms and overall behavioral problems than did those whose traumas were later-onset or noninterpersonal.

Other Trauma and Stressor-Related Disorders

As we have noted, one of the major changes to the *DSM-5* manual was the removal of PTSD from the category of anxiety disorders and its placement in a separate category involving *trauma and stressor-related disorders*. In addition, a new proposed diagnostic classification has been included to assess prolonged grief, which may occur in the context of traumatic stress.

Acute Stress Disorder

The symptoms of acute stress disorder (ASD) parallel those of PTSD, with the essential difference that the onset of symptoms is within the first month following exposure to a traumatic event as defined in Criterion A in the PTSD diagnosis. Consequently, it frequently is the case that youth and adults who go on to develop PTSD demonstrate the acute version in the immediate aftermath of trauma exposure. Unlike the PTSD diagnosis, which requires symptoms to be displayed in each of four clusters, the ASD diagnosis requires the presence of any nine symptoms including intrusions, dissociation, avoidance, and arousal. The symptoms must persist for at least 3 days and cause distress or impairment. A parallel diagnosis proposed for the *ICD-11* is termed acute stress reaction.

Adjustment Disorder

For children and adolescents who do not meet criteria for PTSD or ASD, an alternative diagnosis is that of adjustment disorder (AD), which encompasses clinically significant but less debilitating emotional or behavioral symptoms. AD is defined by three criteria, which specify that (1) the response must occur within 3 months of exposure to an identifiable stressor; (2) that the symptoms cause either significant impairment in functioning or distress that is out of proportion to the stressor; and that (3) the criteria for another disorder are not met. The *ICD-11* draft criteria also include a category of Adjustment Disorder, which is similarly defined.

Reactive Attachment Disorder/Disinhibited Social Engagement Disorder

The diagnoses of reactive attachment disorder (RAD) and disinhibited social engagement disorder (DESD), although frequently confused in the clinical literature with insecure attachment (Allen 2011), apply to extreme cases in which young children have been denied the opportunity to develop a relationship with a specific attachment figure at all, such as the orphaned infants raised in depriving institutions in Romania (Rutter et al., 2012). Although this form of profound social neglect might be considered to be a traumatic experience, the symptoms these children display are quite distinct from those of PTSD and are focused particularly on impaired capacities to form an attachment relationship. This can be displayed in two ways. In RAD, children do not initiate or respond positively to overtures from those offering care or protection and overall display dampened positive affect in social interactions. In DESD, children are indiscriminant in seeking affection, attention, or comfort from others, rather than showing a developmentally appropriate wariness of strangers and preference for a caregiver.

Persistent Complex Bereavement Disorder

Persistent complex bereavement disorder (PCBD) is a new proposed diagnosis currently placed in the *DSM-5* Appendix as a condition for further study. The diagnosis requires that, 12 months or more after the death of someone to whom the individual was close, at least one of the following symptoms is seen: persistent yearning for the lost loved one, intense sorrow, preoccupation with the loved one, or preoccupation with the circumstances of the death. In addition, at least 6 of the following 12 symptoms must be endorsed: difficulty accepting the death, emotional numbness, inability to have positive memories of the deceased, bitterness or anger, maladaptive appraisals such as self-blame, avoidance of reminders, a desire to join the deceased in death, detachment from others, sense of meaningless, loss of identity, and loss of interest in other activities. Not only do these symptoms need to cause distress or impairment, but they must be out of proportion or inconsistent with religious or cultural norms.

There are many overlapping symptoms between PCBD and PTSD, although some research on adults has found that they can reliably be distinguished from one another (Boelen et al., 2010). Deaths that occur in the context of a traumatic event may call for both diagnoses simultaneously but persistent complex grief also can occur in the absence of

PTSD, particularly because the *DSM-5* criteria for PTSD now specifically exclude reactions to deaths that are not accidental, unexpected, or violent. Developmental considerations for applying this proposed diagnosis to children and adolescents are nicely reviewed by Kaplow and colleagues (2012).

A similar diagnosis proposed for *ICD-11*, prolonged grief disorder, focuses on the persistence and pervasiveness of the grief response, including preoccupation with the deceased, difficulty accepting the death, feeling that one has lost a part of the self, and severe impairment in the ability to function, which exceed the norms for the individual's culture, religion, or social milieu.

CHAPTER 2

Conceptualizing PTSD in a Developmental Context

A Note on Terminology

Before beginning our discussion of the developmental literature, some clarification regarding nomenclature is in order (see Table 2.1). Of note, the term "trauma" is often used loosely in the literature in ways that do not always correspond to the accepted *Diagnostic and Statistical Manual of Mental Disorders* (*DSM*) or *International Classification of Diseases* (*ICD*) definitions. For example, in some studies, parental divorce is included on lists of traumatic experiences, whereas the absence of a life threat component makes this more likely to be a painful or stressful event than one which rightly would be expected to lead to posttraumatic stress disorder (PTSD). In addition, other terms are used that overlap with, but are not identical to, the concept of trauma. For example, inspired by Anda and colleagues' (2006) classic studies on the effects of *adverse childhood experiences* (ACEs) on physical and emotional development, many researchers have utilized the ACEs checklist, which includes both experiences that meet diagnostic criteria for trauma exposure (e.g., witnessing family violence) and others that likely would not, even though they certainly would be considered unhappy or stressful (e.g., living with a depressed family member). Similarly, research on *victimization* (Finkelhor, Ormrod et al., 2005), and *polyvictimization* (when more than one form of victimization has been endured) includes traumatic experiences (e.g., physical assault) but others that would not meet the diagnostic system's definition (e.g., having one's property vandalized). In turn, there is a separate literature on childhood *maltreatment* that includes some experiences clearly fitting within the diagnostic definitions of trauma (e.g., physical and sexual abuse) but others that are not so clear (e.g., emotional abuse in the absence of physical threat or violence).

Table 2.1 Terminology in the child PTSD literature

Trauma	Term loosely applied to a range of experiences that are assumed to result in psychological distress and/or psychopathology; not all traumatic events or types of trauma exposure (even those that meet *DSM*'s and *ICD*'s definitions) result in PTSD
Potentially traumatic events	Given that not all events labeled as "traumatic" result in a "traumatized" response, some authors prefer to use the term "*potentially* traumatic" to refer to the event itself, with the term "trauma" reserved for when evidence shows that the individual has been traumatized (i.e., via posttraumatic reactions)
Adverse childhood experiences (ACEs)	Anda and colleagues' (2006) term for negative childhood experiences, some of which meet standard definitions of trauma (e.g., physical or sexual abuse) and others that do not (e.g., living with an unsupportive family or a family member who abused drugs), are shown by research to be associated with significant negative physical and psychological health outcomes, particularly in accumulation
Victimization/ polyvictimization	Finkelhor's (1995) term for harmful (e.g., assault, robbery, bullying) and exploitative (e.g., missocialization) experiences that are harmful to children's development but that may or may not meet the definition of trauma and may or may not be associated with PTSD per se. Polyvictimization (Finkelhor, Ormrod, & Turner, 2007) refers to the all-too-common childhood experience of co-occurring forms of interpersonal victimization (e.g., physical and emotional abuse)
Revictimization	Refers to a repeated experience of a particular form of victimization, usually in a later developmental epoch. For example, children who experience sexual abuse are at heightened risk for later sexual assault in adolescence and adulthood (Fergusson, Horwood & Lynskey, 1997).
Maltreatment	Term used for a range of ways in which caregivers might fail to provide an "average expectable environment" (Cicchetti & Lynch, 1995) for children, including physical abuse, sexual abuse, emotional/psychological abuse, neglect, and exposure to interparental violence. Some of these have been demonstrated to result in PTSD (e.g., physical and sexual abuse, exposure to violence), and others predict other kinds of symptoms and dysfunctions (e.g., emotional abuse is more strongly related to depression, and neglect to social withdrawal; see Kerig et al., 2012)
PTSD	Posttraumatic stress disorder; defined by meeting all the criteria in the *DSM* or *ICD* diagnostic manual
PTSS	Posttraumatic stress symptoms; often measured in research as continuous scales that may or may not meet full diagnostic criteria
Type I trauma	Terr's (1991) label for single-episode traumatic experiences, also known as "short, sharp, shocks" (Kerig et al., 2009) for which the *DSM* criteria for PTSD were originally devised

Type II trauma	Terr's (1991) label for chronic, enduring stressors, such as growing up in an abusive family. These kinds of traumas are believed to result in a different symptom picture, involving pervasive and subtle symptoms that might be misinterpreted as signs of personality disorder, for example.
Simple PTSD	Label introduced by Herman (1992) for symptoms that typically follow from Terr's Type I traumas and map onto DSM criteria.
Complex PTSD	Label introduced by Herman (1992) for a constellation of symptoms arising from chronic victimization, including affect dysregulation (e.g., dysphoria, self-harming, intermittent explosive or inhibited rage); alterations in consciousness (e.g., dissociation, depersonalization), self-perception (e.g., shame, guilt, alienation), relations with others (e.g., isolation, distrust, search for rescuer), and systems of meaning (e.g., hopelessness, loss of faith); Complex PTSD (C-PTSD) is now a disorder with its own criteria in ICD-11 Some of the symptoms Herman observed have now been incorporated into the DSM diagnosis of PTSD (e.g., negative cognitions; dissociative subtype)
DESNOS	Disorders of extreme stress not otherwise specified; an earlier proposed diagnostic category for complex PTSD
Developmental Trauma Disorder	Proposed diagnostic category not accepted for DSM-5, developed to take into account symptoms presented by children who repeatedly have been exposed to interpersonal violence as well as attachment disruptions, which result in PTSD symptoms along with disruptions in regulatory capacities across multiple developmental domains (van der Kolk et al., 2009)

A Developmental Perspective on Traumatic Experiences

In Chapter 1, we discussed the idea of a "child's eye" view of trauma, in that the kinds of appraisals of an event that result in a posttraumatic response—"Is it horrible, or gruesome, or disgusting?"; "Does it threaten my life or that of a loved one?"; "Is my 'safe base' and the security of the attachments upon whom I depend in jeopardy?"; "Am I to blame?"— will be filtered through the child's developmentally based understanding of the event and the world. But there also are a number of other dimensions that are helpful to be considered when assessing the likelihood that a specific experience will be perceived as traumatic, and thus result in posttraumatic stress, for a child or adolescent.

One such dimension can be termed **proximity** (proximal↔distal) and concerns the extent to which the child is a direct victim, versus an eyewitness, versus a remote witness (e.g., one who merely hears about it) to an event (see Table 2.2). As we have discussed, it is new to *DSM-5* to recognize that vicarious trauma arising from learning about a traumatic event can genuinely result in posttraumatic reactions. Such distal events may be quite impactful to children, particularly when they involve harm to a loved one. Indirectly experienced events are especially likely to affect older children and adolescents, whose cognitive skills allow them to engage in imaginal reconstructions and ponder the meanings of events they have not directly undergone. In turn, witnessing certain events may be even more traumatic for children than directly experiencing them—again, attachment figures provide an important example, in that some studies show that preschool children are equally, and sometimes more, distressed by witnessing their mothers' abuse than by being the victims of their own abuse in maltreating families (Kitzmann et al., 2003).

A second dimension concerns **chronicity** (acute↔chronic) and concerns the extent to which the traumatic event consists of a single episode, versus a series of events, versus an enduring pattern. This dimension is related to a distinction Lenore Terr (1991) has made between Type I versus Type II traumas, which Judith Herman (1994) associates with outcomes related to simple versus complex PTSD.

A third dimension involves **dispersion** (child↔family↔community), which refers to the extent to which the trauma impacts the individual child, versus his or her family system, versus his or her entire community. Parents who also are traumatized by an event may be less able to respond to their children's needs; moreover, emotional or physical separation from a caregiver during or following a traumatic event can be devastating for a child. Furthermore, when the entire community is unsafe or in chaos, as in the case of a widespread natural disaster such as a hurricane, and all those surrounding the family are similarly traumatized—sometimes including the relief workers families turn to for help—it is more difficult for parents and children to establish both physical safety and psychological security.

Table 2.2 Developmentally relevant dimensions of traumatic experiences

		Individual	Family	Community
Proximal	Acute	Child is bit by a dog on his or her way home from school one day	There is a fire in the family home and the entire family is evacuated in the middle of the night	Child lives in New Orleans during Hurricane Katrina
	Chronic	Child is sexually abused by a neighbor over a period of years	Abusive father habitually batters his wife and children	Child lives in the middle of a war zone
Distal	Acute	Child sees a dog hit by a car	Child's mother was involved in a serious car accident	Child watches the planes crashing into the towers over and over on TV news on 9/11
	Chronic	Child observes other kids being beaten up every day at school	Child's brother is family scapegoat and is habitually abused by parents	Child lives in a violent neighborhood and hears about atrocities every day

Other dimensions that increase the impact of trauma on children and adolescents:

Intensity

Duration

Preexisting/cumulative trauma

Repeated experience/revictimization

Extent of life threat to self or other

Gruesomeness, disgustingness, graphic violence

Suddenness, unexpectedness, uncontrollability

Stigmatization

Co-optation: Extent to which the child was "groomed," seduced, brainwashed, or co-opted into believing he or she was complicit, voluntary, chose to participate, could have stopped it, is blameworthy

Interpersonal vs. noninterpersonal

Betrayal (Freyd, 1996): Victimization by a person one should be able to turn to for care and protection

Malevolence: Extent to which an event was a result of intentional human cruelty

Caregiver/family members' distress, reactions, supportiveness

Culturally specific meanings and perceptions

Disruptiveness/uncertainty: Extent to which the event or its aftermath disrupt child and family's ongoing day-to-day life and sense of security (e.g., requiring a move, change of schools, living apart, etc.)

Legal or other system involvement: Extent of immediate or ongoing investigations or interventions by law enforcement, child protective services

Age/developmental stage

A Developmental Psychopathology Perspective on Child and Adolescent Trauma

Developmental psychopathology offers a powerful and useful framework for understanding the impact of trauma exposure on the developing young person and his or her interpersonal world (Becker-Blease & Kerig, 2016; Cicchetti, 2016; Cicchetti and Toth, 2005; Kerig, Ludlow, & Wenar, 2012). Developmental psychopathology is an integrative perspective that attends to the ways in which the various domains of development—affective, cognitive, social, and biological—interact dynamically with one another and transact with the environment in ways that are dynamic and reciprocal. Thus, outcomes are the products of complex interactions of factors that may tip an individual's trajectory toward risk or protection at various turning points in the developmental process. The fact that psychopathology is not a matter of a simple "bad input = bad output" formula is seen in the developmental psychopathology constructs of *equifinality*, referring to the fact that a number of different pathways might lead to the same outcome, and *multifinality*, the idea that a single risk factor may lead to diverse outcomes. For example, equifinality helps us to recognize that exposure to trauma is only one possible catalyst that might send an adolescent down the pathway toward delinquency; in turn, multifinality encourages us to remember that PTSD is only one possible consequence of trauma exposure; depression also is a common sequela. Moreover, above all, a key to the developmental psychopathology approach is the idea that psychopathology is best understood as a matter of "normal development gone awry" (Kerig, Ludlow, & Wenar, 2012) and, therefore, as with any disorder, PTSD in childhood cannot be understood outside of its developmental context.

How Might Development Matter?

From a developmental psychopathology perspective, age-related differences play an important role in our understanding of trauma in three respects. First, there are developmental differences in the way that trauma symptoms are expressed across childhood and adolescence. In other words, there may be *developmental transformations* in the way a given

PTSD symptom is expressed (e.g., irritability commonly takes the form of temper tantrums in toddlers but of noncommunicative and isolative behavior in adolescents) (Kerig, Ludlow, & Wenar, 2012).

A second developmental dimension that affects the child's processing of trauma and expression of posttraumatic stress concerns the *stage-salient issues* or developmental tasks that youth are attempting to master at each stage of life (Becker-Blease & Kerig, 2016; Cicchetti et al., 1988; Forehand & Wierson, 1993; Holmbeck, Devine, & Bruno, 2010; Kerig, Ludlow, & Wenar, 2012). In this regard, particular posttraumatic symptoms may come to the fore at specific ages (e.g., separation anxiety in a preschooler versus risk-taking in adolescence) as a function of the developmental tasks the child is attempting to navigate. Moreover, failure to resolve or successfully master these important tasks at one stage of development can carry over into the next stage and shape the way we approach future life challenges (Bowlby, 1988a). According to *developmental cascade* models, the effects of trauma are cumulative across development in that derailment of a trajectory at an early stage of life sets a child up to fail to master subsequent stages in ways that increasingly disrupt functioning over time (Masten and Cicchetti, 2010). For example, a preschooler whose response to trauma exposure is dominated by avoidance may exhibit socially withdrawn behaviors that interfere with the formation of the kinds of positive peer relationships that are of increasing importance to adaptive functioning across the school-age and adolescent years.

Another important developmental psychopathology concept in this regard is that of *transactions*. As active agents in their worlds, continuingly striving to construe events, respond to them, and adapt to their environments, through their actions, children can come to have an impact on their environments that have consequences on the next link in the developmental chain, for better or for worse. For example, in the context of family violence–related trauma, children whose posttraumatic reactions feature hyperarousal or irritability are more likely to stress their parents, resulting in more aversive parent–child interaction, which, in turn, fuels further child problem behavior. Or, to take another example, the boy whose posttraumatic response features avoidance and withdrawal may be a less attractive playmate, resulting in neglect by the peer group and poorer social relations, which, in turn, increase his avoidance.

Thus, exposure to trauma can set in motion a complex set of transactions in which children's appraisals, emotions, and behaviors reciprocally influence their environments' influence on them and their influence on their environments. Transactional processes also may derail development at successive stages when, for example, peer rejection of the avoidant boy triggers him to engage in negative interpersonal behaviors that further isolate him in the adolescent years, a time when the importance of social acceptance to well-being is at its height.

The concept of stage-salient issues also helps us to understand so-called *sleeper effects*, when the effects of earlier trauma reemerge, or even emerge for the first time, at a later developmental period when the child is confronting stage-salient issues that are newly challenged by trauma-related vulnerabilities. For example, the onset of romantic relationships in adolescence may trigger new forms of distress and conflict for a heretofore asymptomatic survivor of childhood sexual abuse, just as the apparently high-functioning preschooler who acts as an emotional caregiver to her family may struggle in new ways with setting boundaries in her relationships with peers in middle childhood. In short, when the stage-salient tasks of development do not (yet) tax a child's emerging capacities, youth may appear to be symptom free and well functioning even though they have been left with vulnerabilities that will be acted upon by the challenges of a subsequent stage.

Third, and related to the earlier discussion, age may come into play when there are *sensitive periods* for the development of particular psychological capacities. Developmental cascade theories suggest that early exposure to trauma imparts a particular risk because it disrupts the development of capacities that are fundamental to adaptive functioning—such as self-regulation—upon which so many subsequent developmental attainments are built. Sensitive periods also have a biological underpinning in that "early exposure to [traumatic] stress during developmental critical periods has been shown ... to reduce brain plasticity and neurogenesis through increasing sensitivity to stress hormones" (McCoy, 2013, p. 265). Once the sensitive period has passed, and neurological and behavioral development become *canalized* into specific pathways, the degrees of freedom may become more constrained and as a result it may be more difficult (albeit not impossible, especially with intervention) for a child to acquire the capacities that have been disrupted by trauma.

A fourth way in which age matters is that children's developmental level can influence their processing of an event, which, as we discussed in Chapter 1, can in turn determine the impact of that event on the child. For example, with advancing age, children have the cognitive complexity to appreciate, or to imagine, the broader implications of a traumatic experience for their future lives. For example, it was only in adolescence that a girl disfigured in early childhood by an accidental burn on her chest comprehended its implications with the distressing thought that she would never be able to wear the style of wedding dress that she was admiring in a magazine. However, cognition is only one facet of development that comes into play in the processing of trauma: language, memory, attachment, self, emotional, moral, interpersonal, and family systemic developmental processes all affect, and may be affected by, experiences of violence, threat, or victimization (Becker-Blease & Kerig, 2016; Kerig, Ludlow, & Wenar, 2012).

A fifth way in which development is important to consider is that, with age, children become increasingly active agents in operating upon, transacting with, and choosing their social environments. Not only do youths' emerging cognitive, emotional, and interpersonal capacities allow them to play an increasingly sophisticated, autonomous, and agentic role in their interactions with others but they also are increasingly able to initiate actions that may help protect them from the adverse effects of trauma. For example, in the case of maltreatment:

> [a]ge opens up expanding opportunities for children to become engaged with extrafamilial activities and peer associations that emotionally and physically separate them from and potentially create a buffer against family stress. Thus, it may be that, over the course of development, the impact of maladaptive family system processes is weakened for those resilient children who enjoy prosocial activities and relationships outside the home. (Kerig, 2016, p. 600)

However, there may be a dark side to this coin that places adolescents in their own "driver's seat" (Kerig, 2014) in that adults tend to attribute greater responsibility to adolescents for managing their own traumatic stress adaptively, and thus may be less patient and supportive than they are with younger children. In addition, adults may even tend to erroneously attribute responsibility to adolescents for bringing those traumas about (Ryan et al., 2007); this is a phenomenon that will be discussed further in the section of this chapter on trauma in the adolescent period.

Last, developmental differences are important to consider related to treatment. Children's or adolescents' capacity to understand and benefit from particular treatment strategies depends upon their present developmental level (Harter, 1983, 1988; Shirk, 1988, 1999). For example, preschoolers need interventions delivered in concrete, present-oriented language. In addition, however, an intriguing proposition that has guided clinical thinking about the treatment of trauma, albeit not one that has yet been put to empirical test, is that children's emotional and cognitive processing of traumatic events may be "frozen" at the developmental stage in which they experienced them (O'Connor, 2000). Thus, when triggered by a trauma reminder, the 12-year-old child may reason about an event experienced at age five years at a preoperational level. If this proposition is valid, recognition of both cases in which the child was in development at the time of trauma exposure and in which the child is in development currently is important for informing our comprehension of that child's reactions to recent stressors as well as the residual effects of past traumas, and intervention techniques may need to be gauged at the level at which the child is processing the trauma as well as at the child's current age. In sum, for all of these reasons, considerations of the developmental dimensions that might be impacted by trauma, and that might need to be addressed in treatment, require our attention.

The Biological Dimension

The human system's response to the threat of a traumatic stressor—the oft-called fight-or-flight response—engages psychophysiological, biochemical, and neuropsychological processes that are highly adaptive in that they increase readiness to respond and ensure survival. These include activation of the sympathetic nervous system (SNS), hypothalamic–pituitary–adrenal (HPA) axis stimulation and the release of cortisol, with accompanying increases in heart rate, blood pressure, and mental and behavioral arousal (De Bellis, 2001). What is characteristic of PTSD, however, is that, rather than returning to a state of homeostasis, the organism recalibrates its set-point and establishes a new baseline level of functioning that is "primed" and thus hyperresponsive to perceived threat. Termed allostatic load (McEwen, 1998), the overtaxed stress response system ultimately is unable to recover, adapt, and function efficiently, and the long-term exposure to increased secretion of stress hormones can be damaging to brain functioning, physical health, and mental health (De Bellis & Crowson, 2003). Studies of maltreated children, for example, have documented decreased intracranial volumes and neuronal densities that are directly proportional to the duration of the abuse and the extent of PTSD symptoms (De Bellis et al., 2010). On the other hand, studies of children rescued from severely abusive environments strike a hopeful note in that there is evidence of recovery of brain function.

The past decade has seen an explosion of research on biological, genetic, and epigenetic processes in PTSD. The developmental implications of this research are detailed in particularly rich and accessible ways in the following sources: Nader, 2008; Ford et al., 2015; Pratchett and Yehuda, 2014; Van Horn, 2011. Nevertheless, there are a number of limitations of the extant research for our present discussion of development. First, the majority of this work has been derived from samples of adults, looking retrospectively at the effects of trauma exposure (Kirsch, Wilhelm, & Goldbeck, 2011). This limits our understanding in that the observed effects of traumatic stress on the developing biology of a child may be quite distinct from that of an adult. For example, studies of adults in emergency rooms have found that low levels of the stress hormone cortisol in the immediate aftermath of exposure to a traumatic stressor are predictive of PTSD, whereas studies including children have found the opposite result, with *higher* levels of cortisol predicting a greater risk of developing PTSD (Delahanty et al., 2005). Similarly, studies on adults have reliably found that PTSD is associated with a small hippocampus, the area of the brain crucial for processing memories, whereas studies of children either have not found this difference (Woon & Hedges, 2008) or have associated PTSD with a *larger* hippocampus (Tupler & De Bellis, 2006).

A further limitation of the extant research is that little attention is paid to accounting for or controlling the effects of the time since trauma exposure—a child who is assessed in the first month after a traumatic event is in a very different phase of psychophysiological reactivity and recovery than the child whose exposure occurred several months ago (Kirsch, Wilhelm, & Goldbeck, 2011). For example, one study that followed children for over a year after trauma exposure found that it was not a small hippocampus at one time point but a *shrinking* hippocampus volume over time that was implicated in the development of PTSD (Carrion, Weems, & Reiss, 2007); moreover, this research team also found that traumatized children evidenced lower levels of activation of the hippocampus during a memory task, as compared to their nontraumatized peers, suggesting that there are indeed deficits in the functioning of the memory circuits in the traumatized child's brain (Carrion et al., 2010).

Another limitation of the biological research on PTSD to date is that little has attended to age-related differences nor has this research been truly developmental by following children over time. However, emerging evidence suggests that there are "critical windows of vulnerability to traumatic stress in brain development" (Gerson & Rappaport, 2012, p. 138) related to time-sensitive phases of myelination, synaptic development, and neural pruning, all of which can be disrupted by stress hormones in ways that may differ for boys and girls. Genes that are disrupted by methylation during these periods can lead to epigenetic effects that further disrupt the stress response system. Some recent work suggests that adolescence may be a particularly sensitive period for trauma exposure, at least in part because of the dramatic hormonal and neuropsychological changes undergone during that period of life; yet little work is available that tracks those changes in a developmentally informed way (Kerig, 2014). Yet an additional caveat is that much of the research on the biology of posttraumatic stress in children has been drawn from those who have experienced maltreatment (Kirsch, Wilhelm, & Goldbeck, 2011). Maltreatment is a chronic interpersonal stressor that is associated with a host of other forms of childhood adversity and thus may have effects that are divergent from those following other forms of trauma exposure, particularly single-event traumas such as accidents, disasters, or medical events.

Despite these limitations, biologically based research and theory on posttraumatic stress strongly implicates deficits in brain and psychophysiological systems that are critical to emotional, cognitive, behavioral, and interpersonal regulation over the life span (Ford, 2009; McCoy, 2013). The outcome is, as Ford (2015) terms it, a "survival brain" that is dominated by primitive mental systems, which ensure rapid responding in response to threat but at the expense of engaging the more complex executive functions needed for healthy adaptation.

> A survival brain operates automatically to defend against external threats, but in so doing, it diverts crucial resources from brain/body systems that are essential in order to prevent the body from succumbing to exhaustion, injury, or illness and to promote learning (e.g., reward seeking, distress tolerance, emotion awareness, problem solving, narrative memory). PTSD represents a dominance of the survival brain over the learning brain. PTSD, therefore, is a biological tradeoff in which avoiding harm takes priority over facilitating healthy growth, rejuvenation, and learning. (Ford et al., 2015, p. 212)

Developmental Differences in the Expression and Consequences of Posttraumatic Stress Across Childhood and Adolescence

In addition to a small amount of extant empirical research that compares the expression and course of PTSD across the epochs of infant, preschool, middle childhood, and adolescent development, a wealth of clinical observation is available to help us paint a developmental psychopathology portrait of trauma across the span of childhood. In the following section, we summarize and integrate information from a number of developmentally oriented sources (Becker-Blease & Kerig, 2016; Brown, Becker-Weidman, & Saxe, 2014; Cicchetti, 1991; Cicchetti et al., 1988; Cicchetti & Toth, 1992; Cicchetti & Valentino, 2006; Connolly, 2014; Forehand & Wierson, 1993; Harter, 1983, 1986; Holmbeck, Devine, & Bruno, 2010; Kerig, Ludlow, & Wenar 2012; Kerig & Schulz, 2012; Kerig et al., 2000; Lehmann & Carlson, 1998; Lieberman & Knorr,

2007; O'Connor, 2000; Osofsky, 2011; Putnam, 1997; Pynoos, 1993; Pynoos & Nader, 1988, 1993; Pynoos et al., 2009; Shirk, 1988; Sroufe & Rutter, 1984). These works, while mostly theoretical and conceptual rather than empirical, help us to create a portrait of how, over each successive epoch of life, trauma may intersect with key dimensions of cognitive, emotional, self, interpersonal, moral, and attachment development (see also Tables 1.1 to 1.3 in Becker-Blease & Kerig [2016, pp. 106–115]).

Before we proceed, one further caveat is worth mentioning regarding the developmental perspective. Although a child's age is typically our metric for determining that child's stage of development, there is an important difference between mental age and chronological age. Some teenagers, for example, never reach the formal operational stage of cognitive development, while, conversely, some school-age youth are uncharacteristically precocious and advanced for their years. In addition, development in each of the various domains does not always keep a single pace: a youth may, for example, be cognitively advanced while being delayed in his or her emotional development. By the same token, physical development may be delayed or advanced; over time there has been a steady decline in the age of onset of puberty and this appears to be particularly the case for children who have undergone traumatic stress (Parent et al., 2003); consequently, traumatized children as young as nine years may be coping with some of the hormonal and social implications of puberty far in advance of their psychological readiness to do so. For these reasons, the developmental portraits we paint subsequently should be considered in the context of the possibility of significant individual differences in what accurately describes a given child within each of these developmental epochs.

PTSD in Infancy and Toddlerhood

Can PTSD occur in infancy? Tucked away in the *DSM-5* section describing the development and course of the disorder is the statement, "PTSD can occur at any age, *beginning after the first year of life*" (American Psychiatric Association [APA], 2013, p. 276, emphasis added). The manual does not provide evidence substantiating the inapplicability of the diagnosis to children in their first year and in fact very few studies have examined

PTSD in children younger than six years; nonetheless, evidence is strong that trauma exposure in infancy is not rare and is associated with the development of significant pathology in the early years of life (Van Horn, 2011). For example, in one of the rare studies including very young children, exposure to violence in infancy was associated with trauma-related symptoms at age three years, and these symptoms, particularly avoidance and arousal, were predictive of later emotional and behavioral problems at school age (Briggs-Gowan, Carter, & Ford, 2012). Therefore, the traumatic stress response in infancy is deserving of our consideration.

The stage-salient issue central to this earliest epoch in life is the development of a secure attachment and, as Erikson (1950) termed it, a sense of basic trust. Attachment is particularly critical for the development of emotional and self-regulation, which initially is experienced as something provided by the caregiver and only over time internalized into capacities that children can initiate for themselves. Thus, infants are dependent on the caregiver to soothe them and to regulate their emotions and have no mechanism for coping with trauma other than seeking comfort from the caregiver. In consequence, the long-term impact of trauma exposure in infancy is entirely dependent on the caregivers' capacity to regulate the child's emotions and repair the damage done. Should the caregiver be unresponsive or unavailable, an infant will protest vigorously until the stress response system exhausts itself and shuts down, leading to a form of extreme withdrawal, termed *anaclitic* depression (Bowlby, 1980; Spitz, 1946). Furthermore, if trauma exposure is repeated or persists over time, the long-term effects may pervade all of a youth's functioning and become an integral part of his or her basic approach to the world, affecting the capacity to tolerate and regulate emotions, form close relationships, and communicate needs.

Trauma exposure in infancy also has impacts that are especially raw and immediate. Because infants lack language to use in mediating experiences, memories are not labeled or organized but are simply stored as they were directly experienced. Similarly, because infants are in the sensorimotor stage of cognitive development, their understanding of the world is based on direct experience, sensation, and action. Therefore, infants are highly likely to associate distressing emotions with stimuli that were experienced proximal to the event; for example, sounds, colors, and smells associated with the hospital in which the child underwent a painful medical procedure. When they are older, children triggered by reminders of traumas that occurred in infancy are subject to what might appear like phobic or bizarre episodes in which they have intense, primitive, and overwhelming emotional reactions to seemingly unrelated sensations, events, or memories; for example, both the child just mentioned and the adults around him or her may be mystified when he or she becomes distressed at the scent of an antiseptic. The trauma response also may cause a child who is functioning age appropriately in other areas of her life to revert to functioning at the sensorimotor level in reaction to a trigger reminiscent of an event that occurred in infancy.

Regarding the implications of infant development for treatment, given the primacy of the attachment relationship in the life of the infant and the infant's dependency on that relationship for physical and psychological safety, interventions that help parents to provide loving and reliable care are essential. For older children attempting to cope with traumas that occurred in infancy, interventions may need to be more experiential than verbal; for example, a school-age boy who had been traumatized by exposure to chronic, early-onset domestic violence spent much of his sessions on the floor next to his therapist, holding the edge of her skirt while he drifted into a peaceful, and rare, mindful state.

PTSD in the Preschool Years

The primary stage salient issues of the preschool years concern the development of autonomy and self-regulation of emotions and behavior. Consequently, these are developmental attainments that are particularly vulnerable to disruption by trauma. In the realm of autonomy, a preschooler whose traumatic experience is characterized by helplessness and loss of control may attempt to cope either by engaging in excessive self-control, leading to internalizing symptoms such as anxiety and depression, or by attempting to exert excessive control over the environment, leading to oppositionality and aggression. Regression to previous levels of functioning is often seen in preschoolers, including loss of developmental attainments such as toileting or sleeping alone, the return of separation anxiety, and reversion to early modes of coping with upsetting emotions such as temper tantrums. New fears often arise (e.g., of the dark, of strangers) that are not specifically linked to the traumatic event but reflect the preschool child's heightened sense of insecurity and vulnerability (Scheeringa et al., 2003).

In the realm of emotional development, preschool children begin to organize their previously inchoate experiences into schemas that persist over time, with a nascent emotional "tone" or personality beginning to emerge. Nonetheless, their perceptions are based more on immediate experience than stable internal representations and their highly variable emotional world may make the effects of trauma appear to be fleeting even when there are hidden "sleeper effects" lurking that will emerge at other times in extreme and inconsistent ways. A preschooler's memories also are stored together grouped by the type of affects involved (e.g., scary experiences with other scary experiences). Therefore, young children tend to drudge up a number of unhappy memories when they experience a trauma reminder and to conflate traumatic experiences with one another. Moreover, beginning in the toddler and preschool years, one of the most important aspects of emotional development implicated in trauma exposure is its effects on emotion regulation, the capacity to cope with and modulate strong emotions in adaptive ways so as to be able to function adaptively in emotionally arousing situations. The ability to regulate emotions is at the heart of many fundamental developmental attainments: self-esteem, tolerance for uncertainty and the inevitable occasional failure en route to mastery, and the ability to negotiate successful relationships with others. As Sroufe and colleagues (2000) state: "Problems in emotional regulation ... are pervasive markers of psychopathology. Such problems underlie most disorders of children and adults. ... Emotional regulation is the defining feature of all close relationships and the central goal of early primary relationships" (pp. 83–84).

As was the case in infancy, preschool children continue to develop the capacities for emotion regulation within the context of the attachment relationship. However, these capacities are developed most adaptively within a safe and supportive caregiving environment, which is not the case when the family context is colored by violence and overwhelming emotions of distress and terror. Even when the source of trauma comes from outside the family system, "the chronic experience of intense negative emotions interferes with the development of emotion regulation, interfering with the abilities to identify feelings in early childhood, elaborate on affective expression in the latency years, and understand emotions and their consequences in adolescence" (Kerig 2003, p. 159). Children chronically exposed to violence may even gravitate toward dangerous situations and relationships in which the experience of heightened emotional arousal is experienced as syntonic.

As noted previously, another way in which children may attempt to cope with unregulated emotions is through overcontrol of them: preschool children exposed to trauma have been observed to engage in constricting or numbing of emotions, which may carry over into a generalized style of emotional inhibition and avoidance of affect in interactions with others. Avoidant styles of coping with stress can foreclose opportunities for growth, such as by inhibiting the development of relationships with prosocial peers and other supportive adults who might be available in the child's environment.

Although attachment is typically identified as the primary stage-salient issue of the first two years of life, attachment continues to be an important source of risk or protection for children exposed to trauma in the preschool years and well beyond. Attention particularly has been paid to the attachment-related consequences of children's exposure to the trauma of violence within the family system, which undermines children's confidence in the predictability of safety and warmth within the family, resulting in chronic worry, arousal, perceived threat, and emotional distress (Cummings and Davies, 2011). Disruptions in secure attachment related to trauma exposure also have been shown to affect the development of the self-system, including the preschool child's sense of self-worth and perceived competence, as well as the capacities to recognize and communicate about internal states of self and other, which are critical to self-understanding as well as healthy social relations. Trauma-related attachment disruptions also are linked to cognitive deficits, in that insecurely attached children exposed to violence demonstrate inhibited exploration and mastery motivation, which are essential to learning and intellectual growth. Moreover, as indicated in our review of biological factors, another cognitive-related implication of early trauma is its direct negative effects on neuropsychological development and intellectual functioning. Neglect in particular is predictive of cognitive deficits and poor academic achievement, although the research strikes a hopeful note in that early adversities can be overcome with a shift to a nurturing and stimulating home environment.

Another important way in which development is implicated in PTSD concerns the ways in which preschool children cognitively comprehend and process a traumatic event. Preschool-age children reason at a preoperational level, which leaves them prone to magical thinking, distorted appraisals, and cognitive confusions about traumatic events such as "time skew," the reversal of the order of events, and "omen formation," the illusion that they knew what was going to happen before it did. When these misperceptions and misappraisals involve disturbing images that generate distress, they can be traumatizing in and of themselves and further interfere with children's ability to reason about and work through the trauma. For example, as his family was driving away from the scene of a terrible car accident, a preschool-age boy (who had remained calm and unfazed throughout the entire ordeal) became distressed at the sight of the still-burning flares at the side of the road and perseverated on them over the next few days, asking for repeated reassurance about "what happened to the fire?"

Regarding interventions, preschoolers may have difficulty representing their traumatic experiences in words and thus may engage in "traumatic play" in which the theme of the traumatic event is replayed repeatedly but without resolution. However, play also provides a powerful vehicle for engaging young children in therapy and provides opportunities to enact scenarios and explore beliefs that allow for cognitive processing to take place (Cohen, Mannarino, & Deblinger, 2012; Knell & Dasari, 2011). In addition to working to address preschooler's cognitive distortions, therapy often needs to address the underlying developmental processes that have been disrupted, particularly by chronic and early-onset trauma, such as the capacity for emotion regulation, empathic mutuality, and healthy object relations. Collateral work with parents also is essential, given their key role in helping children to learn and internalize self-regulation strategies and fostering secure attachment. As we will see in our discussion of interventions that follow, another helpful strategy is to place in developmental context parents challenging child behaviors, such as oppositionality and aggression, and to trace their origins to the experience of trauma.

PTSD and the School-Age Child

In the school-age years, the primary stage-salient tasks are to gain mastery over increasingly complex social and academic environments, which requires translating the security and self-regulation they learned at home to these new contexts. With emotional development allowing for the experience of affects to become more stable, clearly differentiated, and complex, traumatic experiences are likely to be accompanied by diverse and ambivalent emotions that are experienced simultaneously. In turn, the concrete operational stage of cognitive development allows children to formulate perceptions of traumatic events that are more logical and reality oriented. However, both their concrete reasoning and conventional stage of moral development lead school-age children to tend toward organizing information into unambiguously "black and white" categories and to find shades of grey in meaning to be exasperating. Taken together, school-agers' concerns with achieving mastery and comprehending meanings may lead them to perseverate on trying to understand events from a concrete perspective, asking questions that may sound callous to adults (e.g., "What did they do with our dog's body when he died?"; "What happens inside the coffin if it rains?") (Harter, 1988). Their drive to acquire an understanding of "why" events happened also may cause school-age children to become preoccupied with examining their own actions during the event, questioning what they did or did not do and feeling associated guilt, shame, or self-blame, or may fret over ways in which others played a causal role and should be ascribed blame. For example, following a car accident that occurred while his mother was at the wheel, a 10-year-old boy's most pressing perseverative concern was to determine what his mother had done wrong so as to have caused the accident to happen.

In contrast to the preschooler's use of play to represent the event, school-age children may be driven to repetitively tell their story as a way to process and master it. Moreover, cognitive advancements in representational thought also allow school-age children to experience strong emotions in reaction to events they have only experienced in their minds and not in reality. They may experience intense fear or sadness about things that have been described to them or that they have constructed in their minds. For example, hearing of a friend's father's death may provoke in a boy distress over the thought that his own father might die. Similarly, advances in moral reasoning leave school-age children vulnerable to feeling guilty or responsible for things they have not done in fact but have only thought, such as fantasies of taking revenge on an abusive parent. In short, school-age children do not have to have directly experienced an event to find it traumatizing. By the same token, although memories in school-age children are stored in an increasingly organized manner that allows them to sort and access them more accurately, they tend to recall the actual events and their thoughts and feelings about them as equally solid facts.

Symptoms of PTSD often emerge as school problems for children in middle childhood, especially as they affect attention and concentration, but also behavior. Moreover, given the stage-salient importance of peer relationships to the school-age child, the interpersonal consequences of trauma exposure become particularly acute during this period. Peer relations are challenging to all the emerging developmental capacities of the child, confronting children with situations that can elicit powerful and sometimes negative emotions, from routine tasks, such as entering a new social group, to more stressful experiences, such as managing a conflict or being teased or rejected. The child's capacities for interpersonal trust, ability to recognize emotions in self and other, empathy, modulation of emotion, cognitive schemas, moral reasoning, and social skills all are brought to bear when they are confronted with conflicts and relational dynamics in the world of peers. Consequently, it is not surprising that children from violent families have profound difficulties in peer relations, including inaccurate and negative perceptions of self and others; aggression or withdrawal in response to conflict; and deficits in the understanding, regulation, and expression of socially relevant emotions. Given that their close relationships in the family are also sources of danger and anxiety, "Children from violent families may attach negative connotations ... to affiliative emotions, which might logically lead them to avoid the interpersonal emotional realm whenever possible" (Logan & Graham-Bermann, 1999, p. 55).

In regard to implications for treatment, while the school-age children's increasingly sophisticated level of cognitive development introduces certain vulnerabilities, such as perceived responsibility for the trauma or negative appraisals about themselves and their families, it also allows treatment to access and directly address those problematic cognitions. The stage-salient drive for mastery is also a key theme for treatment and often is a therapist's ally in motivating children to overcome the effects of trauma. Group treatments also can be valuable for helping traumatized school-age children to develop social skills and to prevent the spillover of posttraumatic irritability or avoidance onto peer relations.

PTSD in Adolescence

Stage-salient issues of adolescence include the consolidation of identity, the deepening of intimate friendships and romantic relationships, and balancing the needs for continued attachment with individuation from the family of origin. In keeping with their generally felt experience of being display in front of an imaginary, and judgmental, audience (Elkind & Bowen, 1979), a particular characteristic of adolescents exposed to a traumatic event is self-consciousness about their own emotional responses. Fears of vulnerability and concern over being seen as "abnormal" or different from their peers may cause teens to withdraw from their family and friends. Adolescents also can be idealistic and harsh critics who expect reality to live up to their ideals, and disillusionment of those expectations can inspire feelings of anger and alienation. Consequently, negative alterations in cognitions and mood are a particular risk for teenagers who isolate themselves in the aftermath of trauma exposure.

As do schoolagers, teens often experience feelings of shame and guilt about traumatic events. Teenagers are vulnerable to unrealistic perceptions of their own control and may become preoccupied with fantasies of revenge and retribution that represent misguided attempts to undo what was done. In addition, adolescents enter the formal operations phase in which they are increasingly able to reason abstractly, hypothesize, and philosophize. Consequently, trauma exposure incurs a particular risk for *moral injury* in adolescence (Kerig, Wainryb et al., 2013), when perceived violations of the social contract and expectations that the world should be a just or fair place bring about a radical shift in the way youth perceive and interact with others. Given the increasing peer orientation in the adolescent years, some teens may choose to confide only in their close friends, shutting out their parents and other adults who thus may not even be aware that the youth experienced a traumatic event. Many youth who experience family violence set out on a pathway of precocious autonomy in which they become involved in adult behaviors such as drug use and sex in the context of leaving the family of origin and relying for attachment need on intimate relationships with peers—usually antisocial or other troubled youths.

Regarding interventions, cognitively based treatments are particularly helpful for adolescents to restructure dysfunctional beliefs so that violence and intimacy are intertwined or that their experience of trauma has left them irreparably damaged. Behavioral components can be valuable to address avoidance, hypervigilance, and symptoms of irritability and anger. Increasingly, the adolescent needs to be viewed as an active collaborator in treatment and to be allowed independence in thoughts, behavior, and values not only from his or her parents but also from his or her therapist. Sometimes, for youths growing up in violent homes or with parents whose own untreated traumas have left them unavailable, the goal of therapy must focus on helping the youth to learn how to be "sane in insane places" and not get dragged into the family nexus. Peers also become an important source of information reinforcement for adolescents, and thus group treatments can provide powerful sources of feedback, encouragement of interpersonal perspective taking, as well as challenges to unhelpful beliefs from a source that may be more plausible to teenagers than to adults. Whether in the context of group or individual treatments, interventions that focus on enhancing the quality of interpersonal relationships, including the capacity to trust and to have faith in the possibility of creating mutually gratifying and mutually autonomous intimate relationships with others, become increasingly valuable as late adolescence shifts into emerging adulthood.

Risk Seeking in Adolescence. It is in the adolescent period that we see one of the newest additions to the *DSM-5* diagnosis of PTSD arising—risky behavior—and this is worth some consideration in its own right.

Risky behavior can be understood as a normative part of adolescent identity formation, experimentation, and attempts to gain mastery of the environment (Jessor, 1992). However, extreme levels of risk-taking in the aftermath of trauma have the potential to derail normative adolescent development. In an intriguing theoretical explanation for this phenomenon, Pynoos and colleagues (2009) propose that trauma exposure in early childhood can interfere with the normal development of the fear circuitry that is central to guiding a child's appraisal of and response to danger. Although, ideally, a child can turn to an attachment figure for safety and protection, for many traumatized children the attachment figure is either the source of the threat or has failed to provide the child the necessary protective shield. Given the stage-salient task of developing independence and self-reliance in adolescence, Pynoos and colleagues propose, "the symptom manifestations of PTSD ... reflect developmental disturbances in the maturation-driven balance between the need for protection by others, especially by caregivers, and increasing self-efficacy ... in the face of danger ... [As a consequence,] adolescents may be propelled into [precocious] independence and misjudgments about danger and protective action that can result in reckless or high-risk behaviors and, at the same time, take on self-imposed restrictions in pursuing normative developmental opportunities" (p. 392). Moreover, the experience of achieving safety in the face of these self-imposed dangers may activate reward centers in the brain that also are associated with substance abuse and other risky and sensation-seeking behaviors. As the authors further noted, and were later heeded by the developers of the *DSM-5* criteria, "especially among adolescents ... there should be consideration of including proneness to reckless or thrill-seeking behavior ... the source of this behavior is not likely to be irritability or anger, nor hypervigilance, but instead arises from an arousal-related 'fearlessness' ... and the reward of achieving safety that is associated with thrill-seeking behavior" (p. 395). This intriguing description of the neurological origins and psychological functions of these behaviors, I would propose, suggest that the term *"risk-seeking"* might better capture the functional significance of this behavior than the term "risk-taking."

The consequences of such risky behaviors are dire for youth. Not only may they lead youth into dangerous situations, but such risk-taking may be interpreted by others as signs not of trauma, but of conduct disorder or personality disorders, and thus youth may be responded to in ways that are not helpful or compassionate. Ford, Chapman and colleagues (2006) follow up on this theme, describing the ways in which a youth who is betrayed and angry about the injustice of victimization may act out behaviorally as a cry for help and yet experience a double betrayal when others' reaction to this expression of need is punitive and rejecting.

The idea that trauma is linked to risk-seeking among adolescents has been supported in studies arising from different cultural contexts. For example, one study involved a clinical sample of 3,785 adolescents treated in the aftermath of exposure to traumas, mostly involving traumatic loss, family violence, and maltreatment (Layne et al., 2014). On average, youth had experienced more than four different types of traumatic events and the investigators found that, as the accumulation of traumas increased, adolescents were at significantly higher risk of engaging in risky behaviors such as criminal activity, exchanging sexual acts for resources, suicidality, substance use, running away from home, truancy, and interpersonal distrust. Similarly, in a study of adolescents exposed to ongoing terrorism-related violence in Israel, Pat-Horenczyk and colleagues (2007) found that greater exposure to terrorist threats was linked to higher rates of involvement in risk-taking behaviors (e.g., substance use, breaking laws, hitchhiking, defying parents and teachers, driving dangerously, etc.), especially—but not only—for boys. As Pat-Horenczyk and colleagues propose, when examined through a developmental lens, risk-taking can be viewed as "functional and goal-directed behavior that can play an important part in the developmental tasks of adolescence" (p. 66); however, living under ongoing threat "amplifies the identity dilemmas and other issues that the adolescents are already struggling with … [and extreme levels of] risk-taking behavior can thus be seen as a maladaptive endeavor by an adolescent to regain control and mastery" (p. 71).

Summary: Key Take-Home Points About Developmental Differences

To summarize, above all else, there are two important implications of a developmental perspective on trauma exposure, PTSD, and their consequences for children and adolescents. First, exposure to trauma threatens to compromise the development of fundamental underlying stage-salient capacities that are necessary for navigating a given phase of development. Furthermore, failure to resolve issues at one stage of development will carry on into the next and shape the way children approach future life challenges, thus interfering with the child's "capacity to move forward in development," as Anna Freud (1965) defined the essence of childhood psychopathology. The specific symptoms that arise from these developmental derailments may be quite diverse. For example, an insecure attachment may evidence itself as avoidance of others or as an inability to tolerate separation from them, just as the inability to regulate emotions may be demonstrated in a tendency toward depression or aggression. Thus, in keeping with the developmental psychopathology model, and the conceptualization of childhood trauma proposed in the ill-fated Developmental Trauma Disorder proposal (van der Kolk et al., 2009), a symptom itself is merely the external manifestation of a more fundamental underlying difficulty that needs to be understood as an outcome of trauma exposure.

A second implication of a developmental approach is that traumatic experiences may be processed by the child at two developmental levels simultaneously: at the child's current mental age as well as the child's mental age at the time of trauma exposure. As a consequence, intervention techniques may need to be gauged at the level at which the child is processing the trauma as well as at the child's current age. An understanding of where the child was in development at the time of trauma exposure, as well as where the child is in development currently, also will guide our comprehension of that child's reactions to recent stressors as well as the residual effects of past traumas.

However, despite the cumulative and cascading effects of developmental injuries consequent to trauma, these ill effects are probabilistic rather than deterministic: Many protective factors might intervene at critical turning points in the life course and redirect development to a more adaptive course. It is these factors promoting resilience against trauma to which we turn next.

Risk, Protection, and Resilience

Resick and colleagues (2013) make the compelling point that most individuals will experience a traumatic event at some point in their lives and most will demonstrate acute stress symptoms in the immediate aftermath of such an event; nevertheless, most will recover over the months that follow. Thus, resilience is in fact the norm. PTSD, they argue, is best characterized not so much as descent into psychological illness as a failure to progress toward recovery. Therefore, there is much to learn from the study of individual differences and the factors that contribute to risk, protection, and resilience among children and adolescents who have undergone similar kinds of degrees of traumatic stress.

Risk Factors

What increases the risk that a child will be exposed to traumatic stress? In a nationally representative sample of U.S. adolescents, McLaughlin, Koenen et al. (2013a) found that the risk of experiencing a traumatic stressor, particularly one involving interpersonal violence, was highest among those living in single-parent families and those exhibiting behavioral problems. In turn, risk factors for developing PTSD after trauma exposure included female gender, prior trauma exposure, and preexisting anxiety and depressive disorders. Regarding poor recovery from PTSD, poverty, being born in the United States, bipolar disorder, and subsequent trauma exposure interfered with recovery. In another study of risk factors specific to urban youth, Milan and colleagues (2013) followed a large sample of 1,242 ethnically diverse adolescents in order to examine the factors that predicted the likelihood that youth would experience a traumatic event as well as those that increased the likelihood that youth would develop PTSD symptoms in the aftermath of such an event. Over the course of two years, only 5 percent of those exposed to community violence developed PTSD, striking a hopeful note regarding resilience. A previous history of exposure to interpersonal violence, externalizing behavior problems, and associating with delinquent peers were the strongest predictors of subsequent exposure to a traumatic event. In turn, the youth most vulnerable to developing PTSD symptoms following the event were those who had previously demonstrated thought disorder symptoms and social problems (measured by lack of social support, involvement with delinquent peers, and past exposure to interpersonal violence); these youth also were significantly more likely to be White or Latino rather than African American.

More broadly, Trickey and colleagues (2012) carried out a meta-analysis of 64 studies involving a total of 32,238 youth between the ages of six and 18 years and found that strong predictors of PTSD in children and adolescents exposed to trauma included preexisting PTSD, peritraumatic fear, and perceived life threat at the time of trauma exposure. However, to an even greater extent than pre-trauma factors, subsequent interpersonal difficulties (low social support, family dysfunction), maladaptive coping strategies (social withdrawal, thought suppression, blaming others, distraction), and comorbid psychological problems increased youths' vulnerability to developing PTSD.

Additionally, one of the most consistent risk factors that has been associated with childhood PTSD is the extent to which parents display symptoms of PTSD and other forms of psychological distress (Morris, Gabert-Quillen, and Delahanty, 2012; Nugent et al., 2007). Although in some studies parental distress is measured as a reaction to the traumatic event that has befallen the child, in other studies, parental PTSD has arisen from a preexisting experience, often one in the parent's own childhood, a distinction that is worth considering (Kerig & Alexander, 2013).

Intergenerational Transmission. Another contributor to increased vulnerability to PTSD, albeit one that is not well understood, is intergenerational transmission: Parents who have experienced posttraumatic stress are disproportionately likely to raise children who develop the disorder (De Bellis, 2001; Leen-Feldner et al., 2013; Yehuda, Halligan, & Grossman, 2001). The explanation for this likely is multidetermined, including underlying inherited traits, such as anxiety sensitivity, which increase the susceptibility of members in the same family to the effects of trauma exposure (Koenen, Amstadter, & Nugent, 2009), epigenetic processes (Leen-Feldner et al., 2013), the modeling of PTSD symptoms and their negative sequelae by affected parents (Kerig & Alexander, 2013), and the ways in which PTSD interferes with the capacity of parents to be fully emotionally available and responsive to their children's needs (Appleyard & Osofsky, 2003), particularly when a child's trauma reawakens emotional pain in a traumatized parent (Catherall, 1998; Silverman & Lieberman, 1999). Parents who bear the burden of unresolved trauma may engage in boundary violations, in which they turn to children to meet their own emotional needs in developmentally inappropriate ways (Kerig, 2005; Kerig & Alexander, 2013) or exhibit confusing or frightening behaviors that interfere with the formation of a secure attachment (Lyons-Ruth & Jacobvitz, 2008) and are predictive of children's development of PTSD (MacDonald et al., 2008).

Sensitivity to Context. Biological processes also may account for individual variation in how youth are affected by exposure to traumatic stress. While some children and adolescents appear to thrive even in difficult circumstances—the so-called dandelion children—others are highly sensitive to their environments and either thrive when conditions are ideal or wilt when conditions do not match their needs—these are the so-called orchid children (Boyce & Ellis, 2005). One biological marker of such vulnerability is low vagal tone, which indicates ineffectiveness of the parasympathetic nervous system in regulating arousal and promoting recovery after stress (Beauchaine, 2001; Berntson et al., 1994; Berntson, Boysen, & Cacioppo, 1992). Typically measured as a function of respiratory sinus arrhythmia (RSA), low vagal tone is associated with a higher level of psychopathology in children and adolescents (Beauchaine, 2001; Porges, 2007) but more intriguingly, low vagal tone is associated with *differential* reactivity to a number of stressors in childhood, including interparental conflict (Katz & Gottman, 1995), family violence (El-Sheikh et al., 2009), and traumatic stressors in family, peer, and community contexts (McLaughlin, Rith-Najarian et al., 2013b). While children with low vagal tone are susceptible to these forms of stress and trauma, children with high vagal tone demonstrate adaptive functioning even under those challenging circumstances.

Protective Factors

In the biological realm, the flip side of the research just cited on vagal tone and RSA makes a strong case that high vagal tone exerts a protective influence. Children who exhibit adaptive physiological self-regulation are remarkably resilient against developing internalizing or externalizing problems in the face of exposure to traumatic and other stressors, in comparison to their peers (El-Sheikh et al., 2009; Katz & Gottman, 1995; McLaughlin, Rith-Najarian et al., 2013b).

Other studies of protective factors have focused on those in the interpersonal and psychological realms. In an impressive sample of 7,483 trauma-exposed children and adolescents entering a stabilization program in the Illinois child welfare system, Kisiel and colleagues (2016) used an interview to identify protective factors, which they termed "strengths." Youth with histories of multiple trauma exposures exhibited the least strength, as defined by family and personal variables assessed through an interview (e.g., resilience, coping skills, optimism, talents, and relationship permanence). However, for all children, strengths were bolstered over the two time periods assessed, and increasing strengths were associated with a reduction in posttraumatic stress symptoms, risky behaviors, and emotional and behavioral symptoms.

The role of coping also was highlighted in a study of 141 hurricane-exposed children in grades 4 through 8 (Weems & Graham, 2014). Initially, the authors found that 43 percent of the sample appeared to be resilient to developing PTSD 6 months and 12 months after the disaster; however, many of those youth had low levels of exposure to disaster-related diversities. When the investigators focused on those youth with significant levels of exposure, only 16 percent were classified as resilient, and these youth were characterized by the low use of avoidant coping strategies.

Protective Processes

As Rutter (1990) has argued, research on resilience has tended to focus on variables that represent static characteristics of children or their social environments (e.g., intelligence, economic advantage, positive parenting) rather than attending to the underlying dynamic processes by which those characteristics provide protection against risk. Rutter proposed four such processes. First, *reduction of risk impact* may come into play when protective processes help to buffer children from the most negative effects of a traumatic stressor, for example, when parents instill in children a strong positive ethnic identity that helps to protect children from the negative effects of racial hostility (Kerig, 2016). Second, *interruption of negative chain reactions* may occur when positive family processes prevent a downward spiral from occurring, for example, when one parent steps in to provide help and support to another parent who is overwhelmed by distress at a child's traumatic injury. Third, *self-efficacy and coping* arise when children and families experience themselves as successfully surviving and thriving in the face of trauma. Fourth, *opening of opportunities* refers to the ways in which family members "roll with the punches" and look for ways to turn adversities into opportunities for positive growth and change.

An even more explicitly systemic family process orientation regarding resilience in the face of trauma is offered by Walsh (Walsh, 2006, 2003; Walsh, 2016). Her model focuses on three domains of resilience in the family system. The first of these is the family's level of *organization*, which includes clear boundaries as well as the capacity to be flexible in the face of challenges. The second concerns *communication and problem-solving*, which allow family members to communicate their needs and collaboratively arrive at solutions. The third involves the family *belief systems*, in particular the family's ability to find meaning and preserve hope even in the face of traumatic adversities.

Although these theoretical models of resilience have seldom been put to empirical test, one intriguing study of family processes took advantage of a "naturally occurring experiment" by comparing family narratives around the dinner table before and after 9/11 (Fivush, Bohanek, & Zaman, 2011). The investigators found that, among families in which narratives were characterized by stories involving both the acknowledgment of adversity and the overcoming of it, youth were more resilient and able to modulate the effects of stress in their lives.

Posttraumatic Growth

Beyond resilience, and in keeping with the saying, "that which does not kill us makes us stronger," the idea also has been proposed that overcoming adversity and making meaning of it can be associated with the emergence of new strengths and capacities, termed posttraumatic growth (PTG; Tedeschi, Park, & Calhoun, 1998). In contrast to resilience, which refers to adaptive functioning in the face of adversity, specific to the construct of PTG is the idea of an active struggle to adapt, which may be accompanied by symptoms of psychological distress such as PTSD. Nevertheless, it is through this struggle that an individual arrives at a new belief system that buoys the spirit. The construct of posttraumatic growth has been successfully translated downward to children and adolescents in several studies (Kilmer, 2006; Meyerson et al., 2011), including the development of a measure, the *Posttraumatic Growth Inventory for Children-Revised* (Cryder et al., 2006), which reliably assesses the key domains of *appreciation of life* (e.g., "I appreciate each day more"); *relationships with others* (e.g., "I learned how nice people can be"); *new possibilities in life* (e.g., "I have new ideas about how I want things to be"); *personal strength* (e.g., "I can deal with more"); and *spiritual change* (e.g., "My faith is stronger").

Consistent with the theory that PTG develops out of distress and the challenge to adapt, studies in diverse cultures have found that, among U.S. youth exposed to hurricanes in Louisiana (Kilmer et al., 2009), Norwegian youth exposed to tsunamis in Southeast Asia (Hafstad, Kilmer, & Gil-Rivas, 2011), and Japanese youth exposed to diverse traumas (Taku et al., 2012), posttraumatic stress is positively correlated with PTG. Furthermore, in keeping with the notion that PTG involves a struggle to find meaning, children's ruminative thinking, whether that involves distressing or constructive thoughts, is predictive of increasing PTG over time (Kilmer & Gil-Rivas, 2010). More recently, in a study of middle-school students followed 6 months after a devastating earthquake in China, Zhou et al. (2016) investigated processes underlying the development of PTG. The investigators found that youths' self-report ratings of PTG were predicted by the level of social support they received, which, in turn, was associated with increased positive cognitive appraisals over time. In addition, the investigators found that PTSD symptoms and PTG were predicted by different variables, confirming that the two constructs are discriminable and independent of one another.

CHAPTER 3

Evaluation and Assessment of PTSD in Children and Adolescents

Case Formulation Versus Diagnosis

Although establishing whether youth meet criteria for the diagnosis of posttraumatic stress disorder (PTSD) is an important part of a clinical assessment, the ultimate goal is not to place a label on the child but rather to develop a case formulation that can guide intervention planning (Friedberg & McClure, 2002; Kerig, Ludlow, & Wenar, 2012; Shirk & Russell, 1996). Thus, a case formulation has many components that go beyond mere diagnosis, including understanding the family context in which the child is growing up; cultural factors that might affect the child and important people in the child's life, guiding their reactions to the traumatic event and their responses to interventions; and assessing sources of competency, strengths, and resilience that might be enlisted in order to help the youth and family overcome exposure to trauma. Table 3.1 presents an outline of a comprehensive case formulation approach as applied to the assessment of child and adolescent PTSD.

In describing the case formulation approach as applied to children and adolescents, Shirk and Russell (1996) liken it to a hypothesis-creating enterprise in which the clinician strives to develop a plausible theory regarding the *pathogenic processes* that led to the problem and the accompanying *change processes* that might be effective in alleviating it. The child's presentation and the subsequent data derived from an assessment may lead the clinician to posit that the key pathogenic processes derive from the *cognitive* realm, such as cognitive distortions and maladaptive schemas that interfere with recovery from trauma. In the *emotional* realm, pathogenic processes might involve lack of access to feelings or

Table 3.1 *Components of a case formulation for child and adolescent PTSD*

1. Current presenting problem, its manifestations, and its impact on youth functioning:
   a. Physiological/health
   b. Emotional/mood
   c. Behavioral
   d. Cognitive
   e. Interpersonal

2. Characteristics and context of the traumatic event (see Table 2.1)

3. History, developmental milestones, competencies
   a. Temperament; emotional or behavioral dysregulation
   b. Developmental delays, deviations, or precocity
   c. Cognitive vs. emotional developmental level in relation to age
   d. Prior experiences of trauma (age of onset, chronicity, revictimization)
   e. Functioning in extrafamilial environments (e.g., school, peer relationships, interests/hobbies, extracurricular activities)
   f. Strengths, skills, and competencies

4. Family relationships and attachments
   a. Dyadic parent–child relationships: Closeness, role clarity, boundary maintenance versus dissolution
   b. Parent–child attachment: Secure, preoccupied, dismissing, disorganized
   c. Individual parenting styles: Warmth, supportiveness, structure, overprotectiveness, demandingness, parenting competence versus anxiety, parenting stress
   d. Individual parents' past trauma history and current posttraumatic stress reactions
   e. Interparental relationship: Conflict, coparenting cooperation
   f. Whole-family systemic processes: Cohesion vs. enmeshment, distancing, or triangulation; cross-generational coalitions, scapegoating
   g. Family protective factors, sources of resilience (Walsh, 2003): Belief systems (meaning-making, positivity, spirituality); organization (flexibility, connectedness, access to resources); communication and problem-solving (clarity, openness, collaboration)
   h. Extended family and social network sources of protection, support, or stress

5. Cultural and ethnic context variables
   a. Ethnic identity
   b. Acculturation
   c. Ethnocultural and religious beliefs, values, and practices
   d. Cultural beliefs related to the traumatic event
   e. Cultural beliefs and practices related to mental health and treatment
   f. Family experiences of adversity, prejudice, marginalization, minority stress, or historical trauma

6. Cognitive variables
   a. Automatic thoughts
   b. Schemas
   c. Cognitive distortions

7. Behavioral antecedents and consequences

8. Testing data and differential diagnosis considerations

9. Provisional formulation
    a. Coordinate the components in a dynamic and interrelated way
    b. Paint a portrait of the child's environment and inner world
    c. Relate pathogenic processes (those that are hypothesized to have led to the
        problem) to the change processes that could be used to intervene

10. Treatment plan
11. Expected obstacles and impediments to treatment

Sources: Friedberg and McClure (2002); Kerig et al. (2012); Shirk and Russell (1996); Walsh (2003).

the inability to regulate and cope with emotional states. In the *interpersonal* realm, pathogenic processes for traumatized youth might include nonsupportive caregivers or stigma deriving from judgmental peers. Each of these "theories of the problem" might lead to a different intervention focus—in the aforementioned examples, respectively to a cognitively based, affect-regulation focused, or relational type of trauma therapy, each of which will be described in greater detail in Chapter 4.

Best Practices in Multimethod Assessment

As is true of diagnosis and case formulation in all child and adolescent disorders, best practices call for conducting multimethod assessments that integrate various sources of information, including youth, their caregivers, and other important observers such as teachers (Nader, 2008). However, in the case of PTSD, there are particularly challenging issues that arise when assessors attempt to integrate information from various sources.

Challenges in Obtaining and Interpreting Youth Reports

In addition to the limitations inherent from obtaining reports from children who are preverbal, as we have discussed in relation to developmental differences, in their younger years even verbal children may have difficulty identifying and describing their internal experiences. Yet, many of the symptoms of PTSD require access to such kinds of private information as thoughts, feelings, and intentions. For example, avoidance is a behavior that might be associated with many disorders—phobias, social anxiety, even oppositional defiant disorder—but its association with PTSD is predicated on the motivation to avoid people, places, and things that are reminiscent of a trauma. A child—especially but not only a young child—may not have the insight needed to make that connection and to report it accurately.

Based on Piaget's observations of the stages of cognitive development, Witkin (2005) suggests that, as a general rule, children younger than four years of age cannot be called upon as reliable reporters, given their limited language and abstract reasoning skills. In turn, children from four to seven years of age are able to provide reliable information regarding events and their timing if the questions and inferences expected are concrete and consistent with their developmental level. Next, in the age range of 8 to 12 years, children are able to provide information about more abstract constructs and can draw inferences, including describing their internal states and intentions, as long as questions are framed in ways that are developmentally appropriate. Finally, children aged 12 years and older with age-appropriate cognitive skills generally can provide reliable and accurate information. It must be noted, however, that these age ranges provide only a rough guide in that chronological age is not always consonant with developmental age—children may have cognitive and verbal skills that are either highly advanced or delayed in comparison to those expected at their age.

Challenges in Obtaining and Interpreting Caregiver Reports

Caregiver reports can be highly valuable in the assessment of child and adolescent PTSD. Parents, for example, may have knowledge about traumatic experiences that occurred in the very early years of life about which children themselves would be poor reporters. Even in the case of older children and adolescents who, unlike younger children, are able to introspect and describe their inner states and reflect upon their actions, caregivers' observations can flesh out and fill in gaps in the picture that are helpful in arriving at a correct diagnosis. In particular, caregivers' observations can be critical in linking shifts in youths' moods and behaviors to "triggers" that could implicate trauma. For example, caregivers (whether they are biological parents, foster parents, or institutional staff) may be able to detect patterns that warrant further enquiry, such as the youth who systematically reacts with extreme distress to being taken by surprise by physical contact—is this a youth for whom this is a reminder of a traumatic encounter?

However, one of the complicating factors in obtaining caregiver reports of children's PTSD symptoms is that, when the whole family has been affected by the event, such as in the case of a house fire or a natural disaster, trauma-exposed caregivers may themselves be experiencing disruptions in functioning that make it difficult for them to accurately observe or report on their children's behavior. Even when the parent is not causally involved or present during the traumatic event, such as if a child is hit by a car while walking home from school, research shows that trauma to a child can be traumatizing for his or her caregiver (Balluffi et al., 2004). The accuracy of a caregiver report is particularly challenging in the case of a disorder such as PTSD, whose symptoms involve not just observable behaviors but unobservable inner experiences, such as thoughts and feelings and efforts to avoid those thoughts and feelings. Some research suggests that a positive and supportive bond can increase parents' accuracy in reporting their sons' and daughters' posttraumatic reactions, perhaps because of the greater sharing and empathic connection that are fostered by a secure attachment (Holman et al., 2016). Nonetheless, as Cohen and Mannarino (2014) find in their extensive clinical experience, this is not the norm:

> However, most parents of traumatized children do not recognize or seek mental health treatment for their children's PTSD symptoms. Most typically, these parents seek mental health intervention for their children's concerning behavioral problems (e.g., irritability, anger, noncompliance) because these are the symptoms that parents or adults can most easily observe. In some cases, parents may be aware that their children experienced past trauma, but in other cases, they have no knowledge of the extent or impact of the child's trauma experiences. In either situation, parents are often surprised to receive referrals for trauma-focused treatment. (p. 438)

Thus, the diagnosis of PTSD carries with it particularly challenging issues related to differential diagnosis, given that trauma often is not even raised by referral sources as a potential issue of concern and thus is easily overlooked by the assessor who is not vigilant about it.

An even greater challenge in the case of PTSD is that sometimes it is the caregiver himself or herself who is the source of trauma. Maltreating parents may be motivated to underreport or to provide alternative explanations for children's problem behavior. For example, in one case, abusive parents were able to disguise their neglect and maltreatment of their son over the course of several years, successfully convincing teachers and pediatricians that the source of his behavior problems was attention-deficit hyperactivity disorder (ADHD) (Kerig, Sink et al., 2010).

Challenges in Obtaining and Interpreting Other Observers' Reports

Just as with parents, other adults involved in the life of a child, particularly teachers, can be valuable sources of information about the child's functioning in "real world" daily contexts. This is particularly useful for assessing Criterion F in the *Diagnostic and Statistical Manual of Mental Disorders*, 5th Edition (*DSM-5; APA, 2013*), which requires that the child's symptoms be significant enough to create distress or to interfere with functioning in important developmental contexts, such as school and peer relationships. Teachers and other school staff, such as playground monitors, bus drivers, and cafeteria workers, may be able to provide helpful observations about how the child is managing to meet age-relevant task demands in each of these contexts. However, again, these adults may not be in a position to make the necessary inferences about how and why the child's behavior is associated with trauma. The child who stares off into space because he or she is bored and inattentive is difficult for a teacher to discern from the child who is experiencing moments of traumatic intrusions; similarly, the child whose negativity with peers is borne of conduct disorder or delayed social skills is not easily discriminated from the one who is reacting on the basis of posttraumatic irritability.

Cultural and Ethnic Considerations
in PTSD Assessment

As Nader (2007) notes, cultural, religious, and ethnocentric beliefs and practices can affect a youth and his or her family's reactions to trauma exposure, expressions of posttraumatic reactions, and interpretations of PTSD symptoms. Thus, it is important for clinicians to be thoughtful about the ways in which culture might come to bear on the assessment of trauma exposure and PTSD. Highly recommended is preparatory work directed to understanding cultural preferences regarding hierarchies (requiring consideration regarding whom in the family should be approached first and respected as the "gatekeeper"), comfort with openness of expression with those outside the family (which may suggest the need to begin with indirect solicitations for information until rapport and trust are established), and concerns about stigma regarding mental health services (which might be addressed by reframing the assessment as a way of helping others in the present or the future). In addition, cultural and religious beliefs have profound implications for the interventions that will be consonant with family members' beliefs about acceptable ways of healing from trauma (Wilson, 2007).

As Lewis and Ippen (2004) add, there are multiple dimensions of cultural influences on children's and adolescents' responses to trauma. One is their own level of acculturation versus assimilation into mainstream society. In addition, at the family level, influences operate at the level of the culture of origin, which guides both the meaning made and the child's responses to a traumatic event, as well as the larger context of historical trauma, when a wound suffered by a child occurs against an intergenerational background of loss, oppression, and pain (e.g., cultural genocide). These authors differentiate between four kinds of trauma experienced by children: those based on an individual child's developmental status (e.g., abuse, neglect, exposure to interparental or community violence); those experienced as part of a cohort (e.g., natural disasters, terrorism, wars, forcible placement in residential schools); historical traumas experienced by members of their race, culture, or ethnicity (e.g., slavery, racism); and intergenerational legacies of ongoing hatreds and violence (e.g., the Irish "troubles," Arab–Israeli conflicts). In the light of these larger backdrops to the experience of trauma, the authors stress the importance of assessors understanding and inquiring about events that the individual family—as well as their cultural group—have undergone. To this end, the authors advise assessing the sociocultural context by asking four questions: (1) Where did the family come from? (e.g., country of origin, rural or urban background); (2) How did they get here? (e.g., was their migration voluntary or involuntary, stressful or traumatic, or joyous and celebratory?); (3) What is their environment like now? (e.g., do they have access to social support and the protective factors provided by opportunities to continue engaging in their culture's customs?); and (4) How do they view and cope with traumatic events they have experienced? (e.g., how does culture affect their views of the event and are there culturally prescribed methods for healing that can be brought to bear?).

Lewis and Ippen (2004) further point out the importance of assessors understanding culturally mediated beliefs regarding socialization goals, expectations for children at different developmental stages, behaviors that are acceptable or unacceptable, and traits that are promoted or seen as undesirable. Complications may arise particularly for bicultural youth, whose own preferences and aspirations may derive in part or whole from dominant and peer cultures and thus differ from those of their parents. Culture also plays an important role in family members' constructions of what is "traumatic," with some experiences (e.g., painful coming-of-age rituals) and methods of discipline (e.g., physical punishment) seen as culturally appropriate and normative. Language also presents another important consideration for youth of immigrant or refuge families. Not only may they be the "language brokers" of the family given their more well-developed English skills, but these may be children who are bilingual in a particular sense, with English being the language they use for talking about academics but the family's native language remaining the one used for speaking of feelings and their inner life.

Screening Versus Assessment

Screening for trauma exposure or posttraumatic stress symptoms can be differentiated from formal *assessment* on a number of dimensions (Kerig,

Ford, & Olafson, 2015). Screening is a brief process intended to identify youth who may be in need of a more thorough mental health evaluation. Because it does not involve establishing a diagnosis or determining whether services are needed, screening can be conducted by individuals with minimal training and can be carried out universally; for example, school staff could administer a trauma-screening measure to all children in a school who were affected by a peer's suicide. In contrast, assessment refers to a formal mental health evaluation whose purpose is to establish or rule out a diagnosis, and thus requires referral to a trained professional. Because of the time and expense involved, assessment is generally targeted to specific youth suspected to be in need rather than being applied universally to all children in a setting.

Screening for Trauma Exposure

Screening measures differ in terms of their purpose and target. One potential target is to determine whether or not a youth has been exposed to traumatic stress. Some screening measures take a comprehensive approach to documenting a youth's trauma history and inquire about a wide range of types of trauma exposure. For example, the University of California Los Angeles (UCLA) Trauma History Profile (Pynoos & Steinberg, 2014) documents whether a youth experienced each of the 18 different forms of trauma as well as the ages at which these events occurred. The resulting information can then be graphed in ways that show quite effectively the extent, onset, and secession of cumulative trauma. Similarly, the Structured Trauma Related Experiences and Symptoms Screener (STRESS; Grasso, Felton, & Reid-Quiñones, 2015) includes a list of 25 different types of potentially traumatic experiences, including child abuse, community violence, traumatic deaths, accidents, disasters, and illnesses. Many comprehensive measures also include adverse experiences that do not fit the *DSM-5* or *International Classification of Diseases, 11th Edition* (*ICD-11*) criteria for traumatic events; for example, the Traumatic Events Screening Inventory for Children (jford@uchc.edu) includes events such as homelessness, seeing a parent get arrested, or having a parent with substance abuse problems; similarly the Juvenile Victimization Questionnaire (Finkelhor et al., 2011) includes items inquiring about being a victim of theft or bullying. Clinicians conducting assessments on the basis of these screening tools will need to attend to whether the presence of trauma exposure has been established as per the diagnostic criteria.

In contrast to obtaining a comprehensive history of all forms of trauma the youth has undergone, a second approach to screening for trauma exposure is to simply establish its presence. For example, the Massachusetts Youth Screening Inventory (Grisso & Quinlan, 2005) is a screening measure designed specifically for youth entering juvenile justice settings and includes a Trauma Exposure subscale comprising five questions regarding whether the youth has undergone traumatic experiences both generally (e.g., "something very bad or terrifying") and specifically (e.g., "raped or in danger of getting raped"). However, establishing the presence of trauma exposure also can be accomplished with as little as one question. For example, the University of Minnesota's Traumatic Stress Screen for Children and Adolescents (TSSCA; Donisch, Bray, & Gewirtz, 2015) includes one question, to which the youth is asked to respond with "yes" or "no": "Have you ever experienced a bad or upsetting event?," which is followed by a space for the youth to describe that event or events. Similarly, the PTSD Screening Inventory (PSI; Kerig, 2012) asks a single question designed to capture "bad, scary, or violent" experiences that would qualify as traumatic stressors according to the diagnostic criteria but protects against violations of the youth's privacy and the possibility of vicarious trauma that might follow from having screening staff inquire as to the specific nature of those experiences.

No matter how comprehensive they are, a limitation of trauma history measures is that their sensitivity is limited by the accuracy and completeness of the list of traumatic experiences they inquire about. For example, sources of extreme stress that occur in specific contexts, such as refugee families undergoing adversities during forced migrations, or inner city youth hearing gunshots in their neighborhoods, are not routinely captured on these lists. In addition, the language used may limit youths' endorsement of screening items. For example, many girls and boys do not use the word "rape" to label unwanted sexual experiences, and children from maltreating families often do not recognize their parents' behavior as "abuse" (Kerig, Arnzen Moeddel, & Becker, 2011). Measures that use concrete language to describe specific behaviors (e.g., "Has an adult touched your private body parts?"; "Did a caregiver ever hit you with an object?") are more likely to obtain a reliable and valid response from youth.

Screening for Posttraumatic Stress Symptoms

A second target of trauma screening is to determine whether youth are showing evidence of symptoms that might be related to posttraumatic stress. Typically, screening measures for PTSD begin by establishing the presence of traumatic experiences before going on to inquire about posttraumatic reactions following from those events. For example, the most widely used and well-validated screening measure for child and adolescent PTSD is the UCLA PTSD-Reaction Index, which has recently been revised for the *DSM-5* (Pynoos & Steinberg, 2014). After presenting youth with a list of 13 potentially traumatic experiences and one open-ended "other" option, the PTSD-RI asks youth to identify whether in the past month they had experienced any of the 31 symptoms that are drawn directly from the *DSM-5* criteria, including the dissociative subtype. With this level of comprehensiveness, the measure allows the evaluator to determine whether the youth likely meets criteria for the PTSD diagnosis and in which symptom clusters he or she does or does not, which is an extensive amount of information to obtain with a screening instrument. There also is a parent-report version of the measure available to provide collateral information from caregivers.

Again, however, screening measures targeting PTSD symptoms vary widely in whether they are comprehensive or selective. For example, similar to the PTSD-RI, the STRESS includes questions about 21 different posttraumatic symptoms keyed to the *DSM-5* clusters, in addition to assessing whether these symptoms are interfering with the youth's functioning. In contrast, the TSSCA includes a list of only five PTSD symptoms, which inquire about intrusions, avoidance, numbing of positive emotions, and hypervigilance. In between these two extremes, the PSI selectively includes questions about 13 posttraumatic symptoms that have emerged as particularly salient in studies of traumatized youth. Different instruments will be most suitable for different contexts and purposes, with brevity and comprehensiveness each having potential virtues as well as potential limitations.

Diagnostic Interviews

Once a youth has been "screened in" and referred to a qualified mental health professional, diagnostic interviews are considered to be the "gold standard" for establishing the presence of PTSD. At the time of this writing, diagnostic instruments for children are going through an "awkward age," with revised versions keyed to the *DSM-5* criteria still undergoing construction or validation. Moreover, in some cases, child and adolescent diagnostic interviews have been the "neglected step-child" of the PTSD literature. For example, the most well-validated adult diagnostic measure, the Clinician Administered PTSD Scale (CAPS), was downwardly extended to a child and adolescent version for *DSM-IV* (CAPS-CA; Nader et al., 1998); that version did not undergo validation and thus there was no psychometric information nor norms made available; hopefully the version in progress for *DSM-5* will be more fully developed. Those diagnostic measures that exist or are in progress for the assessment of PTSD using *DSM-5* criteria are listed in detail in Table 3.1.

Questionnaire Measures

In addition to the measures designed explicitly for screening purposes already described, a number of other questionnaire measures have been developed, for both clinical and research contexts, in order to obtain youth and parent reports of posttraumatic symptoms. These are also described in Table 3.1. The table also identifies the purpose of each measure and whether its focus is on assessing trauma exposure versus posttraumatic stress reactions. In regard to the first purpose, measures also differ according to whether they are designed to assess comprehensive trauma histories, exposure to a specific form of traumatic stressor (e.g., child abuse or victimization), or whether their aim is simply to establish the presence of exposure to traumatic stress. Measures of trauma exposure also vary in how wide a net they cast in regard to events that strictly adhere to the *DSM* Criterion A versus inquiring about adverse experiences that do not meet formal definitions of "trauma." With regard to the second purpose, measures also range widely in how comprehensive they are in assessing the array of posttraumatic reactions as well as how closely they adhere to the *DSM* criteria for PTSD. Another important dimension along which these questionnaires differ is the availability of caregiver and youth report versions so as to allow the assessment of multiple perspectives.

Measures of Dissociation

Although the *DSM-5* diagnostic criteria for PTSD include a dissociative subtype, and consequently questions about dissociation are included in comprehensive screening measures and diagnostic assessments, the symptoms listed represent a narrow band of what has been described and measured in the dissociation literature more broadly (Putnam, 1997, 2006). Thus, a clinician concerned that a youth's functioning is being affected by dissociative phenomena may wish to employ a measure that assesses the construct in a more broadband way than the presence of depersonalization and derealization alone. The Adolescent and Child versions of the Dissociative Experiences Scale (Armstrong et al., 1997; Putnam & Peterson, 1994) provide one such tool. Validation studies indicate that the measure captures three dimensions of dissociation: depersonalization/derealization (e.g., feeling as though one is in a "fog" or things are unreal), amnesia (e.g., going someplace and not remembering how one got there), and loss of conscious control (e.g., catching oneself "waking up" in the middle of doing something) (Kerig, Charak, et al., 2016; Yoshizumi et al., 2010).

Measures of Other Trauma-Related Symptoms and Processes

PTSD is only one of the disorders that can follow from exposure to traumatic stress and adversity; trauma in childhood has been described as a "gateway" to the development of a range of disorders, either in addition to or aside from PTSD (Kenardy, De Young, and Charlton, 2012). For example, in a sample of trauma-exposed youth in detention, Ford et al. (2008) found that only 19 percent met criteria for PTSD; instead, substance abuse and suicidal ideation were the more prominent concerns. Even when criteria for PTSD are met, a youth's functioning—and response to treatment—may be affected by other co-occurring disorders.

Therefore, a comprehensive assessment will cast a wide net that goes well beyond PTSD-specific symptoms. These particularly include measures of depression, anxiety, and suicidality.

Underlying Processes Related to Trauma and Psychopathology

Consistent with the developmental psychopathology perspectives' focus on underlying dimensions of development that are disrupted by trauma, another recent contribution to our thinking about assessment is suggested by the National Institute of Mental Health's Research Domain Criteria (RDoC) initiative (Insel et al., 2010). Rather than thinking in terms of discrete diagnostic categories, the RDoC criteria point researchers and clinicians toward identifying transdiagnostic domains of biological and psychological functioning that are related to psychopathology (Franklin et al., 2014).

In the context of traumatic stress, a number of such dimensions have been identified by theory and research that consider the underlying mechanisms that link trauma exposure to distress and problem behavior in children and adolescents (Kerig & Becker, 2010). Foremost among these are disruptions in biological, emotional, cognitive, and behavioral self-regulatory processes (Ford, 2009). In this regard, psychophysiological measures of parasympathetic and sympathetic nervous symptom functioning (i.e., respiratory sinus arrhythmia and electrodermal response) and the coordination of these two systems (Berntson et al., 1994; El-Sheikh et al., 2009; Kerig, in press), as well as questionnaire measures of dysregulation such as the *Abbreviated Dysregulation Inventory* (Cruz-Katz, Cruise, & Quinn, 2010) can shed light on youths' posttraumatic reactions and also can guide assessment, case conceptualization, and treatment planning (Aldao & De Los Reyes, 2015). In turn, cognitive models of trauma point to the important role of fundamentally altered appraisals about the self, other people, and the future; measures of traumagenic beliefs, such as the *Child Post-Traumatic Cognitions Inventory* (Meiser-Stedman et al., 2009), as well as measures of trauma-related stigma and alienation (Feiring, Miller-Johnson, & Cleland, 2007) can be valuable in this regard. Particularly, for adolescents, measures that probe for posttraumatic symptoms of hopelessness and futurelessness, such as the *Hopelessness Scale for*

Children (Kazdin, Rodgers, & Colbus, 1986) as well as risky behavior, such as Pat-Horenczyk and colleagues' (2007) *Risk Taking Behavior Questionnaire*, can allow assessors to uncover and address potentially dangerous behaviors. In turn, disruptions in youths' internal working models of self and other, which have significant consequences for their capacity to engage in positive and mutual close personal relationship, are worth assessing, such as with the *Comprehensive Adolescent-Parent Attachment Inventory* (Moretti, McKay, & Holland, 2000). Finally, as we noted in the section of this chapter on posttraumatic growth, measures such as the *Posttraumatic Growth Inventory for Children-Revised* (Cryder et al., 2006) can be used to assess positive changes in the aftermath of trauma exposure.

In addition to the instruments described in Table 3.2, other reviews of measures assessing PTSD and related disorders and processes in children and adolescents can be found in Beidas et al. (2015); Ford (2011); Nader (2008); Strand, Sarmiento, and Pasquale (2005) and online at the following websites:

- National Child Traumatic Stress Network: http://www.nctsn. org/resources/online-research/measures-review
- Veteran Affairs PTSD Resource for Child Trauma Measures: http://www.ptsd.va.gov/professional/assessment/child/index. asp
- International Society for Traumatic Stress Studies: http:// www.istss.org/assessing-trauma.aspx
- National Youth Screening and Assessment Partners: www. nysap.us/Review%20of%20Trauma%20Screening%20 Tools%20for%20Children%20&%20Adolescents.pdf

Differential Diagnosis of PTSD and Other Disorders of Childhood

The definitions of PTSD in both the *DSM* and *ICD* diagnostic systems include symptoms that are seen in other childhood disorders that can be particularly challenging to distinguish from one another. Therefore, differential diagnosis is essential to directing youth and parents to the

Table 3.2 *Measures for the assessment of trauma history, trauma exposure, and PTSD in children and adolescents*

Name	Format	Length	Age range (years)	Reporter(s)	Construct(s) and subscales measured	Psychometric properties
History of exposure to trauma (and other adversities)						
Traumatic Events Screening Inventory-Children (TESI-C; National Center for PTSD, 2011); ncptsd@ncptsd.org	Questionnaire or Interview	24 items	6–18 for youth; 0–18 for parent report	Youth or caregiver	Number of lifetime trauma types Scales: Total Trauma Victimization Nonvictimization	Interrater reliability: kappa = .73 to 1.00; Test–retest reliability: r = .50 to .70 over 2–4 months
Childhood Trauma Questionnaire (CTQ; (Bernstein & Fink 1998); http://www.pearsonassessments.com	Questionnaire	28 items	12 to adult	Youth	Level of lifetime maltreatment (none to severe) Scales: Emotional Physical Sexual abuse Emotional neglect Physical neglect	Internal consistency: a = .66 to .95; Test–retest reliability: r = .79 to .86; Construct validity: Clinical samples score higher (Bernstein & Fink, 1998)
Juvenile Victimization Questionnaire, Screener Sum Version (JVQ; Finkelhor et al., 2011); www.unh.edu/ccrc/jvq/index.html	Questionnaire or interview	34 items	8–17	Youth or caregiver	Number of types of victimization experienced Scales: Total Score Conventional Crime Maltreatment Peer/Sibling Victimization Sexual Victimization Witnessing Violence/Indirect Victimization	Internal consistency: .80; Test–retest reliability: r = .63 (Cuevas et al., 2007; Finkelhor, Hamby et al., 2005)

Adverse Childhood Experiences (ACES); http://acestudy.org/ ace_score	Questionnaire	10 items	0–19 for parent report, 13–19 for youth report	Youth	Number of types of childhood adversity experienced Scales: Total Score	Test–retest reliability: r = .46 to .86 (Dube et al., 2004)
Trauma History Profile (Pynoos & Steinberg, 2014); asteinberg@mednet.ucla.edu	Paper and pencil questionnaire	18 items	6–18	Clinician rating based on interviews, case records	Number of types of trauma and ages at which they occurred	Psychometric data not yet available
Trauma history and PTSD symptoms						
UCLA PTSD-Reaction Index for DSM-5 (UCLA-PTD-RI; Pynoos & Steinberg, 2013); asteinberg@mednet.ucla.edu	Paper and pencil questionnaire	46 items	6–18	Youth, caregiver, or clinician	Trauma exposure and PTSD symptoms as per DSM-5 Scales: DSM-5 criteria met overall DSM-5 criteria on individual clusters Total symptom severity Symptom severity in each cluster	Psychometric data not yet available for DSM-5 version For DSM-IV version: Internal consistency: a = .88 to .91 (Steinberg et al., 2013); Test–retest reliability: r = .84 (Roussos et al., 2005); Convergent validity: .82 w/ Child and Adolescent Version of the CAPS
Child Welfare Trauma Referral Tool	Paper and pencil questionnaire	56 items	1–20	Youth, caregiver	Trauma exposure and PTSD symptom assessment tool to determine if referral warranted Scales: Trauma exposure/reminders	Psychometric data not available

(Continued)

Table 3.2 Measures for the assessment of trauma history, trauma exposure, and PTSD in children and adolescents (Continued)

Name	Format	Length	Age range (years)	Reporter(s)	Construct(s) and subscales measured	Psychometric properties
Child Welfare Trauma Referral Tool—*Continued*					Traumatic stress Externalizing symptoms Relationships/attachment	
Structured Trauma-Related Experiences and Symptoms Screener (STRESS; Grasso, Felton, & Reid-Quiñoines, 2015); dgrasso.uchc.edu	Computer-administered or paper and pencil questionnaire	22	7–17	Youth	Trauma exposure and PTSD symptoms based on *DSM-5* Scales: Adverse Experiences and Trauma History (types and total) *DSM-5* Symptoms (total in each cluster) Dissociative Symptoms Functional Impairment	Internal consistency: α = .92 (Grasso, Felton, & Reid-Quiñones, 2015)
NCTSN CANS Comprehensive- Trauma Version (National Child Traumatic Stress Network Child and Adolescents Needs and Strengths) Trauma Exposure and Symptoms Domains (http://cctasp.northwestern.edu/pdfs/CANS-Trauma-Comprehensive-Manual-3-22-13.pdf)	Clinician semi-structured interview	22 items	0–18	Youth, clinician, chart review	Lifetime Trauma Exposure/Reminders Traumatic Stress Traumatic Grief/Loss	Internal consistency (= .78) (Kisiel et al., 2011)

					Trauma History and History of Treatment Services	Convergent/concurrent validity, discriminant validity, and sensitivity to change described by authors
CANS Trauma Module; http://www.ctbhp.com/providers/rescareteam/CANS_MANUAL.pdf	Paper and pencil questionnaire	12 items	0–18	Youth, clinician		
Trauma Exposure Only						
Structured Clinical Interview for DSM-5 PTSD Trauma Screen www.appi.org/File%20Library/Products/AH1522-Comparison-SCID-RV-vs-CV.pdf	Semi-structured interview, or questionnaire	1 item	All	Youth	Single question assessing exposure to Criterion A stressor	Sensitivity: 75.6 percent (patients) and 65.5 percent (students); Specificity: 67.4 percent (patients) and 87.2 percent (students) (Elhai, Franklin, & Gray, 2008)
Massachusetts Youth Screening Inventory Trauma Exposure scale (MAYSI-TE; Grisso & Barnum, 2003); http://www.nysap.us/MAYSI2.html	Computer-administered or paper and pencil questionnaire	5 items	12–17	Youth	Trauma exposure (One question does involve PTSD symptoms]	Modest correlations (r = .20) with total PTSD symptoms on the UCLA PTSD-RI; Moderately accurate correspondence with diagnosis (AUC = .75, .76); Cut-off score of 3 has sensitivity = 62 and specificity = .25 (Kerig, Arnzen Moeddel, & Becker, 2011)
Exposure to Community Violence (SCECV; Richters & Saltzmann, 1990)	Paper and pencil	18 items	6 to adult	Youth	Exposure to violence	Internal consistency: α = 0.87 (Ceballo et al., 2001); Test–retest reliability: κ = .97 (Thomson et al., 2002)

(Continued)

Table 3.2 Measures for the assessment of trauma history, trauma exposure, and PTSD in children and adolescents (Continued)

Name	Format	Length	Age range (years)	Reporter(s)	Construct(s) and subscales measured	Psychometric properties
PTSD symptoms only						
Pediatric Emotional Distress Scale (PEDS; Saylor et al., 1999); conway.saylor@citadel.edu	Questionnaire	21 items	2–10	Caregiver	Emotional distress following trauma exposure Scales: Anxious/Withdrawn Fearful Acting Out	Internal consistency (α = .72 to .85); Test–retest reliability: 6–8 weeks (r = .55 to .61) Concurrent validity with the Eyberg Child Behavior Inventory (Eyberg, Boggs, & Reynolds, 1980) Discriminant validity discriminating trauma- and non-trauma-exposed children
Child PTSD Symptom Scale (CPSS; Foa et al., 2001); foa@mail.med.upenn.edu	Questionnaire	24 items	8–18	Youth or clinician report	Frequency of past-month symptoms as per DSM-IV Scales: Total Symptoms Functional Impairment (DSM-5 version in progress)	Internal consistency: α = .89; Test–retest reliability 1–2 weeks (r = .63 to .85); Convergent validity with Child PTSD–RI (Foa et al., 2001); Confirmatory factor analyses show construct validity for English version (Meyer et al., 2015)
Trauma Symptom Checklist for Young Children (TSCYC; (Briere, Weathers, & Runtz, 2005); www.parinc.com	Questionnaire	90 items	3–12	Caregiver	Assessment of posttraumatic stress symptoms Subscales: PTS-Intrusion	Internal consistency: α = .87; Test–retest reliability: r = .79;

Instrument	Format	Length	Age	Age	Scales / Description	Psychometrics
Trauma Symptom Checklist for Young Children (TSCYC; (Briere, Weathers, & Runtz, 2005); www.parinc.com—*Continued*					PTS-Avoidance PTS-Arousal PTS-Total Sexual Concerns Dissociation Anxiety Depression Anger/Aggression	Convergent/concurrent validity with Child Behavior Checklist and Trauma Symptom Checklist for Children
Trauma Symptom Checklist for Children (TSCC; Briere, 1996); http://www4.parinc.com/Products/Product.aspx?ProductID=TSCC	Paper and pencil questionnaire	54 items/44 items	8–16	Youth	Posttraumatic stress, symptoms, and other behavior problems over the life span Scales: Validity (Under- and Hyper-response) Anxiety Depression Anger PTSD symptoms Dissociation Sexual Concerns	Internal consistency: α = .85 to .87 (Hawkins & Radcliffe, 2006)
Triggers and Coping Strategies (Kerig, 2004)	Pictorially based interview or self-report form	4 pages	School-age to adult	Youth	Screener to assess posttraumatic reactions, trauma triggers, and coping strategies	Clinical tool designed to identify a youth's trauma triggers, signs of being triggered (posttraumatic reactions), and effective coping strategies
Screening Tool for Trauma and Symptomatic Behaviors (Benamati, 2015); drjoebenamati@gmail.com	Questionnaire	15 items	School-age to adult	Youth	Screening tool for PTSD Scales: Total PTSD Symptoms (14)	Psychometric data not available

(Continued)

Table 3.2 Measures for the assessment of trauma history, trauma exposure, and PTSD in children and adolescents (Continued)

Name	Format	Length	Age range (years)	Reporter(s)	Construct(s) and subscales measured	Psychometric properties
Screening Tool for Trauma and Symptomatic Behaviors (Benamati, 2015); drjoebenamati@gmail.com—Continued					Reexperiencing (2) Avoidance (3) Arousal (4) Alterations in cog/mood (5) Current danger (1)	
Trauma exposure and PTSD symptoms						
Primary Care PTSD Screen for DSM-5 (PC-PTSD; Prins et al., 2016)	Interview	6 items	All ages	Youth	Screening for trauma exposure (1 item) and select DSM-5 PTSD symptoms from each cluster (5 items)	Good diagnostic accuracy when compared to the MINI (AUC = 0.941); Sensitivity = .93; Specificity = .70
University of Minnesota Traumatic Stress Screen for Children and Adolescents (Donisch et al., 2015)	Questionnaire or Interview	5 items	3–18	Youth	Brief screening measure to assess trauma exposure (1 item) and select PTSD symptoms	Correspondence with UCLA PTSD-RI Sensitivity = .90; specificity = .70 (Donisch, Bray, & Gewirtz, 2015)
PTSD Screening Inventory (PSI; Kerig, 2012)	Computer-administered/self-scoring or paper and pencil questionnaire	15 items	School-age to adult	Youth	Brief screening measure Scales: Trauma Exposure (one item) Symptoms consistent with DSM-5 PTSD Immediate danger	In progress

Diagnostic instruments: DSM-5 criteria					
Mini International Neuropsychiatric Interview for Children and Adolescents (MINI-Kid); http://medical-outcomes.com/index/mini7fororganizations	Diagnostic interview		6–17 for parent report; 13–17 for youth report	Parent (if youth under age 13 years) or youth	PTSD diagnosis (DSM-5)	Psychometric data not yet available for DSM-5 version DSM-IV version: Sensitivity = .61 to 1.00 Specificity = .73 to 1.00 Interrater reliability = .64 to 1.00 (Sheehan et al., 2010)
Clinician Administered PTSD Scale for Children and Adolescents for DSM-5 (CAPS-CA-5; Pynoos et al., 2015); http://www.ptsd.va.gov/professional/assessment/child/caps-ca.asp	Structured clinical interview	30 items	7–18	Youth	DSM-5 PTSD diagnosis Symptom levels on each cluster	Psychometric data not available for DSM-5 version Psychometric properties for DSM-IV version: Internal consistency: α = .75 to .81; Interrater reliability = .80 (Erwin et al., 2000)
Structured Clinical Interview for DSM-5 PTSD trauma screen–Research Version, Module L : Trauma and stressor-related disorders (SCID-5); www.appi.org/File%20Library/Products/AH1522-Comparison-SCID-RV-vs-CV.pdf	Semi-structured interview or questionnaire	Not available	All	Youth	DSM-5 PTSD diagnosis Subscales: Acute Stress Disorder PTSD Adjustment Disorder Other Trauma/Stressor Related Disorder	Psychometric data not yet available for DSM-5 version Psychometric properties for DSM-IV version: Sensitivity = .66 to .76 Specificity = .67 to .87 Interrater reliability = .77 (Elhai, Franklin, & Gray, 2008; Lobbestael, Leurgans, & Arntz, 2011)

(Continued)

Table 3.2 Measures for the assessment of trauma history, trauma exposure, and PTSD in children and adolescents (Continued)

Name	Format	Length	Age range (years)	Reporter(s)	Construct(s) and subscales measured	Psychometric properties
Kiddie-SADS PTSD screen and Trauma-Related Disorders Supplement, DSM-5 version (K-SADS-PL); https://www.kennedykrieger.org/patient-care/faculty-staff/joan-kaufman	Semi-structured interview	23 items (includes both primary screen and supplemental module)	6-18	Parent, youth	DSM-5 diagnosis Subscales PTSD (lifetime) Acute Stress Disorder (lifetime)	Psychometric data not yet available for DSM-5 version Psychometric Properties for DSM-IV version: Interrater reliability = .98 Test–retest reliability for PTSD = .67 for present diagnoses and .60 for lifetime diagnoses; (Kaufman et al., 1997)
Anxiety Disorders Interview Schedule Child/Parent Version (ADIS-C/P; Albano et al., in press)						Not yet available

Complex PTSD/developmental trauma disorder					
Structured Interview for Disorders of Extreme Stress-Adolescent (SIDES-A; (Pelcovitz et al., 2004)	Semi-structured clinical Interview	45 items	12–18	Youth	Criteria for disorders of extreme stress NOS proposed diagnosis Subscales: Affect Dysregulation, Somatization, Attention/Consciousness, Self-Perception, Relations With Others, Systems of Meaning	Psychometric data not yet available for adolescent version For adult version: Interrater reliability = .81; internal consistency: α = .53 to .96 (Pelcovitz et al., 1997)
Developmental Trauma Disorder-Structured Interview (DTD-SI; Ford et al., 2011)	Semi-structured Interview	15 items	All	Youth	Developmental trauma disorder proposed diagnosis Subscales: Emotional Dysregulation, Behavioral Dysregulation, Self/Relational Dysregulation	Interrater reliability established; 3-factor structure confirmed; internal consistency: α = .61 to .72; Construct validity established through relations with theoretically relevant types of trauma exposure and parent ratings of dysregulation (Ford et al., 2014)

most helpful interventions. Although two or more disorders may genuinely co-occur, and a correct diagnosis involve "all the aforementioned," the dangers to confusing PTSD with another disorder include not only inappropriate treatments but, in the case of unrecognized PTSD, the possibility that we might fail to rescue a child from a toxic situation. Some research also suggests that a preexisting or comorbid diagnosis is a risk factor that increases the vulnerability of a child to the development or exacerbation of PTSD (Pappagallo, Silva, & Rojas, 2004) and so other disorders are important to consider in case formulation and treatment planning with a trauma-exposed youth, ideally with the goal of integrating interventions for any comorbid disorders (Cohen, 2010).

PTSD Versus Childhood Anxiety Disorders

As the *DSM-5* notes, there are symptoms of PTSD that have potential overlap with childhood disorders in the anxiety spectrum. However, in general, what most clearly differentiates the anxiety disorders from PTSD is that, in addition to lacking the other symptoms of PTSD, they are not related to a specific traumatic event. For example, *obsessive compulsive disorder* involves intrusive thoughts (Criterion B in *DSM-5*, reexperiencing in *ICD-11*), albeit not regarding a specific traumatic event, and *separation anxiety disorder* can produce hypervigilance (Criterion E in *DSM-5*, threat perceptions in *ICD-11*), although this is specific to threats of separation. In turn, *phobias* involved avoidance of a feared stimulus (Criterion D in *DSM-5*, avoidance in *ICD-11*) but are not accompanied by intrusions or arousal (Pappagallo, Silva, & Rojas, 2004). Furthermore, among older children and adolescents who are able to introspect and report about their reasons for wanting to avoid certain places, people, or things, a clinician should suspect PTSD instead of phobia when the rationale is related to a traumatic theme (Schillaci et al., 2009); for example, one boy expressed fear of going to school because the sound of the bell was reminiscent of the fire alarm he heard the night his house burned down.

PTSD Versus Mood Disorders in Childhood

Depression may involve symptoms related to negative cognitions and mood (Criterion D in *DSM-5*, negative feelings about the self in *ICD-11*'s definition of Complex PTSD), including guilt and self-recrimination, lack of interest in previously enjoyed activities, detachment from others, and constricted emotions. Similarly, depression may involve symptoms associated with *DSM-5*'s Criterion E, such as poor concentration, irritability, and sleep disturbance, especially among adolescents (Gerson & Rappaport, 2012). But again, these occur not in relation to a specific traumatic event and without the accompaniment of other key symptoms of PTSD, such as intrusions. Unfortunately, however, in the *DSM-5* revisions to the diagnosis, another change was made that muddies the waters a bit in regard to the differential diagnosis of PTSD and depression. In previous versions of the *DSM*, the PTSD symptom of emotional numbing was described broadly as difficulty accessing a range of emotions. In the DSM-5 criteria, however, the symptom was restricted to the inability to experience *positive* emotions, which sounds a lot like depression. In a study of trauma-exposed adolescents in detention, my students and I looked into this issue by assessing the correspondence among PTSD symptoms, depression, and youths' ratings on a scale that measured a range of forms of emotional numbing, including the numbing of general, fearful, angry, sad, and positive emotions. Our findings showed that only numbing of general emotions and anger were related to PTSD; as we suspected, numbing of positive emotions was related only to depression, not PTSD, as was numbing of sadness (Kerig et al., 2016).

Another mood disturbance that children frequently have received on their journey to a correct diagnosis, especially those with symptoms of C-PTSD or developmental trauma disorder, is *bipolar disorder* (van der Kolk et al., 2009). Hyperarousal and risky behaviors in particular might be mistaken for signs of juvenile mania (Cohen et al., 2010). Affect dysregulation is a common dimension underlying both bipolar and trauma-related disorders, which can result in similar-appearing symptoms, particularly in the realms of impulsivity, reactivity, and emotion dyregulation. However, as van der Kolk and colleagues (2009) point out, the dysregulated affect in PTSD, C-PTSD, and DTD does not include states of mania but rather is characterized by pervasively negative or suppressed emotion. Furthermore, behaviors indicative of impulsivity have unique features in PTSD, C-PTSD, and DTD that are not seen in bipolar disorder, including the functions that serve as a source of maladaptive self-soothing (e.g., deliberate self-harm) and risk-seeking (e.g., intentionally defying death).

In addition, the components of self and relational dysregulation seen in C-PTSD and DTD, such as self-loathing, impaired trust, and lack of reciprocity, are not inherent in bipolar disorder. Finally, differentiating the two is the fact that the onset of the mood disturbance in PTSD is abrupt and is tied specifically to a traumatic event (Miller, 2015).

Psychotic Disorders

Acutely distressed youth in the aftermath of trauma may display disorganized behaviors, in addition to hypervigilance, intrusions, sleep disturbances, and social withdrawal, which may be mistaken for the onset of a psychotic episode (Cohen, 2010). Young children may report unusual sensory experiences, perceptions, and fantasized ideas that need to be differentiated from psychotic delusions or hallucinations. The dissociative subtype in particular requires careful evaluation in this regard. However, research also suggests that trauma exposure may be associated not only with symptoms that are in danger of being mistaken for psychosis but, particularly among youth with a genetic vulnerability, may actually be associated with the development of genuine psychotic thought disorder, loose associations, and hallucinations (Varese et al., 2012).

Physical Illness

Many youth with PTSD also suffer from physical illnesses, including muscle aches, headaches, stomachaches, and gastrointestinal distress (Afari et al., 2014; McCall-Hosenfeld et al., 2014). There are a number of pathways leading to these negative health outcomes. For some children and adolescents, somatic complaints are a way of expressing emotional distress, one that is particularly appropriate to certain cultures. It also is the case that exposure to trauma, particularly chronic trauma, negatively affects the functioning of the immune system and thus leads to not only somatic complaints but also actual somatic dysfunctions (Cohen, 2010). Third, exposure to adverse childhood experiences is associated with engagement in health-risking behaviors, including substance use, disrupted eating, and poor-quality sleep, which in turn lead to negative physical outcomes (Anda et al., 2006).

PTSD Versus Attention Deficit Hyperactivity Disorder (ADHD)

Interestingly, although *DSM-5* includes a discussion of differential diagnosis with many other disorders, the manual is silent regarding a challenge that has been of major concern in the clinical child and adolescent psychology and psychiatry literature, and that is differentiating between PTSD and *ADHD*. To take an extreme example, one study found that 54 percent of sexually abused children also met criteria for a diagnosis of ADHD (McLeer et al., 1994)—the question is, do these two disorders actually co-occur so frequently, or are the symptoms of the one being confused with the other? Other studies evidence far lower levels of comorbidity but do find that symptom overlap—particularly regarding physical and psychological reactivity—can lead to misdiagnosis between the two disorders (Ford & Connor, 2009).

On the side supporting comorbidity, Biederman and colleagues (2013) found that the prevalence of PTSD was higher among a sample of youth with ADHD than in a sample of healthy controls (5.2 percent versus 1.7 percent). Furthermore, those with the dual diagnosis were significantly more likely to evidence serious functional impairments, including psychiatric hospitalizations, school failures, poor social functioning, and other disorders. The investigators also found a high correspondence among siblings regarding the presence of ADHD, whether or not the target child also exhibited PTSD, suggesting that the comorbidity was genuine. Given that ADHD shows a strong familial heritability, the investigators point out that, had symptoms of PTSD merely been mistaken for ADHD in the dually diagnosed youth, they would not have expected to find elevated levels of ADHD in the siblings of youth so erroneously diagnosed. Furthermore, the onset of PTSD was significantly later than the onset of ADHD, suggesting the possibility that ADHD is a risk factor for the development of PTSD. Clinical observations of the impulsive and careless behavior of youth with ADHD (e.g., the child who dashes into traffic on a busy street without first looking to see whether it is safe) do suggest the potential for the disorder to increase the risk for encountering traumatic events.

On the other hand, Weinstein and colleagues (2000) express concern about the potential confusion of the two disorders, and note that symptoms of arousal in PTSD may take the form of sleeplessness, irritability, poor concentration, and being distracted by intrusive thoughts, all of which also are indicators of inattention in youth with ADHD. Similarly, PTSD symptoms of irritability and physiological and psychological reactivity upon exposure to trauma cues could be construed as signs of hyperactivity in ADHD. The American Association of Child and Adolescent Psychiatry (AACAP) Practice Parameters for PTSD (Cohen et al., 2010) similarly point out that PTSD-related restless, overactive, disorganized, and agitated behavior, as well as poor concentration and difficulty sleeping, can be mistaken for symptoms of ADHD. The consequences of an erroneous diagnosis are serious, in that inappropriate interventions might be applied, particularly given the common use of stimulant medication to treat youth with ADHD. Further contributing to the problem is that children often are diagnosed with ADHD on the basis of brief behavioral checklists or visits to the pediatrician that do not involve a careful rule out of exposure to posttraumatic stress. As Weinstein and colleagues state: "An ADHD assessment that does not obtain information about trauma history cannot provide clinicians with the information they need to make accurate differential diagnosis" (p. 374).

In order to clarify this question, best practices call for the implementation of comprehensive assessment procedures, including reports from multiple sources, including the parent, teachers, the child himself/herself; as well as observation of the child in real-world settings (e.g., in the classroom, on the playground, or in the clinician's office) and laboratory tasks that measure sustained attention and impulsivity in objective ways (American Academy of Pediatrics, 2000). Paramount among the assessments are measures or interviews that inquire directly about exposure to trauma. In addition, Weinstein and colleagues (2000) propose a set of strategies for assessing whether a child's apparent inattention or hyperactivity comprises reactions to any such trauma exposure. As a general rule, a differentiating factor is that attention problems in ADHD are pervasive to situations in which low stimulation is present (e.g., when a child feels bored such as in the schoolroom, while doing homework, and during religious services), whereas PTSD-related attention problems are specific to moments of intrusions or perceived threat in relation to a traumatic stressor (van der Kolk et al., 2009). In order to ascertain this distinction,

Weinstein and colleagues suggest that clinicians probe children's thoughts and feelings about their symptoms in order to better differentiate whether they arise from PTSD or ADHD. For example, an inattentive child might be asked if these difficulties paying attention "occur at certain times of the day or night, or with particular people, or in specific places" or are "related to particular people, places, or memories" (p. 374), which might show that they are associated with posttraumatic intrusions. Simply asking a child what thoughts are going through his or her mind while he or she is having trouble sitting still might uncover whether these include distressing thoughts or recollections, just as questions about the feelings a child has at those times can uncover whether inattention is related to posttraumatic avoidance. Similarly, asking children how they feel in their bodies when they are engaged in "jumpy" or overactive behaviors can help us to differentiate posttraumatic distress-related physiological arousal from symptoms of hyperactivity. By the same token, parents can be valuable sources of information regarding contextual factors and whether children's symptoms occur in response to particular environmental characteristics or times of day—homework time versus bedtime, for example—and can provide useful observations about whether a child's affect includes emotional expressions of distress, fear, or anxiety during these episodes.

PTSD Versus Disruptive Behavior Disorders

As is noted in the AACAP practice parameters (Cohen, 2010), angry outbursts and irritability are common among children exposed to trauma, especially those under chronic threat, and are easily mistaken for symptoms of oppositional defiant disorder. Moreover, as we know, some of the newest symptoms added to the *DSM-5* criteria for PTSD were informed by clinical observations of youth who, in the aftermath of trauma, display symptoms involving acting-out behavior such as irritability, aggression, and entering into risky situations (Pynoos et al., 2009), which overlap with the diagnosis of conduct disorder. Fueled by research evidencing the highly disproportionate prevalence of trauma exposure and posttraumatic stress symptoms in the juvenile justice population (e.g., Abram et al., 2004), a large literature has sprung up examining the ways in which unrecognized and untreated PTSD might masquerade as, or even develop into, disruptive behavior disorders (see Kerig & Becker, 2010, 2012, 2015 for reviews). On the one hand, trauma-related disruptions in biological, emotional, cognitive, and interpersonal functioning may lead to a pattern of problem behaviors that are in keeping with oppositional defiant or conduct disorder (Ford, 2002). For example, among detained youth, those with PTSD are also those most likely to also show aggression, poor impulse control, and negative affectivity (Cauffman et al., 1998, Steiner, Garcia, & Matthews, 1997), and this is particularly true of youth with complex trauma (Ford, Chapman et al., 2012). Moreover, PTSD symptoms have been shown to mediate the association between trauma exposure and aggression and other conduct problems (Allwood & Bell, 2008; Bennett et al., 2014; Kerig et al., 2009; Kerig, Vanderzee, et al., 2013; Kerig et al., 2012). Thus, trauma may act as a gateway to disruptive behavior disorders.

On the other hand, similarities in the observed symptoms might contribute to one disorder being misinterpreted as the other. Lipschitz, Morgan, and Southwick, (2002) point to the phenomenological overlap in symptoms between PTSD and the *DSM* definitions of disruptive behavior disorders. For example, hyperarousal may involve bouts of irritability, aggression, and rage, which are difficult to distinguish from the oppositional defiance symptoms of "temper tantrums" and "constant arguing," as well as the conduct disorder symptoms of "bullying and threatening" or "recurrent physical fights." By the same token, posttraumatic emotional numbness and a sense of foreshortened future may give the appearance of callousness toward others, impulsive acting out, and a lack of concern for consequences, all of which map onto the conduct disorder diagnostic criterion of "persistent disregard of rules or rights of others." Similarly, Pappagallo, Silva, and Rojas (2004) point out that childhood manifestations of reexperiencing may be perceived as dysregulated behavior, avoidance may look like oppositionality, and hyperarousal may take the form of irritability, all of which could mislead an assessor into diagnosing a disruptive behavior disorder.

Risky Behavior. Another way in which PTSD may be linked to conduct problems and involvement in the juvenile justice system is through risky behavior, which, as we have seen, is one of the newest additions to the DSM-5 Cluster E symptoms. Many youth who end up in the justice system, or whose parents seek treatment for "incorrigible" behavior, do not engage in acts that are overtly harmful to others, but rather acts that incur harm to themselves: examples include reckless driving, promiscuity, drug abuse, and running away from home, as well nonsuicidal self-injury and actual suicide attempts. Although trauma exposure and PTSD are associated with increased risk for these behaviors in adolescents generally (Pat-Horenczyk et al., 2007), some studies indicate that the risks are even more acute for girls, especially those who have been sexually abused or traumatized within the family system (Chaplo et al., 2015; Kerig & Schindler, 2013). The developmental significance of the emergence of risky behavior in adolescence as well as its potential functions within the trauma response system were discussed in Chapter 2.

Substance Abuse. It is also notable that one particular risky behavior, adolescent substance abuse, is heavily implicated in youth conduct problems and justice involvement as well as having strong associations with trauma exposure and PTSD. For example, large-scale studies find that childhood physical or emotional abuse increase the likelihood of early-onset alcohol abuse by more than 12-fold (Lansford et al., 2010; Southwick Bensley et al., 1999) and that the association between trauma exposure and substance abuse is especially strong for girls (Andersen & Teicher, 2009). It should be noted, however, that substance use and abuse may not only be a matter of posttraumatic risk-taking; they also might involve a form of self-medication (Bujarski et al., 2012). This too is especially the case for girls; while boys attribute substance use to thrill-seeking, girls are more likely to report using drugs to help them cope with trauma and distressing emotions (National Center on Addiction and Substance Abuse, 2003). Girls also evidence more serious physical ill effects from substance abuse and fall more rapidly into addition than do boys; therefore, especially but not only for girls, there is a genuine danger of the development of a bona fide substance use disorder, which comprises yet another differential diagnosis of concern.

Substance use also increases the likelihood of that youth will engage in further risky activities, either due to poor judgment deriving from intoxication or as a consequence of their engagement in illegal activities in order to secure drugs, either of which is a potential source of further trauma exposure. Substance use also is a risk factor for sexual revictimization, particularly among adolescent girls and young women. For example, in a study of 469 adolescent girls followed from high school into their first year of college, Testa, Hoffman, and Livingston (2010) found that earlier sexual victimization was associated with risky behaviors in college (e.g., sexual hookups, multiple partners, and heavy drinking), which in turn was associated with an increased risk of sexual revictimization. The link to PTSD was made even more explicitly by Walsh, Latzman, and Latzman (2014), who found that, among young women in emerging adulthood, trauma-related intrusive symptoms and problem drinking mediated the association between childhood abuse and risky sexual behavior.

Limited Prosocial Emotions/Callous-Unemotional Traits. Of particular concern for trauma-informed clinicians is that a subset of conduct disordered youth are identified with a new specifier in the DSM-5 related to their display of a "limited range of prosocial emotions" (Kahn et al., 2012). This specifier is intended to identify those youth who demonstrate callous-unemotional (CU) traits, the juvenile version of psychopathy. Among conduct disordered youth, those with CU traits evidence a lack of empathy for others or remorse for wrongdoing and consequently begin early on to take a pathway to delinquency, commit the most serious offenses, and demonstrate the most intractable course of conduct problems (Frick, 2009; Frick et al., 2014). The concern for trauma-informed clinicians is that, particularly among youth exposed to chronic and repeated traumas, predominant symptoms of posttraumatic emotional numbing might be mistaken for psychopathic callousness (Kerig & Becker, 2010). Studies do find that youth exposed to chronic trauma, such as those growing up in impoverished neighborhoods beset by violence, show a pattern of desensitization and reduced emotional responsiveness (Gaylord-Harden, Cunningham, & Zelencik, 2011; Gaylord-Harden, Dickson, & Pierre, 2015). Particularly among inner-city African American youth, for whom the "code of the street" promotes the maintenance of a "tough" façade, such desensitization can serve as an adaptive coping mechanism but might be misinterpreted as callousness by culturally uninformed observers. Although empirical research on the differential diagnosis of PTSD-linked emotional numbing and conduct disorder with CU traits is not yet available, Ford and colleagues (2006) provide a set of helpful clinical observations, which can be summarized as follows:

> Traumatic victimization, the[se authors] propose, is an assault to the self that involves a loss of personal integrity and control. In an attempt to regain a sense of agency and to seek redress for the injustices done to them, traumatized youth may adopt a "survival coping" mode in which a tough façade of defiance and callousness masks an inner sense of hopelessness and shame. If the environment does not respond to the youth's disguised and muted calls for help, defiance gives way to desperation and a perceived justification to take any means necessary to defend the self against a hostile world. In this mode, termed "victim coping," the youth's stance toward the world is colored by a sense of distrust in relationships and pessimism about the future, leading to a tendency to gratify impulses immediately with disregard for the consequences either for the self or others. The continual effort at self-protection from external threats of harm and internal threats of unwanted thoughts and feelings is emotionally and mentally exhausting, and the demoralizing effects of the victim coping mentality come to feel like "an escapable life sentence" (p. 40) ... By articulating the perspective of the victimized youth, the trauma coping model also specifically addresses how the ostensible callousness borne of PTSD can be differentiated from true psychopathy. The distinction, Ford and colleagues (2006) argue, is seen in the persistent defiance of traumatized youth and their repeated desperate attempts to redress the injustice of their victimization—a far cry from the cynical coolness of the delinquent youth whose emotional makeup truly is callous and shallow. (Kerig & Becker, 2010, p. 25)

An alternative possibility is that, rather than callousness and PTSD needing to be distinguished from one another, they may co-occur in some youth. In fact, some theories propose that trauma exposure may be one of the pathways by which youth come to be callous and unemotional. As Karpman (1941) originally suggested, research in both youth and adult samples has identified two types of individuals with callous traits. The first, termed primary, demonstrates an inherent *deficit* in emotional responsiveness to others; the second, termed secondary or acquired (Kerig & Becker, 2010), reflects an affective *disturbance* that arises in reaction to trauma such as parental rejection or abuse (Skeem et al., 2007). Porter (1996) expanded further on this theory, suggesting that, in the face of exposure to inescapable trauma, youth may cultivate emotional detachment as a self-protective strategy. A growing body of research has substantiated that there are two subtypes among youth who demonstrate high levels of CU traits and that one is characterized by high levels of exposure to trauma (Kahn et al., 2013; Vaughn et al., 2009) and symptoms of posttraumatic stress (Bennett & Kerig, 2014; Krischer & Sevecke, 2008; Tatar et al., 2012).

A question the research has not fully answered, however, is whether youth in the secondary, or acquired, category are "truly" callous or whether their callousness is a self-protective mask underneath which they have the full range of emotional expressiveness and capacities, as Porter (1996) suggested. Some studies indicate that youth in the secondary category exhibit empathic responses to images of others' distress in ways that youth in the primary category do not (Kimonis et al., 2012). In contrast, other research suggests that, even if acquired rather than inherited, youth in the secondary group do evidence impairments in emotion processing, including their abilities to regulate their affect and to recognize their own and others' emotions (Bennett & Kerig, 2014). Research also has confirmed that posttraumatic numbing accounts for the association between trauma exposure and callousness in young offenders (Allwood, Bell, & Horan, 2011; Kerig et al., 2012). In sum, although possibly an adaptive strategy in the short term, withdrawal of empathy and emotional responsiveness in reaction to trauma can have maladaptive consequences in the longer term, especially when overgeneralized into a callous and desensitized interpersonal style.

CHAPTER 4

Treatment of PTSD in Children and Adolescents

Defining Evidence-Based Interventions

There are many promising and potentially helpful interventions that have been developed for traumatized children, adolescents, and their families. For example, the National Child Traumatic Stress Network's online resource list (http://www.nctsn.org/resources/topics/treatments-that-work/promising-practices#q4) lists more than 40 such interventions. However, in the present review, we will focus attention on those interventions that are evidence based. As Allen (2014) points out, the term "evidence-based" is not used consistently in the literature and is sometimes confused with other poorly defined concepts, such as "evidence-informed" practices. As derived from Sackett and colleagues' (1996) original model, the American Psychological Association's Task Force on Evidence Based Practices (EBP; Levant, 2005) proposes that EBP is comprised of three components: use of the best available empirical evidence regarding what treatments are effective for the client's presenting problem; therapist competence to carry out those interventions; and attention to client characteristics, values, and preferences that might require tailoring and individualization of the treatments. Thus, in contrast to concerns sometimes expressed that evidence-based practice requires rigid adherence to a manual and a "one size fits all" approach (Bernal & Jimenez-Chafey, 2008), the EBP model encourages individualization and flexibility within the context of fidelity to the treatment model (Forehand et al., 2010; Kendall & Beidas, 2007; Kerig, Volz et al., 2010).

However, what clearly differentiates the EBP approach from others is the first component of the model, that the choice of intervention to be implemented must be based on good scientific evidence. That means, in short, that interventions should be able to offer clear confirmation that they have been proven to be efficacious, safe, and feasible. The highest standard of proof is that provided by a randomized controlled trial (RCT), in which two equivalent groups of clients are randomly assigned to conditions in which they either receive the treatment being evaluated or placed in a control group. Control groups may be of three types: a no-treatment waiting list; "treatment as usual" as typically provided in the community; or, in the most methodological rigorous design, assignment to an alternative treatment that already has been established to be effective. According to the criteria adopted by American Psychological Association's (APA) Division 53, the Society of Clinical Child and Adolescent Psychology (Southam-Gerow & Prinstein, 2014), the best empirically validated interventions, those that earn the label, *well-established*, are those that have been studied in clinical trials that meet rigorous scientific criteria (i.e., a randomized controlled design, the treatment steps described in a manual in sufficient detail that it can be replicated by others, clear inclusion criteria for the population for whom the treatment is to be applied; reliable and valid measures used to assess outcomes; and appropriate data analytic strategies used with sufficient statistical power), and that have established either equivalence to an existing treatment or superiority over a placebo or other active treatment in at least two independently conducted randomized trials. Even more compelling are studies that have "dismantled" the treatment in order to show that the "effective ingredients"—that is, the mechanisms that account for the treatment's good outcomes—are specific to the theoretically derived components of the treatment rather than to nonspecific effects (e.g., the passage of time, the warmth of the therapist) that any other, and possibly simpler and cheaper, intervention could have provided (Kazdin, 2007).

A recent exhaustive review of the research base for interventions for child and adolescent trauma, using the Division 53 criteria, was conducted by Dorsey and colleagues (2016). In addition, a number of organizations have developed comprehensive reviews of the interventions that have approached or reached this standard for the practice of psychotherapy with children, adolescents, and families, all of which are accessible online. These include Effective Child Therapy, sponsored by the American Psychological Association Division 53's Society of Clinical Child and Adolescent Psychology (www.effectivechildtherapy.com); Blueprints for Violence Prevention (http://www.colorado.edu/cspv/blueprints/ratings.html); California Evidence-Based Clearinghouse for Child Welfare (www.cedb+cs.org); National Registry of Evidence-Based Programs and Practices (www.nrepp.samhsa.gov); and Office of Juvenile Justice and Delinquency Prevention (OJJDP) Model Programs Guide and Database (www.ojjdp.gov.mpg). Among the interventions that have been proven effective for child and adolescent posttraumatic stress disorder (PTSD), several have garnered particularly strong research evidence although their targets (e.g., the child, the parent, or the family), modality (e.g., individual, group), and the contexts in which they are delivered (e.g., outpatient clinics, schools, detention centers) differ widely.

Evidence-Based Interventions with Young Children and Their Parents

Parent–Child Interaction Therapy

Although not a treatment that was developed specifically for traumatized children, Parent–Child Interaction Therapy (PCIT) (Eyberg & Boggs, 1998) is a highly effective intervention for a range of child behavior problems and parenting challenges that can arise in the context of trauma exposure. Designed for parents and children ages two to seven years, PCIT is a behaviorally based treatment whose goal is to provide parents with effective strategies for managing their children's behavior and promoting a positive attachment (Borrego, Klinkebiel, & Gibson, 2014). The first stage of the treatment, the child-directed interaction phase, focuses on enhancing the quality of the parent–child relationship through helping parents to develop PRIDE skills (Praise, Reflection, Imitation, Description, and Enthusiasm) and to decrease non-facilitative behaviors (e.g., commands, questions, and criticisms) while being engaged in mutually enjoyable play activities with their children. The intervention is highly structured, with the clinician observing the interaction from behind a one-way mirror and providing live coaching to the parent via an audio "bug in the ear" device regarding how to apply the PRIDE skills by attending to and reinforcing positive child behaviors while differentially ignoring and thus diminishing negative behaviors.

Once parents have demonstrated competence in carrying out the PRIDE skills, the second stage, the parent-directed interaction phase, involves teaching parents to use behavior modification techniques, such as time out from positive reinforcement, issuing clear commands, and effectively handling noncompliance. The average course of treatment generally lasts between 11 and 16 weeks, but is variable depending on the pace at which the parent learns the requisite skills.

Although clinical trials of PCIT have not targeted children who evidence symptoms of PTSD, its effectiveness has been demonstrated in samples of children known to have been exposed to the traumatic stressors of maltreatment (Herschell & McNeil, 2007; Timmer et al., 2005) and interparental violence (Timmer et al., 2010). For example, an RCT comparing PCIT to a standard community parenting group for physically abusive parents found that rates of subsequent reports for maltreatment were substantially reduced for parents who received PCIT (19 percent versus 49 percent) (Chaffin et al., 2004). A cautionary note is offered by another study, however, in which, among the maltreating parents in the sample, PCIT was associated with improvements in child behavior, parenting stress, and other predictors of child abuse; however, PCIT also was associated with attrition in that 63.5 percent of the maltreating parents whose children had significant behavior problems left the treatment before completing it (Timmer et al., 2005). Because these studies typically involve a parent who is abusive—and thus is the source of the child's trauma—the challenges to engaging and retaining them in treatment are significant.

Child–Parent Psychotherapy

Child–Parent Psychotherapy (CPP) (Lieberman & Van Horn, 2005, 2008) is a dyadic intervention that focuses on enhancing the relationship between the parent and his or her young child (ages one to five years) so as to promote attachment security in the aftermath of trauma exposure. The underlying theory derives from psychodynamic theory, particularly John Bowlby's (1988b) integration of psychoanalysis and attachment, and builds on the groundbreaking work of Selma Fraiberg's (1980) application of attachment theory to clinical work with mothers and young children.

Several clinical trials have evidenced the effectiveness of CPP. In one RCT, CPP was demonstrated to be superior to community treatment as usual in reducing PTSD symptoms and problem behavior in a sample of preschool children who had been witnesses to domestic violence (Lieberman, Van Horn, & Ippen, 2005). Moreover, the benefits of the treatment continued to show improved functioning for six months after the treatment ended (Lieberman, Ghosh Ippen, & Van Horn, 2006). These good effects were replicated by an independent group of clinical researchers who compared the effectiveness of CPP to more commonly utilized parenting-skill interventions in a sample of maltreated preschoolers and their mothers, and found that CPP was associated with greater increases in attachment security as evidenced by a story task designed to assess internal working models of the self and other (Toth et al., 2002).

Evidence-Based Interventions with School-Age Children and Adolescents

Trauma-Focused Cognitive Behavioral Therapy

Trauma-Focused Cognitive Behavioral Therapy (TF-CBT) (Cohen, Mannarino, & Deblinger, 2017) is the most well-validated intervention to date for children and adolescents who have experienced traumatic stress. Building upon the earlier work of Esther Deblinger (Deblinger & Heflin, 1996), who designed a pioneering intervention for nonoffending parents and their sexually abused children, the underlying philosophy of the model is both cognitive-behavioral and relational. In the behavioral domain, a key feature of the treatment involves countering the tendency toward avoidance that prevents traumatized youth from overcoming trauma and engaging in new learning and, in the realm of cognition, the focus is on identifying and modifying unhelpful thoughts that are keeping the youth (and possibly the caregiver and family) "stuck" in the trauma. In the relational domain, the focus is on increasing the capacity of the parent to provide for the traumatized child's needs. In addition, the implementation of the treatment also incorporates clinical wisdom from other perspectives, as summarized by the acronym CRAFTS, referring to the fact that the treatment is Components-based, Respectful of cultural values, Adaptable and flexible, Family-focused, views the Therapeutic relationships as central, and emphasizes Self-sufficiency.

The acronym PRACTICE identifies each of the components of the TF-CBT model: Psychoeducation and parenting; Relaxation skills; Affective identification and modulation; Cognitive coping; Trauma narrative and cognitive processing; In vivo exposure; Conjoint caregiver–child sessions; and Enhancing safety and future planning. Therapists generally divide sessions between individual time with the caregiver, individual time with the child, and dyadic or family-wide meetings in which skills are reviewed and information is shared. The intervention begins with developmentally appropriate psychoeducation on trauma and posttraumatic stress in order to normalize family members' responses. Another important goal of this phase is to provide both parent and child with the rationale for the treatment, particularly the role that avoidance plays in perpetuating PTSD symptoms and the value of the trauma narrative and open discussion of the traumatic event for counteracting that avoidance. Caregivers also receive guidance and skills for managing difficult child behaviors that may have arisen as part of the posttraumatic response and require immediate attention.

Relaxation skill training equips children with strategies for reducing symptoms of psychophysiological arousal, introduced in playful and enjoyable ways, such as deep-belly breathing and "flopping" like a rag doll. Caregivers also are taught to use these skills and to practice them regularly with the child. Affective identification and modulation, in turn, support children in identifying, coping with, and expressing their emotions in helpful ways. Children are taught to use a thermometer to rate their subjective units of distress in order to identify when they are becoming distressed and need to employ their relaxation skills. Cognitive coping, the next phase, introduces caregivers and children to the "cognitive triangle" connecting thoughts, feelings, and behaviors and how changing one's appraisals of a situation (e.g., "This happened to me because I deserved it" versus "It was an accident") can change one's feelings (e.g., worthlessness versus regret) and subsequent behavior (e.g., self-harm versus self-care).

Each of these skills comes into play during the next stage, which involves the development of a narrative of the traumatic experience. The narrative serves two purposes: first, as a method of graded exposure to the traumatic material, and second, as an opportunity to uncover and process the child's unhelpful cognitions regarding the experience. In order to keep the child engaged and motivated, the narrative itself can take many forms: a written story, a picture book, a play, a rap song, a poem, and so on. The development of the narrative generally takes place over several sessions, with careful monitoring of the child's distress thermometer and use of relaxation techniques as needed. As unhelpful thoughts are brought to the surface, the therapist and child examine them together and, using Socratic questioning, the therapist invites the child to "think like a scientist" and question those assumptions. A useful technique is the "blameberry pie," in which the child is invited to investigate the certainty of his or her ideas by assigning portions of responsibility to all the possible causes for the traumatic event. For example, a boy who felt 100 percent responsible for a car accident because he distracted his mother while she was driving might be invited to consider all the other possible contributors to the crash (e.g., the rain, the speed the other car was going, the tree partially hiding the stop sign). New and more helpful ways of understanding the traumatic event are then incorporated into a revised narrative. Parallel sessions with the caregiver provide them with information about their child's developing narrative as it emerges each week, allow the therapist to gauge and process any unhelpful cognitions the parent may have developed about the training, and provide the opportunity to plan for how the caregiver will be helpful and supportive in the upcoming joint session with the child in which the narrative will be shared. In vivo exposure, the next component of the treatment, supports children in facing trauma reminders as they occur in real-life settings. The caregiver and the child are assisted in developing a plan for graded exposure to people, places, or things that might have become associated with the trauma and thus be a stimulus for avoidance or otherwise trigger trauma symptoms.

Conjoint caregiver–child sessions, the next component, are a feature of TF-CBT and occur at many points, such as when relaxation skills are reviewed and practiced, but key is the session (or sessions) during which the child shares his or her trauma narrative and the caregiver and the child can talk openly about the experience and their thoughts and feelings about it. This often is a very emotional session in that it may be the first time that such an open conversation has taken place and that the child has experienced the caregiver's supportive, nonblaming, and emotionally modulated response to this difficult material. Finally, the last component involves safety planning, both to prevent future recurrences of the traumatic experience and to plan for how the child and caregiver will cope with future trauma reminders, such as anniversary reactions.

The extensive research support, including several RCTs involving hundreds of children and adolescents, which demonstrates TF-CBT's superiority over nondirective "treatments as usual," is summarized in Cohen and colleagues' revised manual (2017) as well as a recent meta-analysis (Cary & McMillen, 2012) and literature review (Dorsey et al., 2016). A number of "dismantling" studies also have been conducted that have confirmed the therapeutic value of specific components of the treatment, including changing unhelpful cognitions (Jensen et al., 2013; Nixon, Sterk, & Pearce, 2012; Ready et al., 2015) and increasing caregivers' behavioral management skills and supportiveness toward the child (Deblinger, Lippmann, & Steer, 1996). Although the creation of the trauma narrative has been deemed an effective way of addressing parental concerns and changing youths' unhelpful beliefs (Deblinger et al., 2011), two studies have found that youth randomly assigned to a TF-CBT condition in which they engage in cognitive processing without a trauma narrative benefit equally in comparison to those who completed a narrative (Deblinger et al., 2011; Nixon, Sterk, & Pearce, 2012).

An intriguing study coding caregivers' in-session emotion processing during the trauma narrative phase found that caregivers' avoidance, blaming, and self-blame were associated with negative child outcomes, whereas caregiver support predicted improvements in children's internalizing symptoms (Yasinski et al., 2016). Another RCT found not only that adolescents who received TF-CBT achieved more significant reductions in posttraumatic stress symptoms than those assigned to standard "treatment as usual" in a community mental health center (Ormhaug et al., 2014), but also that the quality of the therapeutic alliance between the youth and the therapist was a significant moderator of the effectiveness of TF-CBT. Perhaps a positive alliance helped traumatized youth to overcome their pervasive tendency toward avoidance and instead collaborate with the therapist on key therapeutic tasks that require actively engaging with trauma-related material, such as the trauma narrative. Another recent clinical trial randomly assigned clinicians working with traumatized youth in a juvenile justice facility to one of two conditions: web-based training in TF-CBT versus live training. Although youth in both conditions reported significant improvements in PTSD and depressive symptoms, clinicians who received the live training evidenced greater fidelity to the manual and treatment completions (Cohen et al., 2016).

TF-CBT also has been adapted and implemented in a wide range of ages, settings, ethnically diverse populations, Spanish-speaking families, and youth demonstrating traumatic grief, as well as other highly challenging youth, including those with complex trauma symptoms (Cohen, Mannarino, & Deblinger, 2012). In another innovation, Smith and colleagues (2013) integrated TF-CBT into the treatment of extremely behaviorally disruptive girls engaged in multidimensional treatment foster care (Chamberlain, 1996). The results of a small-scale pilot study were encouraging, with girls receiving the combined intervention evidencing lower levels of both PTSD symptoms and delinquent behavior following treatment.

Cognitive Processing Therapy

Cognitive Processing Therapy (CPT) is a brief (12-session) structured therapy originally developed as a treatment for rape victims (Resick & Schnicke, 1993), but now extended to scores of different samples and kinds of traumas. With several independently conducted RCTs to its credit, CPT is considered to be one of the most well-validated approaches for addressing PTSD (Galovski et al., 2015). As the name implies, CPT derives from a cognitive perspective and focuses on identifying and resolving the cognitive "stuck points" or unhelpful appraisals that interfere with recovery from trauma exposure. In the CPT model, PTSD is conceptualized as a failure to cognitively accommodate—to adjust our view of ourselves or the world—in order to come to terms with the traumatic experience. There are two ways a failure of accommodation can take place. In the first case, assimilation, the experience is incorporated into our belief systems in ways that match either preexisting positive schemas (e.g., "Life is fair, so if something bad happened to me, I must have deserved it") or preexisting negative schemas (e.g., "I knew people can't be trusted, so I was a fool to have trusted her"). In the second case, overaccommodation, people radically change their belief systems and reappraise themselves and the world in the light of the traumatic experience (e.g., "I used to think I had some personal control over what happened to me, but now I know I am completely powerless"). Either of these failures of accommodation serves to keep the person "stuck" in the traumatic experience.

In its original version, CPT focused on the generation of a trauma narrative as a way of bringing to light the client's unhelpful beliefs. However, parallel to the research on TF-CBT cited previously, subsequent dismantling studies showed equally effective to the trauma narrative was a modified version of the treatment that elided recounting the upsetting details of the experience in preference to having clients create an "impact statement" regarding their beliefs about how the experience had impacted themselves, their world, and their future. In fact, this modified version has been associated with more rapid therapeutic gains and fewer dropouts from treatment (Resick et al., 2008; Walter et al., 2014). Whether focused on a trauma account or impact statement, the goals of the therapist are to use the narrative to decrease avoidance by encouraging open discussion of the experience, to identify the individual's "stuck points," and to use gentle Socratic questioning and a series of structured worksheets to help clients challenge assimilated or overaccommodated thoughts.

Although most of the empirical evidence supporting CPT has emerged from studies on adults, the approach has proven successful in samples including teenagers (Ahrens & Rexford, 2002; Chard, Weaver, & Resick, 1997). Moreover, recently, the treatment has been revised with a manual that provides an explicit downward extension to adolescents (Matulis et al., 2014). In a pilot study involving 12 sexually or physically abused adolescents with PTSD, Matulis and colleagues found that the adapted treatment was effective in reducing PTSD as well as symptoms of dissociation, depression, and borderline personality pathology.

Trauma Affect Regulation Guide for Education and Therapy

Trauma Affect Regulation Guide for Education and Therapy (TARGET) is a downward extension of an intervention originally designed for adults with complex PTSD (Ford & Russo, 2006), which has been achieving good results in studies including adolescents with histories of exposure to multiple traumas and symptoms related to C-PTSD and DTD. The adolescent version of the intervention can be delivered in a number of formats: as an individual therapy (Ford, Steinberg, et al., 2012), group therapy (Ford & Hawke, 2012), or a milieu treatment in juvenile justice facilities in which youth and staff are both the targets of the intervention (Marrow et al., 2013).

TARGET begins with psychoeducation, using jargon-free and non-stigmatizing language to introduce youth to the concept of an "alarm" in the brain (i.e., the amygdala). Although valuable and necessary for alerting us to danger, an alarm constantly triggered by exposure to repeated traumas can become "stuck" in the on position and no longer communicate with or be guided by the "filing" (e.g., hippocampus) and "thinking" (e.g., prefrontal cortex) centers of the brain. Youth then are involved in learning seven steps that will assist them in turning down the alarm, reengaging the filing and thinking centers, and recovering a sense of personal control. Spelling out the acronym FREEDOM, the TARGET steps are as follows. The first step, Focus, assists youth in learning strategies for focusing their minds and engaging their thinking centers. Unlike relaxation techniques that promote self-calming, or meditation strategies that emphasize emptying the mind of thoughts, TARGET encourages youth to focus their minds on one personally relevant thought that connects them to their most important beliefs and values as a way of engaging their executive functions. The second step, Recognizing triggers, helps youth to identify the aspects of ordinary stressful experiences that have provoked a posttraumatic reaction (e.g., "When that kid flashed me that look in the hallway, it was just like every time I saw that evil look on my foster father's face just before he hammered me"). The next step, Emotion self-check, assists youth in differentiating emotional reactions that are triggered by trauma reminders from those that arise from their enduring "main" goals and values. Next, Evaluating thoughts helps youth to differentiate the accompanying thoughts that are reactive to the trauma trigger (e.g., "He's disrespecting me and I can't stand that!") from those that derive from the thinking center and their deeper values (e.g., "I am a person who values and deserves respect"). On the basis of that greater clarity about their emotions and thoughts, in the next stage, Defining goals, youth also differentiate between reactive goals (e.g., "I'm going to make him pay!") and main goals that get them closer to their deeper values (e.g., "I want everyone to know that I am a young man who deserves respect"). This then allows youth in the next step, Options, to choose between behaviors that are reactive (e.g., "I'm going to punch his lights out!") and those that are consistent with their main goals and values (e.g., "I'm going to walk right past that fool and make a joke with my friends and then we'll all laugh and they'll know I'm cooler than him"). The last step, Make a contribution, helps youth to see how they have been making, and can make still more, positive contributions to the world and perceive their true value as a person. For example, by keeping his cool and modeling for his friends on how to rise above a provocation, this youth is making a valuable contribution to not only his own well-being but also that of his peers.

Empirical support for the TARGET model to date includes an RCT with a sample of adolescent girls involved in delinquent behavior, most of whom met criteria for PTSD as well as at least one other internalizing or externalizing disorder (Ford, Steinberg, et al., 2012). Results showed that a 10-session version of TARGET delivered as an individual treatment was more effective than a relational psychotherapy at reducing symptoms of PTSD, anxiety, traumagenic cognitions, and emotion dysregulation, with small to medium effect sizes. In open trials, when delivered as a group therapy and milieu intervention in juvenile justice facilities, TARGET has been associated with a decrease in violent incidents and use of restraints, as well as reductions in youth PTSD and depression (Ford & Hawke, 2012; Marrow et al., 2013).

Group Therapies

Trauma and Grief Components Therapy for Adolescents

Trauma and Grief Components Therapy for Adolescents (TGCTA) (Layne et al., in press) is a group intervention originally developed for adolescents exposed to war-related trauma in Bosnia (Layne et al., 2008) and recently extended to traumatized youth in the United States. The treatment is delivered to groups of 8 to 10 youths coled by a trained mental health clinician as well as a teacher or facility staff member. TGTCA comprises 24 sessions divided into four modules. Module I involves psychoeducation regarding trauma and traumatic reactions; strengthening participants' emotion regulation skills, particularly in relation to trauma reminders; improving participants' problem-solving and coping skills related to the ways in which their lives have been negatively impacted by trauma; and enhancing youths' ability to solicit and provide support to one another. Module II comprises trauma-processing work, including selecting a traumatic experience that is appropriate to share in the group, constructing and sharing a trauma narrative, exploring the "worst moments" as a way of fostering therapeutic exposure, and processing intervention and revenge fantasies that can contribute to risky adolescent behavior.

Although the first two modules are very similar to what occurs in other evidence-based trauma treatments, such as TF-CBT, unique to TGCTA is Module III, which directly addresses the psychological aftermath of traumatic loss. Sessions focus on providing youth with insights into loss reminders; identifying their own personal grief reactions evoked by those reminders, as well as the mourning rituals that provide solace; providing psychoeducation about normative grieving versus maladaptive grief; and facilitating a healthy adaptation to the loss. Finally, Module IV involves looking forward and promoting positive adolescent development, with sessions focused reflecting on "lessons learned" from trauma and loss and distinguishing between those that are constructive and those that are destructive, problem-solving about current and anticipated future life adversities, and encouraging the development of realistic and yet positive life goals and aspirations.

Evidence in support of TGCTA includes one RCT in which 127 war-exposed youth in Bosnia were randomly assigned to either TGCTA or a classroom-based psychoeducation and skill-development intervention (Layne et al., 2008). While both groups demonstrated reductions in PTSD and depression following the treatment, only youth who received TGCTA demonstrated reductions in maladaptive grief reactions. Other reports of open trials have shown feasibility and positive results with community violence–exposed youth in California (Saltzman et al., 2001) and traumatized or bereaved youth in Delaware (Grassetti et al., 2014). A more recent pilot project conducted in six residential juvenile justice facilities combined TGCTA with a staff psychoeducational program regarding trauma and its effects on youth functioning (Olafson et al., 2016). Results showed posttreatment reductions in youth self-reports of PTSD symptoms, depression, and anger, as well as in facility reports of violent incidents.

Cognitive Behavioral Intervention for Trauma in Schools

A perennial problem facing clinicians wanting to assist traumatized youth, especially those growing up in adverse environments and disadvantaged families, is the difficulty making interventions affordable and accessible. School-based mental health services offer an alternative that has proven highly effective. For example, in an investigation of services offered to children in New Orleans traumatized in the aftermath of Hurricane Katrina, only 37 percent of the children offered an outpatient clinic–based intervention actually enrolled in the treatment, as opposed to 98 percent of the children offered a school-based intervention (Jaycox et al., 2010). That intervention, Cognitive Behavioral Intervention for Trauma in Schools (CBITS), is a 10-session group treatment comprising an introduction to the model, psychoeducation about trauma and relaxation training, introduction to the links between thoughts and feelings, strategies for combating negative thoughts, countering avoidance through graded exposure, creation of a trauma narrative (two sessions), social problem-solving (two sessions), and a final session devoted to relapse prevention and celebrating completion of treatment. In addition, three parent sessions are offered, which assist parents with noticing their children's thoughts, facing their fears, coming to terms with what has happened to them, and solving their daily problems. Teachers also receive a one-session training to help them become supports and advocates for traumatized children, including tips for managing their emotions and behavior in the classroom (Jaycox et al., 2012).

In an RCT involving middle school children who reported exposure to violence in Los Angeles, Stein and colleagues (2003) found that, compared to those assigned to a waiting list, children who received CBITS exhibited lower scores on measures of PTSD, aggression, and emotional and behavioral problems from the perspective of the youth as well as their teachers. Other open trials have supported the benefits of the program as compared to a wait-list in diverse groups, including immigrant Latino youth, Native American youth, and children in Special Education, as well as delivery of the program by non–mental health professionals in the school setting (Jaycox et al., 2012).

Family-Level Interventions

Families Overcoming and Coping Under Stress

Families Overcoming and Coping Under Stress (FOCUS) (Saltzman et al., 2009) is a promising new intervention for trauma-affected families, which was originally developed to enhance resilience in families with military-involved parents. At present, the intervention is beginning to be extended to other populations, including children with medical traumas and traumatized youth in the justice system. Although research data are not yet available on the effectiveness of the intervention in families in which the child evidences PTSD, the evidence to date is promising and likely soon forthcoming and so it warrants inclusion here.

Although a family systemic treatment, the theoretical underpinnings of FOCUS are most strongly related to trauma theory, and the treatment extends from earlier interventions the developers created to address trauma, grief, and loss (Saltzman et al., 2001) as well as parental depression (Beardslee et al., 2007). The treatment is brief and strategic, comprising eight sessions in total: three with the parents, two with the children, and three with the entire family.

In the initial sessions, family members are provided with psycho-education about the effects of trauma and loss on family functioning, with feedback linked specifically to measures that each person completed about his or her own individual levels of PTSD, depression, anxiety, and grief. Highlighting family strengths and adaptive coping strategies, the therapist then collaborates with the family to arrive at a set of goals for treatment. In the next phase, family members are encouraged to describe ways in which they have been affected by trauma-related reactions in their daily lives, what has triggered those responses, and the coping strategies they have utilized. The therapist then offers them additional tools to place in their toolkits, including relaxation strategies, communication skills, and cognitive restructuring techniques.

An innovative part of the treatment is the creation of a graphic timeline by each individual family member that describes his or her experience of the traumatic event or loss, colorful illustrative examples of which can be found in Saltzman (2016). As the developers (Saltzman et al., 2008) note:

> Family members usually have very different levels of exposure, and different experiences of a traumatic situation ... As a result of their different experiences and reactions, family members typically have very different psychological needs and different courses of recovery. These differences may lead to increased family conflict, decreased empathy and understanding between family members, and decreased family support and tolerance. This becomes especially problematic because most families do not have mechanisms of discourse in place that permit open discussion and acknowledgement of these differences. In many cases, family members frame their silence as a way of protecting each other. (p. 248)

For example, one mother's extreme overprotectiveness after her son's witnessing of an armed robbery was causing a high level of family conflict; the explanation for her behavior came to light in one of the parent sessions, during which she revealed that as a child she had been present at the shooting of her uncle, an upsetting piece of information she had attempted to keep from her family in a misdirected desire to protect them. Thus, offering separate parent sessions provides a critical context for exploring of differences in parents' narratives and uncovering ways in which misunderstandings might be negatively affecting their ability to work together as a parenting team. In general, the focus of the parent-only meetings is kept on the goal of promoting children's welfare, rather than exploring marital problems, in order to maintain parents' engagement and openness. In parallel, in the separate child sessions, the therapist uses developmentally appropriate methods to elicit children's narratives of the event, as well as their questions, concerns, or wishes for the family. Finally, in the joint family sessions, the therapist helps each family member to articulate his or her own perspective and to communicate understanding and empathy for those of others, creating a context in which the family can work altogether to create a shared "family narrative" or "healing theory" (Figley, 1989) of the experience. Family resilience is further promoted in the last session, in which problem-solving for future trauma triggers or stressors is discussed.

Research evidence for the effectiveness of the intervention has emerged from large-scale open trials with over 2,000 military families in which the targets of treatment were not child PTSD but child behavioral and emotional difficulties and parent anxiety and depression (Lester et al., 2012) or parent distress (Saltzman et al., 2016). Results to date have been highly positive and gains have persisted over a period of six months after completion of the treatment (Lester et al., 2016). We likely will be hearing more about this intervention in future.

System-Wide Interventions

Trauma Systems Therapy

Trauma Systems Therapy (TST) (Saxe, Ellis, & Kaplow, 2006) grew out of its developers' experiences providing traditional clinic-based individual therapies to youth beset by complex past trauma histories and living in current circumstances characterized by ongoing family instability, poverty, and community violence (Navalta et al., 2013). Recognizing that high rates of dropout were rife in this population, the developers committed to finding a different treatment strategy for engaging families and delivering services. Inspired by the developmental contextual theories of Bronfenbrenner (1979), one of the innovative aspects of TST is its focus on the interaction of the youth and his or her social environment as the target of treatment. The "trauma system" is characterized by the intersection between a traumatized youth who is unable to regulate his or her emotions and a social environment that is unable to assist the child to cope with this dysregulation.

In response, TST was developed as a multidisciplinary team intervention that brings together home-visiting mental health workers, a psychopharmacologist, a psychotherapist, a legal advocate, and a supervising clinician with expertise in trauma, in order to not only foster a child's emotion regulation capacities but also to intervene in the social environment at the levels of the home, school, and neighborhood. Based on an individualized assessment of the child's and family's needs and readiness, treatment involves various combinations of seven modules. The first, Ready-Set-Go, introduces the treatment program and works to actively engage families. The second, Stabilization on Sight, focuses on addressing sources of stress or trauma reminders that might be affecting the child in home or school contexts. The third, Services Advocacy, involves working directly with social service agencies that might provide the kind of stability that is critical for supporting the child's emotion regulation capacities, such as housing, food, or domestic violence services. Fourth, Psychopharmacology is provided to youth in need. Fifth, Emotion Regulation strategies are taught directly to the youth and family. Sixth, Cognitive Processing provides the youth with more adaptive strategies for coping with current stressors or reminders of past trauma. Finally, Meaning Making engages the youth and family in achieving posttraumatic growth by creating meaning from the traumatic event and marking their overcoming it.

To date, empirical evidence for the effectiveness of the intervention comes from open efficacy trials. Among the 72 percent of youth enrolled in a trial in New York state who completed the treatment, outcomes measured three months later were good, with improvements in youth PTSD and emotional and behavioral dysregulation, as well as caregiver physical and mental health and support, in addition to stability of the social environment (Saxe et al., 2005). Another open trial tracked improvements over the course of 15 months among 124 youth who received TST. In addition to confirming that emotion regulation, child functioning, and social-environmental stability improved, and that there were reductions in needs for crisis management and psychiatric hospitalizations for youth who underwent treatment, the investigators also found that improvements in youth emotion regulation substantially accounted for the improvements in child functioning and social environmental stability, in keeping with the precepts of the model (Ellis et al., 2012).

Common Elements Among Effective Treatments

Dorsey and colleagues' (2016) overview of the evidence supporting specific treatments for child and adolescent PTSD also identified a number of common elements among those that are most well established. In whole or in part, each of the most effective treatments included some combination of the following six "ingredients": (a) psychoeducation about trauma and the intervention itself; (b) coaching in emotion regulation (e.g., relaxation, emotion identification, cognitive coping strategies); (c) imaginal exposure; (d) in vivo exposure; (e) cognitive processing; and/or (f) problem-solving. In addition, in parallel with studies of CPT with adults, evidence suggests that explicit reexposure to the details of the event, such as through producing a trauma narrative, might not be necessary to achieve positive outcomes; instead, cognitive restructuring of unhelpful beliefs can be achieved in other ways that are less stressful for youth, as well as therapists. Other lessons from the literature are not as clear. For example, although parent involvement has been found to enhance the effectiveness of some treatments, others are effective without parent involvement.

CHAPTER 5

Case Studies

Case 1: Lucas, a School-Age Boy With a Complex Trauma History

Initial Presentation

Lucas had recently turned eight years old when his foster mother, Ms. Andell, brought him to the clinic for an evaluation. He had been living with her for just over three months, following the death of his mother of a drug overdose, and Ms. Andell was eager to seek services for him. She described Lucas as a mostly quiet, shy, and intensely introverted boy but also as one also was easily upset when frustrated by small disappointments or unexpected changes in routine and was prone to fits of intense rage that his foster mother found startling in that they reminded her of a two-year-old's temper tantrums. Another concern she expressed was that Lucas refused to sleep in his own bed at night and she often found him curled up on the floor of her room when she woke up in the morning. Lucas also frequently wet himself, both at night and during the school day. Ms. Andell also reported that he often seemed "spaced out" and would sometimes need to hear his name called several times before he realized she was talking to him; his new teacher said the same and recently had referred him for an attention-deficit hyperactivity disorder (ADHD) and learning disabilities evaluation. Lucas also seemed preoccupied by food and not only pressed to be fed as soon as he awakened, the moment he came home from school, and before he went to bed at night, but frequently hoarded food and kept a small stash hidden in the closet in his room. Furthermore, Lucas never spoke about his mother and became distressed and angry if anyone mentioned her. He also walked an extremely circuitous route home from school in order to avoid going past the mobile home in which he and his mother had lived together.

Developmental History

Although Lucas and Ms. Andell had not known one another at the time she agreed to become his foster parent, they not only had been long-term neighbors who lived in the same mobile home park, but Ms. Andell had known Lucas's mother, a former schoolmate in the small community in which they lived. They also shared, as did many of their neighbors, an Appalachian heritage in that their grandparents had migrated to this area to escape multigenerational poverty, only to find themselves thrust back into it with the collapse of the industries in this "rust belt" town. However, Ms. Andell had never been friends with Lucas's mother, and in fact had kept a wide berth given Lucas's mother's well-known drug habit and engagement in illegal activities—including theft and commercial sexual activity—in order to support that habit, as well as her penchant for violent and public altercations with an ever-changing roster of romantic partners. Therefore, Ms. Andell did not know much of Lucas's early history, nor the identity of his biological father, but had a strong suspicion that Lucas had suffered serious neglect and possibly physical abuse earlier in his life. During his mothers' many brief incarcerations he was placed in the care of an aunt who expressed no interest in taking on the full-time care of the boy after his mother's death, and Ms. Andell surmised that that relationship, too, had been a neglectful or at least emotionally unsupportive one. She said that Lucas told her that, in his previous home, he spent most of his time alone in his room watching television and that on most nights his dinner consisted of snacks that he had slipped into his pocket at school and hidden in his room. Ms. Andell was able to show the therapist a class picture that had been taken the year previously, one of the few belongings Lucas brought with him from his mother's home, and it showed a remarkably thinner boy than at present with oddly patchy hair—she wondered whether his hair had fallen out due to malnutrition or whether Lucas had pulled it out due to emotional distress.

The incident that brought Lucas into care three months earlier began when he awoke in the morning in his mother's mobile home to the sound of strange noises coming from the living room. Lucas's mother was slumped unconscious on the coach, moaning and unresponsive, with a needle, candle, and metal spoon next to her. When he was unable to rouse her after several attempts, Lucas picked up the phone and called 911. After the paramedics and police arrived, they determined that Lucas's mother had died and her body was taken for an autopsy. The police report commented that they were struck by the fact that Lucas did not cry or indeed show any emotion. Instead, he stood in a corner holding his mother's cell phone, repeatedly pushing the buttons with a dazed expression on his face. Lucas was taken by a social worker to the local Child Protection Agency and, luckily, that very afternoon was able to be placed with Ms. Andell, who had only recently decided, after an intense religious experience at her fundamentalist church, to become a foster parent and to open her home to a child in need. Ms. Andell also reported that the autopsy later showed the cause of death to be a heroin overdose but that the coroner had ruled it inconclusive—he was not able to determine whether the overdose had been accidental or whether, given the extraordinary amount of heroin that was in her system, the death should be ruled a suicide.

Upon meeting the clinician for the initial intake interview, Lucas presented as a slightly built, shy, nervous, physically and emotionally constricted boy who was avoidant of eye contact and initiated no conversation. However, he responded positively to the assessor's gentle manner and warm interest in him and, over the course of the session, became more willing to explore the interesting toys in her room and to elaborate on his answers to her questions. He reported that he liked living at Ms. Andell's house but worried that someday he might have to go somewhere else that wasn't as nice. He admitted that he frequently had worries and that thoughts he did not like to think about often came into his head, especially when he was at school, but that he did not want to talk about these things.

Assessment and Case Conceptualization

Lucas had recently undergone an ADHD and learning disabilities evaluation at his school, results of which suggested that he demonstrated symptoms of the inattentive type of ADHD but which were not consistent across all context in which the behavioral observations took place; in addition, cognitive testing showed that he evidenced some executive functioning deficits but overall was performing in school below his cognitive capacity. The assessment team utilized this information in conjunction with additional testing specific to the presence of posttraumatic stress. Given Lucas's anxiety and reticence to talk directly about his experiences, and the fact that he had not been receiving regular medical care prior to coming to Ms. Andell's and thus had no pediatrician who knew him well, the team decided that in this instance the best sources of information would be Ms. Andell and Lucas's teacher. Both were asked to complete a general measure of behavioral functioning as well as the University of California Los Angeles (UCLA) PTSD-RI (Pynoos & Steinberg, 2014). Results showed that both informants rated Lucas in the clinical range on scales involving internalizing symptoms, including anxiety and depression; the teacher, but not Ms. Andell, rated Lucas in the clinical range on scales involving externalizing symptoms, most notably inattentiveness and poor self-regulation. Both also rated Lucas as meeting criteria for a diagnosis of PTSD, with elevated symptoms on all clusters, including the presence of dissociation. Lucas's history and presentation further suggested that a screening for symptoms consistent with Developmental Trauma Disorder might be clinically useful, even if this category is not part of the official diagnostic nomenclature. Ms. Andell's responses on the Developmental Trauma Disorder-Structured Interview (DTD-SI) (Ford et al., 2011) revealed a good fit: In addition to meeting the first criterion of exposure to both traumatic stress and attachment disruptions, Lucas evidenced signs of emotional, behavioral, and self/relational dysregulation.

The conceptualization the team arrived at was that Lucas evidenced both simple and complex PTSD as a result of exposure to both an acute stressor (the death of his mother) and longstanding attachment disruptions, emotional neglect, and possibly physical abuse. His ability to grieve for and overcome the loss of his mother was being interfered with not only by the traumatic nature of her death but also his ongoing insecurity about his living situation. Working with Ms. Andell to help her provide Lucas with the necessary support and structure, and to clarify the permanence of their relationship and the nature of her attachment to him, would be critical. The nature of his dysregulated behavior and attention suggested that PTSD was a more likely explanation than ADHD and hence close collaboration with the school psychologist and teacher would be needed to allow for the development of a consistent treatment approach across contexts. Cultural factors to be considered included the foster mother and son's shared Appalachian heritage, with its emphasis on self-reliance and stoicism in the face of adversity, as well as their strong fundamentalist religious faith. Sources of resilience to be capitalized on included the warm relationship that was forming between Lucas and Ms. Andell, her investment in his well-being, and his own positive interpersonal orientation that boded well for his capacity to developing a trusting therapeutic relationship.

Treatment Process

Given the evidence base attesting to its effectiveness for treating youth with presentations similar to those of Lucas, TF-CBT was selected as the treatment of choice. In the assessment feedback session, Lucas's foster mother responded well to this suggestion but also admitted to trepidation about hearing Lucas's trauma narrative, given her own history of significant childhood abuse and neglect, which she feared might be triggering for her. Although she initially expressed great reluctance to the idea of having her own therapist in order to work through these issues, stating that "where I come from, we don't talk to strangers," once this was reframed as an adjunct to the parenting components of TF-CBT, she became enthusiastic about this as a way in which she could actively contribute to Lucas's treatment. Thus, a team approach was taken, in which Lucas and Ms. Andell worked individually with their own therapists for the first part of each session, and then came together for joint meetings, in which Lucas would demonstrate to Ms. Andell what he had learned and she could practice her burgeoning parenting skills.

Early in his treatment, it was clear that a major impediment to Lucas's ability to learn and practice emotion regulation skills was that he had limited access to his own emotions—his emotion lexicon and recognition of his own emotional states were limited to the two terms "good" and "yucky." Therefore, his therapist took advantage of the flexibility and modularization of PTSD to expand significantly on this module, taking several additional sessions to help build Lucas's emotion awareness and vocabulary by engaging him in enjoyable activities such as "emotion charades" and creating a "drawing dictionary" of emotion expressions with which he and his therapist created increasingly elaborated cartoon storyboards. Ms. Andell also was enlisted in helping Lucas practice these skills at home, and they together came up with the idea of having a "feelings time" when he came home every afternoon, in which they would tell one another about their day and see if each could guess all the emotions the other person had experienced. Ultimately, Lucas was able to utilize these skills in generating drafts for what would become his trauma narrative, by drawing an outline of himself and placing on the drawing color-coded labels for all the different ways he felt on the day of his mother's death—"scared" when he could not wake her, "confused" when he didn't know what to do, "mad" when the 911 operator at first did not understand him, "sick to his stomach" when he saw where his mother had vomited, "worried" when he didn't know where the social worker was taking him—and the places in his body where he felt those emotions.

Lucas chose to title his narrative, "My Life Then and My Life Now," and much of his reflections on the past were expressed as contrasts to the present—how much more he ate now, how he came home from school eagerly rather than dragging his feet, and how nice Ms. Andell was to him even when he did things that he shouldn't, such as having tantrums or wetting the bed. As he narrated the story of the day his mother died, an important aspect that emerged was in the time span between when he encountered his mother and when he determined to dial 911, which in his mind's eye had expanded to encompass an unbearably long period in which he was awash in uncertainty about what to do—he now found himself perseverating on the thought that, if he had acted more quickly, he could have prevented his mother from dying and thus, he wondered, was he responsible for her death? Another unhelpful cognition emerged later in treatment when, after attending bible studies class, Lucas learned that their fundamentalist church believed that those who commit suicide are damned to eternal hell—if his mother had committed suicide, he wondered, did that mean she was now in hell? Through gentle exploration of the evidence for and against these beliefs and, in the second case, consultation with the deacon of Lucas's church, Lucas was able to develop more realistic and helpful understandings of his mother's death and its causes and consequences.

Outcome

After 20 sessions and the completion and sharing of Lucas's trauma narrative with Ms. Andell, the family felt ready for termination. Lucas's scores on the PTSD-RI were now below clinical cut-offs and his internalizing and externalizing scores were significantly reduced, both from his foster mother's and his teacher's perspectives. Ms. Andell was no longer anxious about talking with Lucas about difficult experiences and emotions, having come to master her own, and she expressed a new sense of self-confidence about her competence as a parent. Together with their therapists they planned for potential trauma reminders and challenges, such as anniversary reactions around the time of his mother's death, or new loss reminders such as her not being present on the day of his 5th grade graduation. Lucas and his foster mother both expressed confidence that they would be able to handle these challenges but, if they could not, that they knew how to reach out for help and whom to call. In fact, four years later, the now-teenaged Lucas was struggling to come to terms with his mother's death and his troubled early life at a new cognitively sophisticated level, particularly in keeping with the adolescent stage-salient tasks of identity and moral development. Therefore, his now-adoptive mother, Ms. Andell, once again sought treatment for him from a therapist with expertise in adolescent trauma.

Case 2: Alejandra—An Adolescent Survivor of Sexual Assault

Initial Presentation

Alejandra was a 16-year-old Latina girl, the eldest of three sisters living in an intact family in a suburb of a large metropolitan area in the Southwest, who was referred to treatment by her juvenile probation officer (PO). Alejandra had a recent spate of minor infractions that had gotten her into trouble with the law—for example, shoplifting, drinking alcohol, vandalism—most of which, the PO thought, had more to do with her hanging out with a "bad crowd" rather than being a "bad kid." However, recently, Alejandra shared with her PO that she had a secret that she had not yet told anyone, including her parents. One night about a year ago, she snuck out of her bedroom window after curfew to meet her friends who were going to a party hosted by a group of fraternity boys at the nearby college. She drank heavily and reported feeling confused when the hour became late and she could not locate any of the friends she had come with. A young man she had been enjoying talking with much of the evening offered to give her a ride home and she accepted. However, instead of taking her home, he drove to a deserted parking lot where he demanded that she have sex with him, berating her in demeaning terms when she resisted. Finally, he used physical force, afterwards pushing Alejandra out of his car, again accompanied by abusive words, forcing her to walk home alone in the dark. Since that time, Alejandra's oppositionality and disruptive behavior had increased at both school and home and her parents were considering sending her away to a "boot camp" for incorrigible youth. Alejandra admitted that she was "terrified" to tell her very strict and traditional parents about the sexual assault for fear that they would disown her and view her as a disgrace to the family. She was surprised when, after the PO revealed her secret to them, they responded with concern and immediately followed up with the PO's suggestion of a referral to a mental health provider with expertise in trauma treatment. However, Alejandra stated that she did not want her parents to participate in her treatment and would only attend sessions if the work were to be completely private between herself and the therapist.

Assessment and Case Conceptualization

After some initial shyness, Alejandra warmed to the clinician and expressed excitement about going through an assessment, saying that her psychology course was one of the few that really fascinated her in high school and that she wanted to learn more about "what makes me tick." The diagnostic interview they completed showed that Alejandra met full criteria for a diagnosis of PTSD, nondissociative subtype. Although she showed elevations on all symptom clusters, particularly notable were the high levels of symptoms in Cluster D (negative cognitions and mood) as well as Cluster E (hyperarousal). Given this potentially toxic combination of negative thoughts and irritability in an adolescent, the therapist also thought it wise to screen for potential suicidality. Although

Alejandra admitted that she "didn't care about anything anymore" and felt there was nothing to look forward to in life, she denied any thoughts or active intentions toward suicide, emphasizing how important her Catholic faith and Mexican heritage were to her in that regard. In turn, the diagnostic interview questions related to conduct disorder also did not show that Alejandra met criteria for this diagnosis—although she did engage in rule breaking, these were recent behaviors that could be linked sequentially and conceptually to her experience of trauma, and did not represent a long-standing pattern involving violations of the rights of others. Similarly, although she joined her peers in drinking and smoking marijuana, and used these substances, as she put it, to "help me with my stress," there weren't indications that she presently met criteria for a substance abuse disorder, although the risk was high. Collateral information from her teachers corroborated these impressions. Alejandra's homeroom teacher in particular expressed appreciation for the opportunity to contribute in any way to helping Alejandra, describing her as a good student and "bright light" whose recent academic withdrawal and misbehavior was "mystifying" to him given her previous high performance and positive attitude.

Alejandra's parents, both second-generation Mexican Americans from working-class backgrounds, also agreed to come to the clinician's office for an intake interview. They completed Spanish-language versions of behavioral measures, as well as a measure of PTSD, and, although some mild levels of problem behavior and posttraumatic symptoms were endorsed, striking was their tendency to minimize any problems and to emphasize their perceptions of Alejandra as, until only recently, a well-functioning girl who was a credit to her family. Both parents expressed grief and shock that their daughter had been sexually assaulted and, although their response was not consistent with Alejandra's fear that they would "disown" her, they did acknowledge that this was a source of great shame for the family and that they were determined that no one outside of their immediate circle should know that this had occurred. They expressed their willingness to support Alejandra's treatment in any way needed but also respected her desire for privacy and agreed to allow her to come to sessions without them being present or receiving reports about what went on in those sessions.

In the context of the assessment, the therapist noted a number of sources of resilience that could be capitalized on in treatment, including Alejandra's intelligence and capacity for thoughtful introspection, her willingness to be open, and her active curiosity about her own psychology. Her religious and ethnic identities were an important source of strength for her, as was her parents' support, although her lack of trust in the latter and unwillingness to harness it in the service of her treatment suggested possible sources of challenge for the therapy.

Treatment Process

Given Alejandra's age and verbal skills, and particularly due to CPT's strong evidence base in the treatment of sexual assault survivors, CPT was identified as the treatment of choice for helping her to overcome the traumatic effects of the rape she had experienced. The treatment started with psychoeducation about the nature of PTSD and its symptoms, which Alejandra absorbed eagerly. Alejandra had many questions and hesitations about writing an impact statement, in particular because she did not want to run the risk that her parents or younger sisters would find it, nor any of the worksheets she completed while investigating and challenging her beliefs. However, she took her therapist's lessons about the negative power of avoidance to heart and proposed an accommodation strategy in which Alejandra would work on these materials in the therapist's waiting room after school and return them to the therapist for safekeeping in her office—"It's my own personal psych study hall!" Alejandra declared.

In analyzing Alejandra's initial impact statement, the therapist noted many indications that Alejandra had arrived at a set of negative appraisals regarding herself and the world around her in her attempt to make sense of the assault. These included both assimilated beliefs (e.g., "I must have done something to deserve this," a legacy of her belief in a just world) as well as overaccommodated beliefs (e.g., "My judgment can never be trusted"; "I can never get close to a guy again"; "Now that I've been violated, no man will ever want me"). To address these, the therapist engaged in a gentle Socratic dialogue that never challenged Alejandra's beliefs directly but rather invited her to be curious about them and to examine the evidence for them, pro and con. One sample dialogue went as follows:

Alejandra: Of course it is my fault, and it just proves I can't trust my own judgment. I'm a stupid idiot. Who takes a ride home from a complete stranger?

Therapist: So I'm hearing you say that you think you are to blame for being raped because you accepted a ride home from a stranger, and that was a dumb thing to do? And that makes you a person with bad judgment—back then as well as now?

Alejandra: Exactly. If only I hadn't gone with him, I wouldn't have gotten hurt!

Therapist: I see. Well, hmm. [Thoughtful pause.] Tell me something, I'm wondering, have any of your friends ever accepted a ride from someone they didn't know well?

Alejandra: Well, yeah.

Therapist: And did each and every one of them get raped?

Alejandra: Well, no ...

Therapist: So, I wonder, what was different about this time, that you got raped?

Following this question, Alejandra and the therapist compiled a list of all the "ingredients" that she believed went into causing this experience. "I was stupid" remained on the list but other causes were added, including "My friends didn't watch my back," "That girl kept pushing me to down shots even though she could see I was already drunk," and "My parents won't let me drive myself places"; moreover, an even bigger portion of responsibility became attributed to a new reason, which Alejandra stated as: "That guy is a creep. He had no right to rape me." All of these elements went into Alejandra's final version of her impact statement and, as she compared it to her first version toward the end of treatment, she expressed surprise that she had ever been, as she phrased it, "so mean to myself" and stated that one of the biggest rewards she had gotten from therapy was to learn, as she put it, "how to be on my own side." A further challenging phase of treatment for Alejandra came toward the end, in which the worksheets focused on issues of trust and intimacy, which were two of the biggest causalities of her traumatic experience.

Outcome

At the end of treatment, Alejandra evidenced significant reductions in PTSD symptoms, although she continued to evidence hypervigilance and reactivity to trauma reminders, such as the all-too-frequent depictions of sexual violence in movies and video games. However, particularly because she now understood the origins of these symptoms in her traumatic experience, and that she was able to label them correctly as PTSD rather than her own "craziness," she felt better able to cope with them. She also continued to express hesitations about becoming physically intimate with a boyfriend in future but no longer held to the beliefs that she had been "ruined," that no one would want her, or that she deserved no better than to be raped. In fact, the lifting of her sense of self-blame and shame allowed her to share her final impact statement with her parents, which she did in a follow-up "booster" session with the therapist three months after her last session. Alejandra's parents expressed pride in how far she had come and acknowledged the ways in which they had inadvertently validated some of her unhelpful beliefs by reinforcing them with their own.

Author Biography

Patricia K. Kerig received her doctorate in clinical psychology from the University of California at Berkeley with a specialization in children and families and currently is a Professor and the Director of Clinical Training in the Department of Psychology at the University of Utah. She is an author of over a hundred books, chapters, scientific papers, and guest-edited special issues devoted to understanding the factors that predict risk, recovery, and resilience among youth and families coping with adversity and traumatic stress. She has been the recipient of numerous research grants, including most recently a four-year grant from the National Institute of Justice to support a longitudinal study of the emotional, cognitive, interpersonal, and psychophysiological mechanisms underlying the link between childhood trauma exposure and adolescent involvement in the juvenile justice system. She recently was named the Editor in Chief of the *Journal of Traumatic Stress* and has been a member of the editorial boards of several other scientific journals. She also has been an active contributor to front-line efforts to create trauma-informed systems and to remediate the effects of traumatic stress exposure on youth and families, including the National Child Traumatic Stress Network's Juvenile Justice Consortium and the Center for Trauma Recovery and Juvenile Justice.

References

Abram, K. M., Teplin, L. A., Charles, D. R., Longworth, S. L., McClellan, G. M., & Dulcan, M. K. (2004). Posttraumatic stress disorder and trauma in youth in juvenile detention. *Archives of General Psychiatry 61*(4), 403–410. doi:10.1001/archpsyc.61.4.403

Afari, N., Ahumada, S. M., Wright, L. J., Mostoufi, S., Golnari, G., Reis, V., & Cuneo, J. G. (2014). Psychological trauma and functional somatic syndromes: A systematic review and meta-analysis. *Psychosomatic Medicine 76*(1), 2–11.

Ahrens, J., & Rexford, L. (2002). Cognitive processing therapy for incarcerated adolescents with PTSD. *Journal of Aggression, Maltreatment & Trauma 6*(1), 201–216. doi:http://dx.doi.org/10.1300/J146v06n01_10

Aldao, A., & De Los Reyes, A. (2015). Commentary: A practical guide for translating basic research on affective science to implementing physiology in clinical child and adolescent assessments. *Journal of Clinical Child & Adolescent Psychology 44*(2), 341–351. doi:10.1080/15374416.2014.895942

Alisic, E., Zalta, A. K., van Wesel, F., Larsen, S. E., Hafstad, G. S., Hassanpour, K., & Smid, G. E. (2014). Rates of post-traumatic stress disorder in trauma-exposed children and adolescents: Meta-analysis. *British Journal of Psychiatry 204*(5), 335–340.

Allen, B. (2011). The use and abuse of attachment theory in clinical practice with maltreated children, part I: Diagnosis and assessment. *Trauma, Violence, & Abuse 12*(1), 3–12.

Allen, B. (2014). Understanding evidence-based treatment for trauma-exposed children: Definition, development, misconceptions. In B. Allen & M. Kronenberg (Eds.), *Treating traumatized children: A casebook of evidence-based therapies*. New York: Guilford.

Allwood, M. A., & Bell, D. J. (2008). A preliminary examination of emotional and cognitive mediators in the relations between violence exposure and violent behaviors in youth. *Journal of Community Psychology 36*(8), 989–1007.

Allwood, M. A., Bell, D. J., & Horan, J. (2011). Posttrauma numbing of fear, detachment, and arousal predict delinquent behaviors in early adolescence. *Journal of Clinical Child and Adolescent Psychology 40*(5), 659–667. doi:10.1080/15374416.2011.597081

American Academy of Pediatrics. (2000). Diagnosis and evaluation of the child with Attention-Deficit/Hyperactivity Disorder. *Pediatrics 105*(5), 1158–1170.

American Psychiatric Association. (1980). *Diagnostic and statistical manual of mental disorders (DSM-III)* (3rd ed.). Arlington, CA: Author.

American Psychiatric Association. (1994). *Diagnostic and statistical manual of mental disorders, Version IV.* Washington, DC: American Psychiatric Association.

American Psychiatric Association. (2013). *Diagnostic and statistical manual of mental disorders, (DSM-5).* Washington, DC: Author.

Anda, R. F., Felitti, V. J., Bremner, J. D., Walker, J. D., Whitfield, C. H., Perry, B. D., Dube, S. R., & Giles, W. H. (2006). The enduring effects of abuse and related adverse experiences in childhood. A convergence of evidence from neurobiology and epidemiology. *European Archives of Psychiatry and Clinical Neuroscience 256*(3), 174–186.

Andersen, S. L., & Teicher, M. H. (2009). Desperately driven and no brakes: Developmental stress exposure and subsequent risk for substance abuse. *Neuroscience & Biobehavioral Reviews 33*(4), 516–524. doi:http://dx.doi.org/10.1016/j.neubiorev.2008.09.009

Andrews, B., Brewin, C. R., & Rose, S. (2003). Gender, social support, and PTSD in victims of violent crime. *Journal of Traumatic Stress 16*(4), 421–427. doi:10.1023/a:1024478305142

Appleyard, K., & Osofsky, J. D. (2003). Parenting after trauma: Supporting parents and caregivers in the treatment of children impacted by violence. *Infant Mental Health Journal 24*(2), 111–125.

Armour, C., Müllerová, J., & Elhai, J. D. (2016). A systematic literature review of PTSD's latent structure in the Diagnostic and Statistical Manual of Mental Disorders: DSM-IV to DSM-5. *Clinical Psychology Review 44*, 60–74.

Armstrong, J. G., Putnam, F. W., Carlson, E. B., Libero, D. Z., & Smith, S. R. (1997). Development and validation of a measure of adolescent dissociation: The Adolescent Dissociative Experiences Scale. *Journal of Nervous and Mental Disease 185*(8), 491–497.

Balluffi, A., Kassam-Adams, N., Kazak, A., Tucker, M., Dominguez, T., & Helfaer, M. (2004). Traumatic stress in parents of children admitted to the pediatric intensive care unit. *Pediatric Critical Care Medicine 5*(6), 547–553. doi:10.1097/01.pcc.0000137354.19807.44

Beardslee, W. R., Wright, E. J., Gladstone, T. R. G., & Forbes, P. (2007). Long-term effects from a randomized trial of two public health preventive interventions for parental depression. *Journal of Family Psychology 21*(4), 703–713.

Beauchaine, T. P. (2001). Vagal tone, development, and Gray's motivational theory: Toward an integrated model of autonomic nervous system functioning in psychopathology. *Development and Psychopathology 13*(2), 183–214. doi:10.1017/s0954579401002012

Becker-Blease, K., & Kerig, P. K. (2016). *Child maltreatment: A developmental traumatology perspective, APA Division 56 Trauma Psychology Book Series.* Washington, DC: American Psychological Association Press.

Beidas, R. S., Stewart, R. E., Walsh, L., Lucas, S., Downey, M. M., Jackson, K., Fernandez, T., & Mandell, D. S. (2015). Free, brief, and validated: Standardized instruments for low-resource mental health settings. *Cognitive and Behavioral Practice 22*(1), 5–19. doi:http://dx.doi.org/10.1016/j.cbpra.2014.02.002

Belknap, J., Holsinger, K., & Little, J. (2012). Sexual minority status, abuse, and self-harming behaviors among incarcerated girls. *Journal of Child & Adolescent Trauma 5*(2), 173–185.

Benamati, J. (2015). Screening Tool for Trauma and Symptomatic Behaviors. Unpublished measure.

Bennett, D. C., & Kerig, P. K. (2014). Investigating the construct of trauma-related acquired callousness among delinquent youth: Differences in emotion processing. *Journal of Traumatic Stress 27*(4), 415–422. doi:10.1002/jts.21931

Bennett, D. C., Modrowski, C. A., Kerig, P. K., & Chaplo, S. D. (2015). Investigating the dissociative subtype of PTSD in a sample of traumatized detained youth. *Psychological Trauma 7*(5), 465–472. doi:http://dx.doi.org/10.1037/tra0000057

Bennett, D. C., Kerig, P. K., Chaplo, S. D., McGee, A. B., & Baucom, B. R. (2014). Validation of the five-factor model of PTSD symptom structure among delinquent youth. *Psychological Trauma 6*(4), 438–447. doi:10.1037/a0035303

Bernal, G., & Jimenez-Chafey, M. I. (2008). Cultural adaptation of psychotherapy for ethnic-minority youth: Beyond one-size-fits-all. *Child and Family Policy and Practice Review 4*, 3–6.

Bernier, M-J. J., Hébert, M., & Collin-Vézina, D. (2013). Dissociative symptoms over a year in a sample of sexually abused children. *Journal of Trauma & Dissociation 14*(4), 455–472. doi:10.1080/15299732.2013.769478

Bernstein, D. P., & Fink, L. A. (1998). *CTQ: Childhood Trauma Questionnaire: A retrospective self-report*. San Antonio, TX: Psychological Corp.

Berntson, G. G., Boysen, S. T., & Cacioppo, J. T. (1992). Cardiac orienting and defensive responses: Potential origins in autonomic space. In B. A. Campbell, H. Hayne & R. RIchardson (Eds.), *Attention and information processing in infants and adults: Perspectives from human and animal research* (pp. 163–200). Hillsdale, NJ: Erlbaum.

Berntson, G. G., Cacioppo, J. T., Quigley, K. S., & Fabro, V. T. (1994). Autonomic space and psychophysiological response. *Psychophysiology 31*(1), 44–61. doi:10.1111/j.1469-8986.1994.tb01024.x

Biederman, J., Petty, C. R., Spencer, T. J., Woodworth, K. Y., Bhide, P., Zhu, J., & Faraone, S. V. (2013). Examining the nature of the comorbidity between pediatric attention deficit/hyperactivity disorder and post-traumatic stress disorder. *Acta Psychiatrica Scandinavica 128*(1), 78–87.

Boelen, P. A., van de Schoot, R., van den Hout, M. A., de Keijser, J., & van den Bout, J. (2010). Prolonged Grief Disorder, depression, and posttraumatic stress disorder are distinguishable syndromes. *Journal of Affective Disorders* *125*(1–3), 374–378. doi:http://dx.doi.org/10.1016/j.jad.2010.01.076

Borrego, J., Klinkebiel, C., & Gibson, A. (2014). Parent-child interaction therapy: An overview. In B. Allen & M. Kronenberg (eds.), *Treating traumatized children: A casebook of evidence-based therapies* (pp. 165–182). New York: Guilford.

Bovin, M. J., & Marx, B. P. (2011). The importance of the peritraumatic experience in defining traumatic stress. *Psychological Bulletin 137*(1), 47–67. doi:10.1037/a0021353

Bowlby, J. (1980). *Attachment and loss, (Vol. 3.) Loss: Sadness and depression.* New York: Basic Books.

Bowlby, J. (1988a). Developmental psychiatry comes of age. *American Journal of Psychiatry 145*(1), 1–10.

Bowlby, J. (1988b). *A secure base: Parent-child attachment and healthy human development.* New York, NY: Basic Books.

Boyce, W. T., & Ellis, B. J. (2005). Biological sensitivity to context: I. An evolutionary–developmental theory of the origins and functions of stress reactivity. *Development and Psychopathology 17*(2), 271–301. doi:10.1017/S0954579405050145

Brewin, C. R., Lanius, R. A., Novac, A., Schnyder, U., & Galea, S. (2009). Reformulating PTSD for DSM-V: Life after Criterion A. *Journal of Traumatic Stress 22*(5), 366–373.

Briere, J. (1996). *Trauma Symptom Checklist for Children.* Odessa, FL: Psychological Assessment Resources, Inc.

Briere, J., Weathers, F. W., & Runtz, M. (2005). Is dissociation a multidimensional construct? Data from the Multiscale Dissociation Inventory. *Journal of Traumatic Stress 18*(3), 221–231.

Briggs-Gowan, M. J., Carter, A. S., & Ford, J. D. (2012). Parsing the effects of violence exposure in early childhood: Modeling developmental pathways. *Journal of Pediatric Psychology 37*(1), 11–22. doi:10.1093/jpepsy/jsr063

Bronfenbrenner, U. (1979). Contexts of child rearing: Problems and prospects. *American Psychologist 34*(10), 844–850. doi:10.1037/0003-066x.34.10.844

Brown, A., Becker-Weidman, E., & Saxe, G. N. (2014). A developmental perspective on childhood traumatic stress. In M. J. Friedman, T. M. Keane & P. A. Resick (Eds.), *Handbook of PTSD* (pp. 331–350). New York: Guilford.

Brunner, R., Parzer, P., Schuld, V., & Resch, F. (2000). Dissociative symptomatology and traumatogenic factors in adolescent psychiatric patients. *The Journal of Nervous and Mental Disease 188*(2), 71–77.

Bui, E., Brunet, A., Olliac, B., Very, E., Allenou, C., Raynaud, J-P. P., Claudet, I., Bourdet-Loubère, S., Grandjean, H., Schmitt, L., & Birmes, P. (2011). Validation of the peritraumatic dissociative experiences questionnaire and peritraumatic distress inventory in school-aged victims of road traffic accidents. *European Psychiatry* 26(2), 108–111. doi:10.1016/j.eurpsy.2010.09.007

Bujarski, S. J., Feldner, M. T., Lewis, S. F., Babson, K. A., Trainor, C. D., Leen-Feldner, E., Badour, C. L., & Bonn-Miller, M. O. (2012). Marijuana use among traumatic event-exposed adolescents: Posttraumatic stress symptom frequency predicts coping motivations for use. *Addictive Behaviors* 37(1), 53–59. doi:http://dx.doi.org/10.1016/j.addbeh.2011.08.009

Cao, X., Wang, L., Cao, C., Zhang, J., & Elhai, J. D. (2016). DSM-5 posttraumatic stress disorder symptom structure in disaster-exposed adolescents: Stability across gender and relation to behavioral problems. *Journal of Abnormal Child Psychology*, 1–12. doi:10.1007/s10802-016-0193-1

Carlson, E. A., Tuppet Yates, M., & Alan Sroufe, L. (2009). Development of dissociation and development of the self. In P. F. Dell & J. A. O'Neil (Eds.), *Dissociation and the dissociative disorders: DSM-V and beyond* (pp. 39–52). New York: Routledge.

Carmassi, C., Akiskal, H. S., Yong, S. S., Stratta, P., Calderani, E., Massimetti, E., Akiskal, K. K., Rossi, A., & Dell'Osso, L. (2013). Post-traumatic stress disorder in DSM-5: estimates of prevalence and criteria comparison versus DSM-IV-TR in a non-clinical sample of earthquake survivors. *Journal of Affective Disorders 151*(3), 843–848.

Carrion, V. G., Haas, B. W., Garrett, A., Song, S. Y., & Reiss, A. L. (2010). Reduced hippocampal activity in youth with posttraumatic stress symptoms: an fMRI study. *Journal of Pediatric Psychology 35*(5), 559–569.

Carrion, V. G., Weems, C. F., & Reiss, A. L. (2007). Stress predicts brain changes in children: A pilot longitudinal study on youth stress, posttraumatic stress disorder, and the hippocampus. *Pediatrics 119*(3), 509–516. doi:10.1542/peds.2006-2028.

Cary, C. E., & McMillen, J. C. (2012). The data behind the dissemination: A systematic review of trauma-focused cognitive behavioral therapy for use with children and youth. *Children and Youth Services Review 34*(4), 748–757. doi:http://dx.doi.org/10.1016/j.childyouth.2012.01.003

Catherall, D. R. (1998). Treating traumatized families. In C. R. Figley (Ed.), *Burnout in families: The systemic costs of caring. Innovations in psychology* (pp. 187–215). Boca Raton, FL: CRC Press,Inc.

Cauffman, E., Feldman, S. S., Waterman, J., & Steiner, H. (1998). Posttraumatic stress disorder among female juvenile offenders. *Journal of the American Academy of Child and Adolescent Psychiatry 37*(11), 1209–1216. doi:10.1353/foc.0.0015

Ceballo, R., Dahl, T. A., Aretakis, M. T., & Ramirez, C. (2001). Inner-city children's exposure to community violence: How much do parents know? *Journal of Marriage and Family, 63*(4), 927–940. doi:10.1111/j.1741-3737.2001.00927.x

Centers for Disease Control. (2010). Youth Risk Behavior Survey. http://apps.nccd.cdc.gov/youthonline/App/Default.aspx

Chaffin, M., Silovsky, J. F., Funderburk, B., Anne Valle, L., Brestan, E. V., Balachova, T., Jackson, S., Lensgraf, J., & Bonner, B. L. (2004). Parent-Child Interaction Therapy with physically abusive parents: Efficacy for reducing future abuse reports. *Journal of Consulting and Clinical Psychology 72*(3), 500–510. doi:10.1037/0022-006X.72.3.500

Chamberlain, P. (1996). Intensified foster care: Multi-level treatment for adolescents with conduct disorders in and out of home care. In E. D. Hibbs & P. S. Jensen (Eds.), *Psychosocial treatments for child and adolescent disorders: Empirically based strategies for clinical practice* (pp. 475–496). Washington, DC: American Psychological Association.

Chaplo, S. D., Kerig, P. K., Bennett, D. C., & Modrowski, C. A. (2015). The roles of emotion dysregulation and dissociation in the association between sexual abuse and self-injury among juvenile justice-involved youth. *Journal of Trauma & Dissociation 16*(3), 272–285. doi:10.1080/15299732.2015.98 9647

Chard, K. M., Weaver, T. L., & Resick, P. A. (1997). Adapting cognitive processing therapy for child sexual abuse survivors. *Cognitive and Behavioral Practice 4*(1), 31–52.

Cicchetti, D. (1991). Fractures in the crystal: Developmental psychopathology and the emergence of self. *Developmental Review 11*(3), 271–287.

Cicchetti, D., & Lynch, M. (1995). Failures in the expectable environment and their impact on individual development: The case of child maltreatment. In D. Cicchetti & D. J. Cohen (Eds.), *Developmental psychopathology: Risk, disorder, and adaptation* (Vol. 2.) (pp. 32–71). New York, NY: Wiley.

Cicchetti, D., & Toth, S. L. (1992). Editorial: The role of developmental theory in prevention and intervention. *Development and Psychopathology 4*(4), 489–494.

Cicchetti, D., & Toth, S. L. (2005). Child maltreatment. *Annual Review of Clinical Psychology 1*(1), 409–438. doi:10.1146/annurev.clinpsy.1.102803.144029

Cicchetti, D., Toth, S. L., Bush, M. A., & Gillespie, J. F. (1988). Stage-salient issues: A transactional model of intervention. In E. D. Nannis & P. A. Cowan (Eds.), *Developmental psychopathology and its treatment* (pp. 123–146). San Francisco: Jossey-Bass.

Cicchetti, D., & Valentino, K. (2006). An ecological transactional perspective on child maltreatment: Failure of the average expectable environment and its influence upon child development. In D. Cicchetti & D. J. Cohen (Eds.), *Developmental psychopathology* (pp. 129–201). New York, NY: Wiley.

Cicchetti, D. (2016). Socioemotional, personality, and biological development: Illustrations from a multilevel developmental psychopathology perspective on child maltreatment. *Annual Review of Psychology 67*(1), 187–211. doi:10.1146/annurev-psych-122414-033259

Cloitre, M., Garvert, D. W., Brewin, C. R., Bryant, R. A., & Maercker, A. (2013). Evidence for proposed ICD-11 PTSD and complex PTSD: A latent profile analysis. *European Journal of Psychotraumatology.* doi:10.3402/ejpt. v4i0.20706

Cohen, J. A., Mannarino, A. J., & Deblinger, E. (2012). *Trauma-Focused CBT for children and adolescents: Treatment applications.* New York: Guilford.

Cohen, J. A., Mannarino, A. J., & Deblinger, E. (2017). *Treating trauma and traumatic grief in children and adolescents* (2nd ed.). New York: Guilford.

Cohen, J. A., & Mannarino, A. P. (2014). Psychosocial treatments for children and adolescents with PTSD. In M. J. Friedman, T. M. Keane & P. A. Resick (Eds.), *Handbook of PTSD.* New York: Guilford.

Cohen, J. A., & Scheeringa, M. S. (2009). Post-traumatic stress disorder diagnosis in children: Challenges and promises. *Dialogues in Clinical Neuroscience 11*(1), 91–99. doi:PMC3181905

Cohen, J. A., Mannarino, A. P., Jankowski, K., Rosenberg, S., Kodya, S., & Wolford, G. L. (2016). A randomized implementation study of trauma-focused cognitive behavioral therapy for adjudicated teens in residential treatment facilities. *Child Maltreatment 21*(2), 156–167.

Cohen, J. A. (2010). Practice parameter for the assessment and treatment of children and adolescents with posttraumatic stress disorder. *Journal of the American Academy of Child & Adolescent Psychiatry 49*(4), 414–430. doi:http://dx.doi.org/10.1016/j.jaac.2009.12.020

Cohen, J. A., Bukstein, O., Walter, H., Benson, R. S., Chrisman, A., Farchione, T. R., Hamilton, J., Keable, H., Kinlan, J., Schoettle, U., Siegel, M., Stock, S., & Medicus, J. (2010). Practice parameter for the assessment and treatment of children and adolescents with posttraumatic stress disorder. *Journal of the American Academy of Child and Adolescent Psychiatry 49*(4), 414–430.

Cohen, J. A., & AACAP Work Group on Quality Issues. (2010). Practice parameter for the assessment and treatment of children and adolescents with posttraumatic stress disorder. *Journal of the American Academy of Child & Adolescent Psychiatry 49*(4), 414–430. doi:http://dx.doi.org/10.1016/j. jaac.2009.12.020

Connolly, J. (2014). Outcomes in emerging adulthood for maltreated youth: A clinical-developmental approach. *Child Maltreatment 19*(3–4), 270–274. doi:10.1177/1077559514557932

Cook, A., Spinazzola, J., Ford, J., Lanktree, C., Blaustein, M., Cloitre, M., DeRosa, R., Hubbard, R., Kagan, R., Liautaud, J., Mallah, K., Olafson, E., & van der Kolk, B. A. (2005). Complex trauma in children and adolescents. *Psychiatric Annals 35*(5), 390–398.

Copeland, W. E., Keeler, G., Angold, A., & Costello, E. J. (2010). Posttraumatic stress without trauma in children. *American Journal of Psychiatry 167*(9), 1059–1065. doi:10.1176/appi.ajp.2010.09020178

Corliss, H. L., Cochran, S. D., & Mays, V. M. (2002). Reports of parental maltreatment during childhood in a United States population-based survey of homosexual, bisexual, and heterosexual adults. *Child Abuse & Neglect 26*(11), 1165–1178. doi:http://dx.doi.org/10.1016/S0145-2134(02)00385-X

Costello, E. J., Erkanli, A., Fairbank, J. A., & Angold, A. (2002). The prevalence of potentially traumatic events in childhood and adolescence. *Journal of Traumatic Stress 15*(2), 99–112. doi:10.1023/a:1014851823163

Cowan, P. A. (1978). *Piaget with feeling.* New York: Holt, Rinehart, and Winston.

Cruz-Katz, S. J., Cruise, K. R., & Quinn, T. A. (2010). The Abbreviated Dysregulation Inventory: Examining the factor structure and testing associations with adolescent aggression. Annual meeting of the American Psychology-Law Society, Vancouver, BC, Canada.

Cryder, C. H., Kilmer, R. P., Tedeschi, R. G., & Calhoun, L. G. (2006). An exploratory study of posttraumatic growth in children following a natural disaster. *American Journal of Orthopsychiatry 76*(1), 65–69. doi:10.1037/0002-9432.76.1.65

Cuevas, C. A., Finkelhor, D., Turner, H. A., & Ormrod, R. K. (2007). Juvenile delinquency and victimization: A theoretical typology. *Journal of Interpersonal Violence 22*(12), 1581–1602. doi:10.1177/0886260507306498

Cummings, E. M., & Davies, P. T. (2011). *Marital conflict and children: An emotional security perspective.* New York: The Guilford Press.

D'Augelli, A. R., Pilkington, N. W., & Hershberger, S. L. (2002). Incidence and mental health impact of sexual orientation victimization of lesbian, gay, and bisexual youths in high school. *School Psychology Quarterly 17*(2), 148–167. doi:10.1521/scpq.17.2.148.20854

D'Andrea, W., Ford, J., Stolbach, B., Spinazzola, J., & van der Kolk, B. A. (2012). Understanding interpersonal trauma in children: why we need a developmentally appropriate trauma diagnosis. *American Journal of Orthopsychiatry 82*(2), 187–200.

Danzi, B. A., & La Greca, A. M. (2016). DSM-IV, DSM-5, and ICD-11: Identifying children with posttraumatic stress disorder after disasters. *Journal of Child Psychology and Psychiatry 57*(12), 1444–1452. doi:10.1111/jcpp.12631

De Bellis, M. D. (2001). Developmental traumatology: The psychobiological development of maltreated children and its implications for research, treatment, and policy. *Development and Psychopathology 13*(3), 539–564.

De Bellis, M. D., & Crowson, M. (2003). The impact of maltreatment on brain development in childhood. *The North Carolina Psychologist*, 10–11.

De Bellis, M. D., Hooper, S. R., Woolley, D. P., & Shenk, C. E. (2010). Demographic maltreatment, and neurobiological correlates of PTSD symptoms in children and adolescents. *Journal of Pediatric Psychology 35*(5), 570–577.

Deblinger, E., & Heflin, A. H. (1996). *Treating sexually abused children and their nonoffending parents: A cognitive behavioral approach.* Thousand Oaks, CA: Sage.

Deblinger, E., Lippmann, J., & Steer, R. (1996). Sexually abused children suffering posttraumatic stress symptoms: Initial treatment outcome findings. *Child Maltreatment 1*(4), 310–321. doi:10.1177/1077559596001004003

Deblinger, E., Mannarino, A. P., Cohen, J. A., Runyon, M. K., & Steer, R. A. (2011). Trauma-focused cognitive behavioral therapy for children: impact of the trauma narrative and treatment length. *Depression and Anxiety 28*(1), 67–75.

Deblinger, E., & Runyon, M. K. (2005). Understanding and treating feelings of shame in children who have experienced maltreatment. *Child Maltreatment 10*(4), 364–376.

Delahanty, D. L., Nugent, N. R., Christopher, N. C., & Walsh, M. (2005). Initial urinary epinephrine and cortisol levels predict acute PTSD symptoms in child trauma victims. *Psychoneuroendocrinology 30*(2), 121–128. doi:http:// dx.doi.org/10.1016/j.psyneuen.2004.06.004

Donisch, K., Bray, C., & Gewirtz, A. (2015). *University of minnesota's traumatic stress screen for children and adolescents.* Minneapolis, MN: University of Minnesota.

Dorsey, S., McLaughlin, K. A., Kerns, S. E. U., Harrison, J. P., Lambert, H. K., Briggs, E. C., Cox, J. R., & Amaya-Jackson, L. (2016). Evidence base update for psychosocial treatments for children and adolescents exposed to traumatic events. *Journal of Clinical Child & Adolescent Psychology*, 1–28. doi:10.1080/ 15374416.2016.1220309

Dube, S. R., Williamson, D. F., Thompson, T., Felitti, V. J., & Anda, R. F. (2004). Assessing the reliability of retrospective reports of adverse childhood experiences among adult HMO members attending a primary care clinic. *Child Abuse & Neglect 28*(7), 729–737.

Dyb, G., Rodriguez, N., Brymer, M. J., Saltzman, W. R., Steinberg, A. M., & Pynoos, R. S. (2008). Emotional reactions, peritraumatic dissociation, and posttraumatic stress reactions in adolescents. *Journal of Child and Adolescent Trauma 1*(1), 63–74. doi:10.1080/19361520801934423

El-Sheikh, M., Kouros, C. D., Erath, S., Cummings, E. M., Keller, P., Staton, L., Beauchaine, T., & Moore, G. A. (2009). Marital conflict and children's externalizing behavior: Interactions between parasympathetic and sympathetic nervous system activity. *Monographs of the Society for Research in Child Development 74*(1), Serial 292.

Elhai, J. D., Franklin, C. L., & Gray, M. J. (2008). The SCID PTSD module's trauma screen: Validity with two samples in detecting trauma history. *Depression and Anxiety 25*(9), 737–741. doi:10.1002/da.20318

Elkind, D., & Bowen, R. (1979). Imaginary audience behavior in children and adolescents. *Developmental Psychology 15*(1), 38–44. doi:10.1037/0012-1649.15.1.38

Ellis, B. H., Fogler, J., Hansen, S., Forbes, P., Navalta, C. P., & Saxe, G. (2012). Trauma systems therapy: 15-month outcomes and the importance of effecting environmental change. *Psychological Trauma: Theory, Research, Practice, and Policy 4*(6), 624-630. doi:10.1037/a0025192

Erikson, E. H. (1950). *Childhood and society.* New York: Norton.

Erikson, E. H. (1964). Clinical observation of play disruption in young children. In M. R. Haworth (Ed.), *Child psychotherapy* (pp. 264–276). New York: Basic Books.

Erwin, B. A., Newman, E., McMackin, R. A., Morrissey, C., & Kaloupek, D. G. (2000). PTSD, malevolent environment, and criminality among criminally involved male adolescents. *Criminal Justice and Behavior 27*(2), 196–215.

Eyberg, S. M., & Boggs, S. R. (1998). Parent-child interaction therapy: A psychosocial intervention for the treatment of young conduct-disordered children. In J. M. Briesmeister and C. E. Schaefer (Eds.), *Handbook of parent training* (pp. 61–97). New York: Wiley.

Eyberg, S., Boggs, S. R., & Reynolds, L. A. (1980). *Eyberg child behavior inventory.* University of Oregon Health Sciences Center.

Fairbank, J. A., Putnam, F. W., & Harris, W. W. (2014). Child traumatic stress: Prevalence, trends, risk, and impact. In M. J. Friedman, T. M. Keane and P. A. Resick (Eds.), *Handbook of PTSD: Science and Practice.* New York: Guilford.

Feiring, C., Miller-Johnson, S., & Cleland, C. M. (2007). Potential pathways from stigmatization and internalizing symptoms to delinquency in sexually abused youth. *Child Maltreatment 12*(3), 220–232.

Fergusson, D. M., Horwood, L. J., & Lynskey, M. T. (1997). Childhood sexual abuse, adolescent sexual behaviors and sexual revictimization. *Child Abuse & Neglect 21*(6), 789–802.

Figley, C. R. (1989). *Treating stress in families.* New York: Brunner/Mazel.

Finkelhor, D. (1995). The victimization of children: A developmental perspective. *American Journal of Orthopsychiatry 65*(2), 177–193.

Finkelhor, D., Hamby, S., Turner, H., & Ormrod, R. (2011). *The Juvenile Victimization Questionnaire: 2nd Revision (JVQ-R2)*. Durham, NH: Crimes Against Children Research Center.

Finkelhor, D., Ormrod, R. K., & Turner, H. A. (2007). Polyvictimization and trauma in a national longitudinal cohort. *Development and Psychopathology 19*(1), 149–166.

Finkelhor, D., Ormrod, R., Turner, H., & Hamby, S. L. (2005). The victimization of children and youth: A comprehensive, national survey. *Child Maltreatment 10*(1), 5–25.

Finkelhor, D., Hamby, S. L., Ormrod, R., & Turner, H. (2005). The Juvenile Victimization Questionnaire: Reliability, validity, and national norms. *Child Abuse & Neglect 29*(4), 383–412. doi:http://dx.doi.org/10.1016/j.chiabu.2004.11.001

Finkelhor, D., Turner, H., Ormrod, R., & Hamby, S. L. (2009). Violence, abuse, and crime exposure in a national sample of children and youth. *Pediatrics 124*(5), 1411–1423. doi:10.1542/peds.2009-0467

Fivush, R., Bohanek, J. G., & Zaman, W. (2011). Personal and intergenerational narratives in relation to adolescents' well-being. *New Directions for Child and Adolescent Development 2011*(131), 45–57.

Foa, E. B., Johnson, K. M., Feeny, N. C., & Treadwell, K. R. (2001). The Child PTSD Symptom Scale: A preliminary examination of its psychometric properties. *Journal of Clinical Child Psychology 30*(3), 376–384.

Ford, Julian D., Spinazzola, J., van der Kolk, B., & Grasso, D. (2014). Developmental Trauma Disorder (DTD) field trial: I. evidence of reliability, structure, and validity of the DTD Semi-structured Interview (DTD-SI). Paper presented at the *International Society for Traumatic Stress Studies Annual Convention*, Miami, FL.

Ford, J. D. (2002). Traumatic victimization in childhood and persistent problems with oppositional-defiance. In R. Greenwald (Ed.), *Trauma and juvenile delinquency: Theory, research, and interventions* (pp. 25–58). Binghamton, New York: Haworth.

Ford, J. D. (2009). Neurobiological and developmental research: Clinical implications. In M. A. Courtois and J. D. Ford (Eds.), *Treating complex traumatic stress disorders: An evidence-based guide* (pp. 31–58). New York: Routledge.

Ford, J. D., Grasso, D. A., Elhai, J. D., & Courtois, C. A. (2015). *Posttraumatic Stress Disorder: Scientific and professional dimensions* (2nd ed.). Kidlington, Oxford, UK: Academic Press.

Ford, J. D., Hartman, J. K., Hawke, J., & Chapman, J. F. (2008). Traumatic victimization, posttraumatic stress disorder, suicidal ideation, and substance abuse risk among juvenile justice-involved youth. *Journal of Child and Adolescent Trauma 1*(1), 75–92. doi:10.1080/19361520801934456

Ford, J. D. (2015). An affective cognitive neuroscience-based approach to PTSD psychotherapy: The TARGET Model. *Journal of Cognitive Psychotherapy* 29(1), 68–91.

Ford, J. D. (2011). Assessing child and adolescent complex traumatic stress reactions. *Journal of Child & Adolescent Trauma* 4(3), 217–233. doi:10.1080 /19361521.2011.897080

Ford, J. D., & Connor, D. F. (2009). ADHD and posttraumatic stress disorder. *Current Attention Disorders Reports* 1(2), 60–66.

Ford, J. D., Chapman, J., Connor, D. F., & Cruise, K. R. (2012). Complex trauma and aggression in secure juvenile justice settings. *Criminal Justice and Behavior* 39(6), 694–724. doi:10.1177/0093854812436957

Ford, J. D., Chapman, J., Mack, M., & Pearson, G. (2006). Pathways from traumatic child victimization to delinquency: Implications for juvenile and permanency court proceedings and decisions. *Juvenile and Family Court Journal* 57(1), 13–26. doi:10.1111/j.1755-6988.2006.tb00111.x

Ford, J. D., Elhai, J. D., Connor, D. F., & Frueh, B. C. (2010). Poly-victimization and risk of posttraumatic, depressive, and substance use disorders and involvement in delinquency in a national sample of adolescents. *Journal of Adolescent Health* 46(6), 545–552.

Ford, J. D., & Hawke, J. (2012). Trauma affect regulation psychoeducation group and milieu intervention outcomes in juvenile detention facilities. *Journal of Aggression, Maltreatment & Trauma* 21(4), 365–384. doi:10.1080/10926771 .2012.673538

Ford, J. D., & Russo, E. (2006). Trauma-focused, present-centered, emotional self-regulation approach to integrated treatment for posttraumatic stress and addiction: Trauma Adapative Recovery Group Education and Therapy (TARGET). *American Journal of Psychotherapy* 60(4), 335–355.

Ford, J. D., Spinazzola, J., Van der Kolk, B., & Grasso, D. (2014, November). Developmental Trauma Disorder (DTD) Field Trial: I. Evidence of Reliability, Structure, and Validity of the DTD Semi-structured Interview (DTD-SI). Paper presented at the *International Society for Traumatic Stress Studies Annual Convention, Miami, FL.*

Ford, J. D., Steinberg, K. L., Hawke, J., Levine, J., & Zhang, W. (2012). Randomized trial comparison of emotion regulation and relational psychotherapies for PTSD with girls involved in delinquency. *Journal of Clinical Child and Adolescent Psychology* 41(1), 27–37. doi:10.1080/15374 416.2012.632343

Forehand, R., & Wierson, M. (1993). The role of developmental factors in planning behavioral interventions for children: Disruptive behavior as an example. *Behavior Therapy* 24(1), 117–141.

Forehand, R., Dorsey, S., Jones, D. J., Long, N., & McMahon, R. J. (2010). Adherence and flexibility: They can (and do) coexist! *Clinical Psychology: Science and Practice 17*(3), 258–264.

Fraiberg, S., Adelson, E., & Shapiro, V. (1980). Ghosts in the nursery: A psychoanalytic approach to the problems of impaired infant-mother relationships. In S. Fraiberg (Ed.), *Clinical studies in infant mental health* (pp. 164–196). New York, NY: Basic Books.

Franklin, J. C., Jamieson, J. P., Glenn, C. R., & Nock, M. K. (2014). How developmental psychopathology theory and research can inform the Research Domain Criteria (RDoC) project. *Journal of Clinical Child & Adolescent Psychology 44*(2), 280–290. doi:10.1080/15374416.2013.873981

Freud, A. (1965). *Normality and pathology in childhood*. New York: International Universities Press.

Freyd, J. J. (1996). *Betrayal trauma: The logic of forgetting childhood abuse.* Cambridge, MA: Harvard University Press.

Frick, P. J. (2009). Extending the construct of psychopathy to youth: Implications for understanding, diagnosing, and treating antisocial children and adolescents. *The Canadian Psychiatric Association Journal/La Revue de l'Association des psychiatres du Canada 54*(12), 803–812.

Frick, P. J., Ray, J. V., Thornton, L. C., & Kahn, R. E. (2014). Annual Research Review: A developmental psychopathology approach to understanding callous-unemotional traits in children and adolescents with serious conduct problems. *Journal of Child Psychology and Psychiatry 55*(6), 532–548. doi:10.1111/jcpp.12152

Friedberg, R. D., & McClure, J. M. (2002). *Clinical practice of cognitive therapy with children and adolescents: The nuts and bolts.* New York: Guilford.

Friedman, M. J., Resick, P. A., & Keane, T. M. (2014). PTSD from DSM-III to DSM-5: Progress and challenges. In M. J. Friedman, T. M. Keane & P. A. Resick (Eds.), *Handbook of PTSD* (pp. 3–20). New York: Guilford.

Friedman, M. J., Resick, P. A., Bryant, R. A., & Brewin, C. R. (2011). Considering PTSD for DSM-5. *Depression and Anxiety 28*(9), 750–769. doi:10.1002/da.20767

Freud, A. (1965). *Normality and pathology in childhood*. New York: International Universities Press.

Galovski, T. E., Wachen, J. S., Chard, K. M., Monson, C. M., & Resick, P. A. (2015). Cognitive Processing Therapy. In U. Schnyder & M. Cloitre (Eds.), *Evidence Based Treatments for Trauma-Related Psychological Disorders: A Practical Guide for Clinicians* (pp. 189–203). Cham: Springer International Publishing.

Gaylord-Harden, N., Cunningham, J., & Zelencik, B. (2011). Effects of exposure to community violence on internalizing symptoms: Does desensitization to violence occur in African American youth? *Journal of Abnormal Child Psychology 39*(5), 711–719. doi:10.1007/s10802-011-9510-x

Gaylord-Harden, N. K., Dickson, D., & Pierre, C. (2015). Profiles of community violence exposure among African American youth: An examination of desensitization to violence using latent class analysis. *Journal of Interpersonal Violence 31*(11), doi:10.1177/0886260515572474

Gerson, R., & Rappaport, N. (2012). Traumatic stress and posttraumatic stress disorder in youth: Recent research findings on clinical impact, assessment, and treatment. *Journal of Adolescent Health 52*(2), 137–143.

Giannopoulou, I., Strouthos, M., Smith, P., Dikaiakou, A., Galanopoulou, V., & Yule, W. (2006). Post-traumatic stress reactions of children and adolescents exposed to the Athens 1999 earthquake. *European Psychiatry 21*(3), 160–166.

Gil-Rivas, V., Silver, R. C., Holman, E. A., McIntosh, D. N., & Poulin, M. (2007). Parental response and adolescent adjustment to the September 11, 2001 terrorist attacks. *Journal of Traumatic Stress 20*(6), 1063–1068. doi:10.1002/jts.20277

Goodman, M. (2012). Complex PTSD is on the trauma spectrum: Comment on Resick et al. (2012). *Journal of Traumatic Stress 25*(3), 254–255. doi:10.1002/jts.21695

Grassetti, S. N., Herres, J., Williamson, A. A., Yarger, H. A., Layne, C. M., & Kobak, R. (2014). Narrative focus predicts symptom change trajectories in group treatment for traumatized and bereaved adolescents. *Journal of Clinical Child & Adolescent Psychology 44*(6), 1–9. doi:10.1080/15374416.2014.913249

Grasso, D. J., Felton, J. W., & Reid-Quiñones, K. (2015). The Structured Trauma-Related Experiences and Symptoms Screener (STRESS): Development and preliminary psychometrics. *Child Maltreatment 20*(3), 214–220. doi:10.1177/1077559515588131

Gray, J. A. (1988). *The psychology of fear and stress* (2nd ed.). New York: Cambridge University Press.

Gray, J. A. (2003). *The neuropsychology of anxiety: An enquiry into the functions of the septo-hippocampal system.* New York, NY: Oxford University Press.

Grisso, T., & Barnum, R. (2003). *Massachusetts Youth Screening Instrument Version 2: User's manual and technical report.* Sarasota, FL: Professional Resource Press.

Grisso, T., & Quinlan, J. C. (2005). Massachusetts Youth Screening Instrument-Version 2. In T. Grisso, G. Vincent and D. Seagrave (Eds.), *Mental health screening and assessment in juvenile justice* (pp. 99–111). New York: Guilford.

Hafstad, G. S., Dyb, G., Jensen, T. K., Steinberg, A. M., & Pynoos, R. S. (2014). PTSD prevalence and symptom structure of DSM-5 criteria in adolescents and young adults surviving the 2011 shooting in Norway. *Journal of Affective Disorders* 169, 40–46. doi:http://dx.doi.org/10.1016/j.jad.2014.06.055

Hafstad, G. S., Kilmer, R. P., & Gil-Rivas, V. (2011). Posttraumatic growth among Norwegian children and adolescents exposed to the 2004 tsunami.

Psychological Trauma: Theory, Research, Practice, and Policy 3(2), 130–138. doi:10.1037/a0023236

Harter, S. (1983). Cognitive-developmental considerations in the conduct of play therapy. In C. E. Schaefer & K. J. O'Connor (Eds.), *Handbook of play therapy* (pp. 95–127). New York: Wiley.

Harter, S. (1986). Cognitive-developmental processes in the integration of concepts about emotions and the self. *Social Cognition 4*(2), 119–151.

Harter, S. (1988). Developmental and dynamic changes in the nature of the self-concept: Implications for child psychotherapy. In S. Shirk (Ed.), *Cognitive development and child psychotherapy*. New York: Plenum.

Hawkins, S. S., & Radcliffe, J. (2006). Current measures of PTSD for children and adolescents. *Journal of Pediatric Psychology 31*(4), 420–430. doi:10.1093/jpepsy/jsj039

Herman, J. L. (1992). *Trauma and recovery: The aftermath of violence—from domestic abuse to political terror*. New York: Basic Books.

Herman, J. L. (1994). Sequelae of prolonged and repeated trauma: Evidence for a complex posttraumatic syndrome (DESNOS). In J. R. T. Davidson & E. G. Foa (Eds.), *Posttraumatic stress disorder: DSM-IV and beyond* (pp. 213–228). Washington, DC: American Psychiatric Press.

Herman, J. (2012). CPTSD is a distinct entity: Comment on Resick et al. (2012). *Journal of Traumatic Stress 25*(3), 256–257. doi:10.1002/jts.21697

Herschell, A. D., & McNeil, C. B. (2007). Parent-child interaction therapy with physically abusive families. In J. M. Briesmeister & C. E. Schaefer (Eds.), *Handbook of parent training: Helping parents prevent and solve problem behaviors* (pp. 234–267). New York: Wiley.

Holman, E. A., Garfin, D. R., & Silver, R. C. (2014). "Media's role in broadcasting acute stress following the Boston Marathon bombings. *Proceedings of the National Academy of Sciences 111*(1), 93–98. doi:10.1073/pnas.1316265110

Holman, K., Chaplo, S. D., Modrowski, C. A., & Kerig, P. K. (2016). Correspondence between mothers' and detained youths' reports of trauma exposure and posttraumatic stress symptoms: The role of attachment quality. Society for Research in Adolescence, Baltimore, MD.

Holmbeck, G. N., Devine, K. A., & Bruno, E. F. (2010). Developmental issues and considerations in research and practice. In J. R Weisz & A. E Kazdin (Eds.), *Evidence-Based Psychotherapies for Children and Adolexcents* (pp. 28–44). New York: Guilford.

Horowitz, M. J. (2011). *Stress response syndromes*. Northvale, NJ: Aronson.

Horowitz, M. J. (1993). Stress-response syndromes. In *International handbook of traumatic stress syndromes*, 49-60. Springer.

Idsoe, T., Dyregrov, A., & Idsoe, E. C. (2012). Bullying and PTSD Symptoms. *Journal of Abnormal Child Psychology 40*(6), 901–911. doi:10.1007/s10802-012-9620-0

Insel, T. R., Cuthbert, B. N., Garvey, M. A., Heinssen, R. K., Pine, D. S., Quinn, K. J., Sanislow, C. A., & Wang, P. S. (2010). Research domain criteria (RDoC): Toward a new classification framework for research on mental disorders. *American Journal of Psychiatry 167*(7), 748–751.

Jaycox, L. H., Cohen, J. A., Mannarino, A. P., Walker, D. W., Langley, A. K., Gegenheimer, K. L., Scott, M., & Schonlau, M. (2010)."Children's mental health care following Hurricane Katrina: A field trial of trauma-focused psychotherapies. *Journal of Traumatic Stress 23*(2), 223–231. doi:10.1002/jts.20518

Jaycox, L. H., Kataoka, S. H., Stein, B. D., Langley, A. K., & Wong, M. (2012). Cognitive Behavioral Intervention for Trauma in Schools. *Journal of Applied School Psychology 28*(3), 239–255. doi:10.1080/15377903.2012.695766

Jaycox, L. H., Stein, B. D., Kataoka, S. H., Wong, M., Fink, A., Escudero, P. I. A., & Zaragoza, C. (2002). Violence exposure, posttraumatic stress disorder, and depressive symptoms among recent immigrant schoolchildren. *Journal of the American Academy of Child & Adolescent Psychiatry 41*(9), 1104–1110. doi:http://dx.doi.org/10.1097/00004583-200209000-00011

Jensen, T. K., Holt, T., Ormhaug, S. M., Egeland, K., Granly, L., Hoaas, L. C., Hukkelberg, S. S., Indregard, T., Stormyren, S. D., & Wentzel-Larsen, T. (2013). A randomized effectiveness study comparing trauma-focused cognitive behavioral therapy with therapy as usual for youth. *Journal of Clinical Child & Adolescent Psychology 43*(3), 356–369. doi:10.1080/15374416.2013.822307

Jessor, R. (1992). Risk behavior in adolescence: A psychosocial framework for understanding and action. *Developmental Review 12*, 374–390.

Kahn, R. E., Frick, P. J., Younstrom, E. A., Youngstrom, J. K., Feeny, N. C., & Findling, R. L. (2013). Distinguishing primary and secondary variants of callous-unemotional traits among adolescents in a clinic-referred sample. *Psychological Assessment 25*(3), 966. doi:10.1037/a0032880

Kahn, R. E., Frick, P. J., Youngstrom, E., Findling, R. L., & Youngstrom, J. K. (2012). The effects of including a callous–unemotional specifier for the diagnosis of conduct disorder. *Journal of Child Psychology and Psychiatry 53*(3), 271–282. doi:10.1111/j.1469-7610.2011.02463.x

Kaplow, J. B., Howell, K. H., & Layne, C. M. (2014). Do circumstances of the death matter? Identifying socioenvironmental risks for grief-related psychopathology in bereaved youth. *Journal of Traumatic Stress 27*(1), 42–49. doi:10.1002/jts.21877

Kaplow, J. B., Layne, C. M., Pynoos, R. S., Cohen, J. A., & Lieberman, A. (2012). DSM-V diagnostic criteria for bereavement-related disorders in children and adolescents: Developmental considerations. *Psychiatry 75*(3), 243–266. doi:10.1521/psyc.2012.75.3.243

Karpman, B. (1941). On the need of separating psychopathy into two distinct clinical types: the symptomatic and the idiopathic. *Journal of Criminal Psychopathology 3*, 112–137.

Katz, L. F., & Gottman, J. M. (1995). Vagal tone protects children from marital conflict. *Development and Psychopathology 7*(1), 83–92.

Kazdin, A. E. (2007). Mediators and mechanisms of change in psychotherapy research. *Annual Review of Clinical Psychology 3*, 1–27. doi:10.1146/annurev.clinpsy.3.022806.091432

Kazdin, A. E., Rodgers, A., & Colbus, D. (1986). The Hopelessness Scale for Children: Psychometric characteristics and concurrent validity. *Journal of Consulting and Clinical Psychology 54*(2), 241–245. doi:10.1037/0022-006X.54.2.241

Keeley, J. W., Reed, G. M., Roberts, M. C., Evans, S. C., Robles, R., Matsumoto, C., Brewin, C. R., Cloitre, M., Perkonigg, A., Rousseau, C., Gureje, O., Lovell, A. M., Sharan, P., & Maercker, A. (2016). Disorders specifically associated with stress: A case-controlled field study for ICD-11 mental and behavioural disorders. *International Journal of Clinical and Health Psychology 16*(2), 109–127. doi:http://dx.doi.org/10.1016/j.ijchp.2015.09.002

Kenardy, J., De Young, A., and Charlton, E. (2012, November). PTSD as a "gateway" disorder in young children. Annual Meeting of the International Society for Traumatic Stress Studies, Los Angeles.

Kendall, P. C., & Beidas, R. S. (2007). Smoothing the trail for dissemination of evidence-based practices for youth: Flexibility within fidelity. *Professional Psychology: Research and Practice 38*(1), 13–20.

Kerig, P. K. (2004). Unpublished measure. University of Utah, Salt Lake City.

Kerig, P. K. (2005). Revisiting the construct of boundary dissolution: A multidimensional perspective. In P. K. Kerig (Ed.), *Implications of parent-child boundary dissolution for developmental psychopathology: Who is the parent and who is the child?* (pp. 5–42). New York: Haworth.

Kerig, P. K. (2003). In search of protective processes for children exposed to interparental violence. *Journal of Emotional Abuse 3*(3–4), 149–182. doi:10.1300/J135v03n03_01

Kerig, P. K. (2012). Unpublished measure. University of Utah, Salt Lake City.

Kerig, P. K. (2014). Maltreatment and trauma in adolescence: A time of heightened risk and potential resilience. *StressPoints 28*(1), 1–21.

Kerig, P. K. (2016). Family systems approaches to developmental psychopathology. In D. Cicchetti (Ed.), *Developmental psychopathology, Vol. I: Theory and method* (pp. 580–630). New York: Wiley.

Kerig, P. K. (in press). Polyvictimization and girls' involvement in the juvenile justice system: Investigating gender-differentiated patterns of risk, recidivism, and resilience, *Journal of Interpersonal Violence*.

Kerig, P. K., & Alexander, J. F. (2013). Family matters: Integrating trauma treatment into Functional Family Therapy with delinquent youth. In P. K. Kerig (Ed.), *Psychological trauma and juvenile delinquency* (pp. 122–140). London: Routledge.

Kerig, P. K., Moeddel, M. A., & Becker, S. P. (2011). Assessing the sensitivity and specificity of the MAYSI-2 for detecting trauma among youth in juvenile detention. *Child & Youth Care Forum 40*, 345–352. doi:10.1007-s10566-010-9124-4

Kerig, P. K., & S. P. Becker. (2012). Trauma and girls' delinquency. In S. Miller, L. D. Leve & P. K. Kerig (Eds.), *Delinquent girls: Contexts, relationships, and adaptation* (pp. 119–143). New York: Springer.

Kerig, P. K., & Becker, S. P. (2015). Early abuse and neglect as risk factors for the development of criminal and antisocial behavior. In J. Morizot & L. Kazemian (Eds.), *The development of criminal and antisocial behavior* (pp. 181–199). New York: Springer.

Kerig, P. K., & Bennett, D. C. (2013). Beyond fear, helplessness, and horror: Peritraumatic reactions associated with posttraumatic stress symptoms among traumatized delinquent youth. *Psychological Trauma 5*(5), 431–438. doi:10.1037/a0029609

Kerig, P. K., Bennett, D. C., Thompson, M., & Becker, S. P. (2012). "Nothing really matters": Emotional numbing as a link between trauma exposure and callousness in delinquent youth. *Journal of Traumatic Stress 25*(3), 272–279. doi:10.1002/jts.21700

Kerig, P. K., Chaplo, S. D., Bennett, D. C., & Modrowski, C. A. (2016). "Harm as harm": Gang membership, perpetration trauma, and posttraumatic stress symptoms among youth in the juvenile justice system. *Criminal Justice and Behavior 43*(5), 635–652. doi:10.1177/0093854815607307

Kerig, P. K., Fedorowicz, A. E., Brown, C. A., & Warren, M. (2000). Assessment and intervention for PTSD in children exposed to violence. In R. Geffner, P. Jaffe & M. Sudermann (Eds.), *Children exposed to family violence: Current issues in research, intervention and prevention, and policy development* (pp. 161–184). Binghamton, NY: Haworth Press.

Kerig, P. K., Ford, J. D., & Olafson, E. (2015). *Assessing exposure to psychological trauma and posttraumatic stress symptoms in the juvenile justice population*. Los Angeles, CA & Durham, NC: National Center for Child Traumatic Stress.

Kerig, P. K., & Schindler, S. R. (2013). Engendering the evidence base: A critical review of the conceptual and empirical foundations of gender-responsive interventions for girls' delinquency. *Laws 2*(3), 244–282. doi:10.3390/laws2030244

Kerig, P. K., & Schulz, M. S. (2012). The transition from adolescence to adulthood: What lies beneath and what lies beyond. In P. K. Kerig, M. S. Schulz & S. T. Hauser (Eds.), *Adolescence and beyond: Family processes in development.* New York: Oxford University Press.

Kerig, P. K., Sink, H. E., Cuellar, R. E., Vanderzee, K. L., & Elfstrom, J. L. (2010). Implementing Trauma-Focused CBT with fidelity and flexibility: A family case study. *Journal of Clinical Child & Adolescent Psychology 39*(5), 713–722. doi:10.1080/15374416.2010.501291

Kerig, P. K., Vanderzee, K. L., Becker, S. P., & Ward, R. M. (2013). Deconstructing PTSD: Traumatic experiences, posttraumatic symptom clusters, and mental health problems among delinquent youth. In P. K. Kerig (Ed.), *Psychological trauma and juvenile delinquency* (pp. 47–62). London: Routledge.

Kerig, P. K., Volz, A. R., Moeddel, M. A. A., & Cuellar, R. E. (2010). Implementing dating violence prevention programs with flexibility, fidelity, and sensitivity to diversity: Lessons learned from Expect Respect. *Journal of Aggression, Maltreatment & Trauma 19*(6), 661–680. doi:10.1080/10926771.2010.502079

Kerig, P. K., Wainryb, C., Twali, M. S., & Chaplo, S. D. (2013). America's child soldiers: Toward a research agenda for studying gang-involved youth in the United States. *Journal of Aggression, Maltreatment & Trauma 22*(7), 773–795. doi:10.1080/10926771.2013.813883

Kerig, P. K., Ward, R. M., Vanderzee, K. L., & Moeddel, M. A. (2009). Posttraumatic stress as a mediator of the relationship between trauma and mental health problems among juvenile delinquents. *Journal of Youth and Adolescence 38*(9), 1214–1225. doi:10.1007/s10964-008-9332-5

Kerig, P. K., & Becker, S. P. (2010). From internalizing to externalizing: Theoretical models of the processes linking PTSD to juvenile delinquency. In S. J. Egan (Ed.), *Posttraumatic stress disorder (PTSD): Causes, symptoms and treatment* (pp. 1–46). Hauppauge, NY: Nova Science Publishers.

Kerig, P. K., Charak, R., Chaplo, S. D., Bennett, D. C., Armour, C., Modrowski, C. A., & McGee, A. B. (2016). Validation of the factor structure of the Adolescent Dissociative Experiences Scale in a sample of trauma-exposed detained youth. *Psychological Trauma: Theory, Research, Practice, and Policy 8*(5), 592–600. doi:10.1037/tra0000140

Kerig, P. K., Ludlow, A., & Wenar, C. (2012). *Developmental psychopathology: From infancy through adolescence* (6th ed.). Maidenhead, UK: McGraw-Hill.

Kessler, R. C., Petukhova, M., Sampson, N. A., Zaslavsky, A. M., & Wittchen, H. -U. (2012). Twelve-month and lifetime prevalence and lifetime morbid risk of anxiety and mood disorders in the United States. *International Journal of Methods in Psychiatric Research 21*(3), 169–184. doi:10.1002/mpr.1359

Kilmer, R. P. (2006). Resilience and posttraumatic growth in children. In L. G. Calhoun & R. G. Tedeschi (Eds.), *Handbook of posttraumatic growth* (pp. 264–288). Mahwah, NJ: Erlbaum.

Kilmer, R. P., & Gil-Rivas, V. (2010). Exploring posttraumatic growth in children impacted by Hurricane Katrina: Correlates of the phenomenon and developmental considerations. *Child Development 81*(4), 1211–1227.

Kilmer, R. P., Gil-Rivas, V., Tedeschi, R. G., Cann, A., Calhoun, L. G., Buchanan, T., & Taku, K. (2009). Use of the Revised Posttraumatic Growth Inventory for Children. *Journal of Traumatic Stress 22*(3), 248–253. doi:10.1002/jts.20410

Kilpatrick, D. G., Resnick, H. S., Milanak, M. E., Miller, M. W., Keyes, K. M., & Friedman, M. J. (2013). National estimates of exposure to traumatic events and PTSD prevalence using DSM-IV and DSM-5 criteria. *Journal of Traumatic Stress 26*(5), 537–547. doi:10.1002/jts.21848

Kilpatrick, D. G., Ruggiero, K. J., Acierno, R., Saunders, B. E., Resnick, H. S., & Best, C. L. (2003). Violence and risk of PTSD, major depression, substance abuse/dependence, and comorbidity: Results from the National Survey of Adolescents. *Journal of Consulting and Clinical Psychology 71*(4), 692–700. doi:10.1037/0022-006X.71.4.692

Kimmerling, R., Weitland, J. C., Iverson, K. M., Karpenko, J. A., & Jain, S. (2014). Gender issues in PTSD. In M. J. Friedman, T. M. Keane & P. A. Resick (Eds.), *Handbook of PTSD* (pp. 313–330). New York: Guilford.

Kimonis, E. R., Frick, P. J., Cauffman, E., Goldweber, A., & Skeem, J. (2012). Primary and secondary variants of juvenile psychopathy differ in emotional processing. *Development and Psychopathology 24*(Special Issue 03), 1091–1103. doi:10.1017/S0954579412000557

Kirsch, V., Wilhelm, F. H., & Goldbeck, L. (2011). Psychophysiological characteristics of PTSD in children and adolescents: A review of the literature. *Journal of Traumatic Stress 24*(2), 146–154.

Kisiel, C. L., Fehernbach, T., Torgersen, E., Stolbach, B., McClelland, G., Griffin, G., & Burkman, K. (2014). Constellations of interpersonal trauma and symptoms in child welfare: Implications for a developmental trauma framework. *Journal of Family Violence 29*(1), 1–14.

Kisiel, C. L., & Lyons, J. S. (2001). Dissociation as a mediator of psychopathology among sexually abused children and adolescents. *American Journal of Psychiatry 158*(7), 1034–1039. doi:http://dx.doi.org/10.1176/appi.ajp.158.7.1034

Kisiel, C., Lyons, J. S., Blaustein, M., Fehrenbach, T., Griffin, G., Germain, J., Saxe, G., & Ellis, H. (2011). *Child and adolescent needs and strengths (CANS) manual: The NCTSN CANS Comprehensive—Trauma Version: A comprehensive information integration tool for children and adolescents exposed to traumatic events.* Chicago, IL: Praed Foundation/Los Angeles, CA & Durham, NC: National Center for Child Traumatic Stress.

Kisiel, C., Summersett-Ringgold, F., Weil, L. E. G., & McClelland, G. (2016). Understanding strengths in relation to complex trauma and mental health symptoms within child welfare. *Journal of Child and Family Studies*, 1–15. doi:10.1007/s10826-016-0569-4

Kitzmann, K. M., Gaylord, N. K., Holt, A. R., & Kenny, E. D. (2003). Child witnesses to domestic violence: A meta-analytic review. *Journal of Consulting and Clinical Psychology 71*(2), 339–352.

Kletter, H., Weems, C. F., & Carrion, V. G. (2009). Guilt and posttraumatic stress symptoms in child victims of interpersonal violence. *Clinical Child Psychology and Psychiatry 14*(1), 71–83.

Knell, S. M., & Dasari, M. (2011). Cognitive-behavioral play therapy. In S. W. Russ & L. N. Niec (Eds.), *Play in clinical practice: Evidence-based approaches* (pp. 236–263). New York: Guilford.

Koenen, K. C., Amstadter, A. B., & Nugent, N. R. (2009). Gene-environment Interaction in posttraumatic stress disorder: An Update. *Journal of Traumatic Stress 22*(5), 416–426. doi:10.1002/jts.20435

Koutsikou, S., Crook, J. J., Earl, E. V., Leith, J. L., Watson, T. C., Lumb, B. M., & Apps, R. (2014). Neural substrates underlying fear-evoked freezing: the periaqueductal grey–cerebellar link. *The Journal of Physiology 592*(10), 2197–2213. doi:10.1113/jphysiol.2013.268714

Krischer, M. K., & Sevecke, K. (2008). Early traumatization and psychopathy in female and male juvenile offenders. *International journal of law and psychiatry 31*(3), 253–262.

Lancaster, S. L., Melka, S. E., & Rodriguez, B. F. (2011). Emotional predictors of PTSD symptoms. *Psychological Trauma: Theory, Research, Practice, and Policy 3*(4), 313–317. doi:10.1037/a0022751

Landolt, M. A., Schnyder, U., Maier, T., Schoenbucher, V., & Mohler-Kuo, M. (2013). Trauma exposure and posttraumatic stress disorder in adolescents: A national survey in Switzerland. *Journal of Traumatic Stress 26*(2), 209–216. doi:10.1002/jts.21794

Lanius, R. A., Brand, B., Vermetten, E., Frewen, P. A., & Spiegel, D. (2012). The dissociative subtype of posttraumatic stress disorder: Rationale, clinical and neurobiological evidence, and implications. *Depression and Anxiety 29*(8), 701–708. doi:10.1002/da.21889

Lansford, J. E., Dodge, K. A., Pettit, G. S., & Bates, J. E. (2010). Does physical abuse in early childhood predict substance use in adolescence and early adulthood? *Child Maltreatment 15*(2), 190–194. doi:10.1177/1077559509352359

Lansing, A. E., Plante, W. Y., & Beck, A. N. (2016). Assessing stress-related treatment needs among girls at risk for poor functional outcomes: The impact of cumulative adversity, criterion traumas, and non-criterion events. *Journal of Anxiety Disorders*. doi:http://dx.doi.org/10.1016/j.janxdis.2016.09.007

Layne, C. M., Greenson, J. K., Ostrowski, S. A., Kim, S., Reading, S., Vivrette, R. L., Briggs, E. C., Fairbank, J. A., & Pynoos, R. S. (2014). Cumulative trauma exposure and high risk behavior in adolescence: Findings from the National Child Traumatic Stress Network core data set. *Psychological Trauma* 6(S1), S40–S49.

Layne, C. M., Saltzman, W. R., Kaplow, J. B., Olafson, E., & Pynoos, R. in press. *Trauma and Grief Component Therapy for Adolescents (TGCTA)*. New York: Cambridge University Press.

Layne, C. M., Saltzman, W. R., Poppleton, L., Burlingame, G. M., Pašalić, A., Duraković, E., Mušić, M., Ćampara, N., Dapo, N., Arslanagić, B., Steinberg, A. M., & Pynoos, R. S. (2008). Effectiveness of a school-based group psychotherapy program for war-exposed adolescents: A randomized controlled trial. *Journal of the American Academy of Child & Adolescent Psychiatry 47*(9), 1048–1062. doi:http://dx.doi.org/10.1097/CHI.0b013e31817eecae

Leen-Feldner, E. W., Feldner, M. T., Knapp, A., Bunaciu, L., Blumenthal, H., & Amstadter, A. B. (2013). Offspring psychological and biological correlates of parental posttraumatic stress: Review of the literature and research agenda. *Clinical Psychology Review 33*(8), 1106–1133. doi:http://dx.doi.org/10.1016/j.cpr.2013.09.001

Lehmann, P., & Carlson, B. E. (1998). Crisis intervention with traumatized child witnesses in shelters for battered women. In A. R. Roberts (Ed.), *Battered women and their families* (pp. 99–128). New York: Springer.

Lengua, L. J., Long, A. C., Smith, K. I., & Meltzoff, A. N. (2005). Pre-attack symptomatology and temperament as predictors of children's responses to the September 11 terrorist attacks. *Journal of Child Psychology and Psychiatry 46*(6), 631–645.

Lester, P., Liang, L. –J., Milburn, N., Mogil, C., Woodward, K., Nash, W., Aralis, H., Sinclair, M., Semaan, A., Klosinski, L., Beardslee, W., & Saltzman, W. (2016). Evaluation of a family-centered preventive intervention for military families: Parent and child longitudinal outcomes. *Journal of the American Academy of Child & Adolescent Psychiatry 55*(1), 14–24. doi:10.1016/j.jaac.2015.10.009

Lester, P., Saltzman, W. R., Woodward, K., Glover, D. A., Leskin, G. A., Bursch, B., Pynoos, R. S., & Beardslee, W. R. (2012). Evaluation of a family-centered prevention intervention for military children and families facing wartime deployments. *American Journal of Public Health 102*(supplement 1), S48–S54. doi:http://dx.doi.org/10.2105/AJPH.2010.300088.

Levant, R. F. (2005). *Report of the 2005 presidential task force on evidence-based practice. Washington, DC.* American Psychological Association.

Lewis, M. L., & Ippen, C. G. (2004). Rainbows of tears, souls full of hope: Cultural issues related to young children and trauma. In J. D. Osofsky (Ed.), *Young children and trauma* (pp. 11–46). New York: Guilford.

Lieberman, A. F., & Van Horn, P. (2008). *Psychotherapy with infants and young children: Repairing the effects of stress and trauma on early attachment*: New York.

Lieberman, A. F., & Knorr, K. (2007). The impact of trauma: A developmental framework for infancy and early childhood. *Pediatric annals 36*(4), 209–215.

Lieberman, A. F., & Van Horn, P. (2005). *Don't hit my mommy!: A manual for child-parent psychotherapy with young witnesses of family violence: Zero to Three.*

Lieberman, A. F., Ippen, C. G., & Van Horn, P. (2006). Child-parent psychotherapy: 6-month follow-up of a randomized controlled trial. *Journal of the American Academy of Child & Adolescent Psychiatry 45*(8), 913–918. doi:10.1097/01.chi.0000222784.03735.92

Lieberman, A. F., Van Horn, P., & Ippen, C. G. (2005). Toward evidence-based treatment: Child-parent psychotherapy with preschoolers exposed to marital violence. *Journal of the American Academy of Child & Adolescent Psychiatry 44*(12), 1241–1248. doi:10.1097/01.chi.0000181047.59702.58

Lindauer, R. J. L. (2012). Child maltreatment—Clinical PTSD diagnosis not enough?!: Comment on Resick et al. (2012). *Journal of Traumatic Stress 25*(3), 258–259. doi:10.1002/jts.21698

Lipschitz, D. S., Winegar, R. K., Nicolaou, A. L., Hartnick, E., Wolfson, M., & Southwick, S. M. (1999). Perceived abuse and neglect as risk factors for suicidal behavior in adolescent inpatients. *Journal of Nervous and Mental Disease 187*(1), 32–39.

Lipschitz, D. S., Morgan, C. A., & Southwick, S. M. (2002). Neurobiological disturbances in youth with childhood trauma and in youth with conduct disorder. *Journal of Aggression, Maltreatment & Trauma 6*(1), 149–174. doi:10.1300/J146v06n01_08

Liu, L., Wang, L., Cao, C., Qing, Y., & Armour, C. (2016). Testing the dimensional structure of DSM-5 posttraumatic stress disorder symptoms in a nonclinical trauma-exposed adolescent sample. *Journal of Child Psychology and Psychiatry 57*(2), 204–212. doi:10.1111/jcpp.12462

Lobbestael, J., Leurgans, M., & Arntz, A. (2011). Inter-rater reliability of the Structured Clinical Interview for DSM-IV Axis I Disorders (SCID I) and Axis II Disorders (SCID II). *Clinical Psychology & Psychotherapy, 18*(1), 75–79. doi:10.1002/cpp.693

Logan, D. E., & Graham-Bermann, S. A. (1999). Emotion expression in children exposed to family violence. *Journal of Emotional Abuse 1*(3), 39–64.

Lyons-Ruth, K., & Jacobvitz, D. (2008). Attachment disorganization: Genetic factors, parenting contexts, and developmental transformation from infancy to adulthood. In J. Cassidy & P. R. Shaver (Eds.), *Handbook of attachment* (pp. 666–697). New York: Guilford.

MacDonald, H. Z., Beeghly, M., Grant-Knight, W., Augustin, M., Woods, R. W., Cabral, H., Rose-Jacobs, R., Saxe, G. N., & Frank, D. A. (2008).

Longitudinal association between infant disorganized attachment and childhood posttraumatic stress symptoms. *Development and Psychopathology* 20(2), 493–508.

Maercker, A., Brewin, C. R., Bryant, R. A., Cloitre, M., Reed, G. M., van Ommeren, M., Humayun, A., Jones, L. M., Kagee, A., Llosa, A. E., Rousseau, C., Somasundaram, D. J., Souza, R., Suzuki, Y., Weissbecker, I., Wessely, S. C., First, M. B., & Saxena, S. (2013). Proposals for mental disorders specifically associated with stress in the International Classification of Diseases-11. *The Lancet 381*(9878), 1683–1685. doi:10.1016/S0140-6736(12)62191-6

Marrow, M. T., Knudsen, K. J., Olafson, E., & Bucher, S. E. (2013). The value of implementing TARGET within a trauma-informed juvenile justice setting. In edited by P. K. Kerig (Ed.), *Psychological trauma and juvenile delinquency* (pp. 174–187). London: Routledge.

Masten, A. S., & Cicchetti, D. (2010). Developmental cascades. *Development and Psychopathology 22*(3), 491–495.

Matulis, S., Resick, P. A., Rosner, R., & Steil, R. (2014). Developmentally adapted Cognitive Processing Therapy for adolescents suffering from posttraumatic stress disorder after childhood sexual or physical abuse: A pilot study. *Clinical Child and Family Psychology Review 17*(2), 173–190. doi:10.1007/s10567-013-0156-9

McCall-Hosenfeld, J., Winter, M., Heeren, T., & Liebschutz, J. M. (2014). The association of interpersonal trauma with somatic symptom severity in a primary care population with chronic pain: Exploring the role of gender and the mental health sequelae of trauma. *Journal of Psychosomatic Research 77*(3), 196–204. doi:http://dx.doi.org/10.1016/j.jpsychores.2014.07.011

McCoy, D. C. (2013). Early violence exposure and self-regulatory development: A bioecological systems perspective. *Human Development 56*(4), 254–273.

McEwen, B. S. (1998). Stress, adaptation, and disease: Allostasis and allostatic load. *Annals of the New York Academy of Sciences 840*(1), 33–44. doi:10.1111/j.1749-6632.1998.tb09546.x

McLaughlin, K. A., Koenen, K. C., Hill, E. D., Petukhova, M., Sampson, N. A., Zaslavsky, A. M., & Kessler, R. C. (2013). Trauma exposure and posttraumatic stress disorder in a national sample of adolescents. *Journal of the American Academy of Child and Adolescent Psychiatry 52*(8), 815–830. e14.

McLaughlin, K. A., Rith-Najarian, L., Dirks, M. A., & Sheridan, M. A. (2013). Low vagal tone magnifies the association between psychosocial stress exposure and internalizing psychopathology in adolescents. *Journal of Clinical Child & Adolescent Psychology 44*(2), 314–328. doi:10.1080/15374416.2013.843464

McLeer, S. V., Callaghan, M., Henry, D., & Wallen, J. (1994). Psychiatric disorders in sexually abused children. *Journal of the American Academy of Child and Adolescent Psychiatry 27*, 650–654.

McNair, R. (2002). *Perpetration-induced traumatic stress*. New York: Praeger.

Meiser-Stedman, R., Smith, P., Bryant, R., Salmon, K., Yule, W., Dalgleish, T., & Nixon, R. D. (2009). Development and validation of the Child Post-Traumatic Cognitions Inventory (CPTCI). *Journal of Child Psychology and Psychiatry 50*(4), 432–440.

Meyer, R. M. L., Gold, J. I., Beas, V. N., Young, C. M., & Kassam-Adams, N. (2015). Psychometric Evaluation of the Child PTSD Symptom Scale in Spanish and English. *Child Psychiatry & Human Development, 46*(3), 438–444. doi:10.1007/s10578-014-0482-2

Meyerson, D. A., Grant, K. E., Carter, J. S., & Kilmer, R. P. (2011). Posttraumatic growth among children and adolescents: A systematic review. *Clinical Psychology Review 31*(6), 949–964. doi:http://dx.doi.org/10.1016/j.cpr.2011.06.003

Milan, S., Zona, K., Acker, J., & Turcios-Cotto, V. (2013). Prospective risk factors for adolescent PTSD: Sources of differential exposure and differential vulnerability. *Journal of Abnormal Child Psychology 41*(2), 339–353. doi:10.1007/s10802-012-9677-9

Miller, L. (2015). *PTSD and forensic psychology: Applications to civil and criminal law*. New York: Springer.

Modrowski, C. A., Chaplo, S. D., Bennett, D. C., & Kerig, P. K. (2016). Screening for PTSD among detained adolescents: Implications of the changes in DSM-5. *Psychological Trauma 9*(1). doi:10.1037/tra000015

Modrowski, C. A., & Kerig, P. K. under review. Investigating factors associated with PTSD dissociative subtype membership in a sample of traumatized justice-involved youth.

Moretti, M. M., McKay, S., & Holland, R. (2000). The Comprehensive Adolescent-Parent Attachment Inventory (CAPAI). *Unpublished measure and data. Simon Fraser University, Burnaby, British Columbia, Canada.*

Morris, A., Gabert-Quillen, C., & Delahanty, D. (2012). The association between parent PTSD/depression symptoms and child PTSD symptoms: A meta-analysis. *Journal of Pediatric Psychology 37*(10), 1076–1088. doi:10.1093/jpepsy/jss091

Nader, K. (2008). *Understanding and assessing trauma in children and adolescents*. New York: Routledge.

Nader, K., Newman, E., Weathers, F. W., Kaloupek, D. G., Kriegler, J. A., Blake, D. D., & Pynoos, R. S. (1998). *Clinician Administered PTSD scale for Children and Adolescents for DSM-IV (CAPS-CA)*. White River Junction, VT: National Center for PTSD.

Nader, K. (2007). Culture and the assessment of trauma in youths. In J. Wilson & C. S. Tang (Eds.), *Cross-cultural assessment of psychological trauma and PTSD* (pp. 169–196). Springer.

Nader, K. (2011). The assessment of associated features important to understanding childhood trauma. *Journal of Child & Adolescent Trauma* 4(4), 259–273. doi:10.1080/19361521.2011.614923

National Center on Addiction and Substance Abuse. (2003). The formative years: Pathways to substance abuse among girls and young women ages 8-22. www.casacolumbia.org/templates/publications_reports.aspx

Navalta, C. P., Brown, A. D., Nisewaner, A., Ellis, B. H., & Saxe, G. N. (2013). Trauma Systems Therapy. *Treating complex traumatic stress disorders in children and adolescents: Scientific foundations and therapeutic models*, 329–348.

Nixon, R., Vandervord, D., Sterk, J., & Pearce, A. (2012). A randomized trial of cognitive behaviour therapy and cognitive therapy for children with posttraumatic stress disorder following single-incident trauma. *Journal of Abnormal Child Psychology* 40(3), 327–337. doi:10.1007/s10802-011-9566-7

Nugent, N. R., Ostrowski, S., Christopher, N. C., & Delahanty, D. L. (2007). Parental posttraumatic stress symptoms as a moderator of child's acute biological response and subsequent posttraumatic stress symptoms in pediatric injury patients. *Journal of Pediatric Psychology* 32(3), 309–318. doi:10.1093/jpepsy/jsl005

O'Connor, K. J. (2000). *The play therapy primer* (Vol. 2.). New York: Wiley.

Olafson, E., Boat, B. W., Putnam, K. T., Thieken, L., Marrow, M. T., & Putnam, F. W. (2016). Implementing Trauma and Grief Component Therapy for Adolescents and Think Trauma for traumatized youth in secure juvenile justice settings. *Journal of Interpersonal Violence*. doi:10.1177/0886260516628287

Ormhaug, S. M., Jensen, T. K., Wentzel-Larsen, T., & Shirk, S. R. (2014). The therapeutic alliance in treatment of traumatized youths: Relation to outcome in a randomized clinical trial. *Journal of Consulting and Clinical Psychology* 82(1), 52–64. doi:10.1037/a0033884

Osofsky, J. D. (2011). Perspectives related to trauma and its impact on young children. In J. D. Osofsky (Ed.), *Clinical Work with Traumatized Young Children* (pp. 9–10). New York: Guilford Press.

Paolucci, E. O., Genuis, M. L., & Violato, C. (2001). A meta-analysis of the published research on the effects of child sexual abuse. *The Journal of Psychology* 135(1), 17–36. doi:10.1080/00223980109603677

Pappagallo, M., Silva, R. R., & Rojas, V. M. (2004). Differential diagnosis of PTSD in children. In R. R. Silva (Ed.), *Posttraumatic stress disorders in children and adolescents: Handbook* (pp. 218–236). New York: Norton.

Parent, A. -S., Teilmann, G., Juul, A., Skakkebaek, N. E., Toppari, J., & Bourguignon, J. -P. (2003). The timing of normal puberty and the age limits of sexual precocity: Variations around the world, secular trends, and changes after migration. *Endocrine Reviews* 24(5), 668–693. doi:10.1210/er.2002-0019

Pat-Horenczyk, R., Peled, O., Miron, T., Brom, D., Villa, Y., & Chemtob, C. (2007). Risk-taking behaviors among Israeli adolescents exposed to recurrent terrorism: Provoking danger under continuous threat? *American Journal of Psychiatry 164*(1), 66–72.

Pelcovitz, D., van der Kolk, B. A., Herman, S., Roth, S., & Kaplan, S. (2004). *Structured Interview for Disorders of Extreme Stress-NOS Adolescent Version (SIDES-A).* New York: New York University School of Medicine.

Pelcovitz, D., van der Kolk, B. A., Roth, S., Mandel, F., Kaplan, S., & Resick, P. (1997). Development of a criteria set and a structured interview for Disorders of Extreme Stress (SIDES). *Journal of Traumatic Stress 10*(1), 3–16.

Perkonigg, A., Kessler, R. C., Storz, S., & Wittchen, H. -U. (2000). Traumatic events and post-traumatic stress disorder in the community: Prevalence,risk factors and comorbidity. *Acta Psychiatrica Scandinavica 101*(1), 46–59. doi:10.1034/j.1600-0447.2000.101001046.x

Porges, S. W. (2007). The polyvagal perspective. *Biological Psychology 74*(2), 116–143. doi:http://dx.doi.org/10.1016/j.biopsycho.2006.06.009

Porter, S. (1996). Without conscience or without active conscience? The etiology of psychopathy revisited. *Aggression and Violent Behavior 1*(2), 179–180.

Pratchett, L. C., & Yehuda, R. (2014). Developmental trauma from a biophysical perspective. In R. Pat-Horenczyk, D. Brom & J. M. Vogel (Eds.), *Helping children cope with trauma* (pp. 3–18). New York: Routledge.

Prins, A., Bovin, M. J., Smolenski, D. J., Marx, B. P., Kimerling, R., Jenkins-Guarnieri, M. A., Kaloupek, D. G., Schnurr, P. P., Kaiser, A. P., Leyva, Y. E., & Tiet, Q. Q. (2016). The Primary Care PTSD Screen for DSM-5 (PC-PTSD-5): Development and evaluation within a veteran primary care sample. *Journal of General Internal Medicine 31*(10), 1206–1211. doi:10.1007/s11606-016-3703-5

Putnam, F. W. (1997). *Dissociation in children and adolescents: A developmental perspective.* New York: Guilford.

Putnam, F. W. (2006). Dissociative disorders. In D. Cicchetti & D. J. Cohen (Eds.), *Developmental psychopathology. Volume III: Risk, disorder and adaptation* (pp. 657–695). New York: Wiley.

Putnam, F. W., & Peterson, G. (1994). Further validation of the Child Dissociative Checklist. *Dissociation 7*(4), 204–211.

Pynoos, R. S. (1993). Traumatic stress and developmental psychopathology in children and adolescents. In J. Oldham, M. Riba and A. Tasman (Eds.), *American Psychiatric Press review of psychiatry* (pp. 205–238). Washington, DC: American Psychiatric Press.

Pynoos, R. S., Fairbank, J. A., Briggs, E. C., Steinberg, A. M., Layne, C. M., Stolbach, B., & Ostrowski, S. A. (2008). Trauma exposure, adverse experiences, and diverse symptom profiles in a national sample of traumatized children. International Society for Traumatic Stress Studies, Chicago, IL.

Pynoos, R. S., & Nader, K. (1988). Psychological first aid and treatment approach to children exposed to community violence: Research implications. *Journal of Traumatic Stress 1*(4), 445–473.

Pynoos, R. S., & Nader, K. (1993). Issues in the treatment of posttraumatic stress in children and adolescents. In J. P. Wilson & B. Raphael (Eds.), *International handbook of traumatic stress syndromes* (pp. 535–549). New York: Plenum.

Pynoos, R. S., & Steinberg, A. M. (2014). UCLA PTSD Reaction Index for DSM-5. Unpublished measure. Los Angeles: University of California Los Angeles.

Pynoos, R. S., Weathers, F. W., Steinberg, A. M., Marx, B. P., Layne, C. M., Kaloupek, D. G., Schnurr, P. P., Keane, T. M., Blake, D. D., Newman, E., Nader, K. O., & Kriegler, J. A. (2015). Available from the National Center for PTSD at www.ptsd.va.gov.

Pynoos, R. S., Steinberg, A. M., Layne, C. M., Briggs, E. C., Ostrowski, S. A., & Fairbank, J. A. (2009). DSM-V PTSD diagnostic criteria for children and adolescents: A developmental perspective and recommendations. *Journal of Traumatic Stress 22*(5), 391–398. doi:10.1002/jts.20450

Ready, C. B., Hayes, A. M., Yasinski, C. W., Webb, C., Gallop, R., Deblinger, E., & Laurenceau, J. -P. (2015). Overgeneralized beliefs, accommodation, and treatment outcome in youth receiving trauma-focused cognitive behavioral therapy for childhood trauma. *Behavior Therapy 46*(5), 671–688. doi:http://dx.doi.org/10.1016/j.beth.2015.03.004

Resick, P. A., Monson, C. M., & Rizvi, S. L. (2013). Posttraumatic stress disorder. In W. E. Craighead, D. J. Miklowitz and L. W. Craighead (Eds.), *Psychopathology*. New York: Wiley.

Resick, P. A., Bovin, M. J., Calloway, A. L., Dick, A. M., King, M. W., Mitchell, K. S., Suvak, M. K., Wells, S. Y., Stirman, S. W., & Wolf, E. J. (2012). A critical evaluation of the complex PTSD literature: Implications for DSM-5. *Journal of Traumatic Stress 25*(3), 241–251. doi:10.1002/jts.21699

Resick, P. A., Galovski, T. E., Uhlmansiek, M. O., Scher, C. D., Clum, G. A., & Young-Xu, Y. (2008). A randomized clinical trial to dismantle components of cognitive processing therapy for posttraumatic stress disorder in female victims of interpersonal violence. *Journal of Consulting and Clinical Psychology 76*(2), 243–258. doi:10.1037/0022-006X.76.2.243

Resick, Pa A., and Mark W. Miller. 2009. "Posttraumatic stress disorder: Anxiety or traumatic stress disorder?" *Journal of Traumatic Stress* 22 (5):384-390. doi: 10.1002/jts.20437.

Resick, P. A., & Schnicke, M. K. (1993). *Cognitive processing therapy for rape victims: A treatment manual, Cognitive processing therapy for rape victims: A treatment manual.* Thousand Oaks, CA: Sage Publications, Inc.

Richters, J. E., & Saltzman, W. (1990). *Survey of children's exposure to community violence.* Rockville, MD: National Institute of Mental Health.

Roberts, A. L., Rosario, M., Corliss, H. L., Koenen, K. C., & Austin, S. B. (2012). Childhood gender nonconformity: A risk indicator for childhood abuse and posttraumatic stress in youth. *Pediatrics 129*(3), 410–417.

Rojas-Flores, L., Clements, M. L., Koo, J. H., & London, J. (2016). Trauma and psychological distress in Latino citizen children following parental detention and deportation. *Psychological Trauma: Theory, Research, Practice, and Policy.* No Pagination Specified. doi:10.1037/tra0000177

Roussos, A., Goenjian, A. K., Steinberg, A. M., Sotiropoulou, C., Kakaki, M., Kabakos, C., Karagianni, S., & Manouras, V. (2005). Posttraumatic stress and depressive reactions among children and adolescents after the 1999 earthquake in Ano Liosia, Greece. *American Journal of Psychiatry 162*(3), 530–537.

Rutter, M. (1990). Psychosocial resilience and protective mechanisms. In J. Rolf, A. S. Masten, D. Cicchetti, K. H. Nuechterlein & S. Weintraub (Eds.), *Risk and protective factors in the development of psychopathology* (pp. 181–214). Cambridge: Cambridge University Press.

Rutter, M., Kumsta, R., Schlotz, W., & Sonuga-Barke, E. (2012). Longitudinal studies using a "natural experiment" design: The case of adoptees from Romanian institutions. *Journal of the American Academy of Child and Adolescent Psychiatry 51*(8), 762–770.

Ryan, J. P., Herz, D., Hernandez, P. M., & Marshall, J. M. (2007). Maltreatment and delinquency: Investigating child welfare bias in juvenile justice processing. *Children and Youth Services Review 29*(8), 1035–1050. doi:http://dx.doi.org/10.1016/j.childyouth.2007.04.002

Sachser, C., & Goldbeck, L. (2016). Consequences of the diagnostic criteria proposed for the ICD-11 on the prevalence of PTSD in children and adolescents. *Journal of Traumatic Stress.* doi:10.1002/jts.22080

Sachser, C., Keller, F., & Goldbeck, L. (2016). Complex PTSD as proposed for ICD-11: Validation of a new disorder in children and adolescents and their response to Trauma-Focused Cognitive Behavioral Therapy. *Journal of Child Psychology and Psychiatry.* doi:10.1111/jcpp.12640

Sackett, D. L., Rosenberg, W. C., Muir Gray, J. A., Haynes, R. B., & Richardson, W. S. (1996). Evidence based medicine: what it is and what it isn't It's about integrating individual clinical expertise and the best external evidence. *British Journal of Medicine 312*(7023), 71–72.

Saewyc, E. M. (2011). Research on adolescent sexual orientation: Development, health disparities, stigma, and resilience. *Journal of Research on Adolescence 21*(1), 256–272. doi:10.1111/j.1532-7795.2010.00727.x

Saltzman, W. R., Lester, P., Pynoos, R., Mogil, C., Green, S., Layne, C. M., & et al., (2009). *FOCUS Family Resilience Enhancement Training Manual (2nd ed.).* Los Angeles: University of California, Los Angeles.

Saltzman, W. R., Babayan, T., Lester, P., Beardslee, W. R., & Pynoos, R. S. (2008). Family-based treatments for child traumatic stress: A review and report on current innovations. In D. Brom, R. Pat-Horenczyk, & J. D. Ford (Eds.), *Treating traumatized children: Risk, resilience and recovery* (pp. 240–254). New York: Routledge.

Saltzman, W. R., Pynoos, R. S., Layne, C. M., Steinberg, A. M., & Aisenberg, E. (2001). Trauma- and grief-focused intervention for adolescents exposed to community violence: Results of a school-based screening and group treatment protocol. *Group Dynamics 5*(4), 291–303. doi:http://dx.doi.org/10.1037/1089-2699.5.4.291

Saltzman, W. R. (2016). The FOCUS family resilience program: An innovative family intervention for trauma and loss. *Family Process.* doi:10.1111/famp.12250

Saltzman, W. R., Lester, P., Milburn, N., Woodward, K., & Stein, J. (2016). Pathways of risk and resilience: Impact of a family resilience program on active-duty military parents. *Family Process.* doi:10.1111/famp.12238

Saxe, G. N., Ellis, B. H., & Kaplow, J. B. (2006). *Collaborative treatment of traumatized children and teens: The trauma systems therapy approach.* New York: Guilford.

Saxe, G., & Wolfe, J. (1999). Gender and posttraumatic stress disorder. In P. A. Saigh & D. Bremner (Eds.), *Posttraumatic stress disorder: A comprehensive text* (pp. 160–179). Boston: Allyn & Bacon.

Saxe, G. N., Ellis, B. H., Fogler, J., Hansen, S., & Sorkin, B. (2005). Comprehensive Care for Traumatized Children-An open trial examines a specialized treatment plan—Trauma systems therapy. *Psychiatric Annals 35*(5), 443–449.

Saylor, C. F., Swenson, C. C., Reynolds, S. S., & Taylor, M. (1999). The Pediatric Emotional Distress Scale: A brief screening measure for young children exposed to traumatic events. *Journal of Clinical Child Psychology 28*(1), 70–81.

Schauer, M., & Elbert, T. (2010). Dissociation following traumatic stress. *Zeitschrift für Psychologie/Journal of Psychology 218*(2), 109–127. doi:10.1027/0044-3409/a000018

Scheeringa, M. S., Zeanah, C. H., Drell, M. J., & Larrieu, J. L. (1995). Two approaches to the diagnosis of posttraumatic stress disorder in infancy and early childhood. *Journal of the American Academy of Child and Adolescent Psychiatry 34*(2), 191–200.

Scheeringa, M. S., Zeanah, C. H., & Cohen, J. A. (2011). PTSD in children and adolescents: Toward an empirically based algorithm. *Depression and Anxiety 28*(9), 770–782. doi:10.1002/da.20736

Scheeringa, M. S., Zeanah, C. H., Myers, L., & Putnam, F. W. (2003). New findings on alternative criteria for PTSD in preschool children. *Journal of Amer Academy of Child & Adolescent Psychiatry 42*(5), 561.

Schillaci, J., Yanasak, E., Adams, J. H., Dunn, N. J., Rehm, L. P., & Hamilton, J. D. (2009). Guidelines for differential diagnoses in a population with posttraumatic stress disorder. *Professional Psychology: Research and Practice* 40(1), 39–45. doi:10.1037/a0013910

Sheehan, D. V., Sheehan, K. H., Shytle, R. D., Janavs, J., Bannon, Y., Rogers, J. E., Milo, K. M., Stock, S. L., & Wilkinson, B. (2010). Reliability and validity of the Mini International Neuropsychiatric Interview For Children And Adolescents (MINI-KID). *The Journal of Clinical Psychiatry* 71(3), 313–326.

Shirk, S. R. (1988). *Cognitive development and child psychotherapy.* NY: Plenum.

Shirk, S. R. (1999). Developmental therapy. In W. K. Silverman & T. H. Ollendick (Eds.), *Developmental issues in the clinical treatment of children* (pp. 60–73). Boston: Allyn & Bacon.

Shirk, S. R., & Russell, R. L. (1996). *Change processes in child psychotherapy: Revitalizing treatment and research.* New York: Guilford.

Silverman, R. C., & Lieberman, A. F. (1999). Negative maternal attributions, projective identification, and the intergenerational transmission of violent relational patterns. *Psychoanalytic Dialogues* 9(2), 161–186.

Skeem, J., Johansson, P., Andershed, H., Kerr, M., & Louden, J. E. (2007). Two subtypes of psychopathic violent offenders that parallel primary and secondary variants. *Journal of Abnormal Psychology* 116(2), 395.

Smith, D. K., Chamberlain, P., & Deblinger, E. (2013). Adapting Multidimensional Treatment Foster Care for the treatment of co-occurring trauma and delinquency in adolescent girls." In P. K. Kerig (Ed.), *Psychological trauma and juvenile delinquency* (pp. 141–155). London: Routledge.

Southam-Gerow, M. A., & Prinstein, M. J. (2014). Evidence base updates: The evolution of the evaluation of psychological treatments for children and adolescents. *Journal of Clinical Child & Adolescent Psychology* 43(1), 1–6. doi: 10.1080/15374416.2013.855128

Southwick Bensley, L., Spieker, S. J., Van Eenwyk, J., & Schoder, J. (1999). Self-reported abuse history and adolescent problem behaviors. II. alcohol and drug use. *Journal of Adolescent Health* 24(3), 173–180. doi:10.1016/S1054-139X(98)00112-8

Spitz, R. A. (1946). Anaclitic depression. *Psychoanalytic Study of the Child 2*, 313–342.

Sroufe, L. A., Sunita, D., Nancy, W.,& Elizabeth, C. (2000). Relationships, development, and psychopathology. In A. J. Sameroff, M. Lewis & S. M. Miller (Eds.), *Handbook of developmental psychopathology* (2nd ed., pp. 75–91). New York: Kluwer.

Sroufe, L. A., & Rutter, M. (1984). The domain of developmental psychopathology. *Child Development 55*, 17–29.

Stallard, P., Velleman, R., & Baldwin, S. (1998). Prospective study of post-traumatic stress disorder in children involved in road traffic accidents. *Bmj* *317*(7173), 1619–1623.

Stein, B. D., Jaycox, L. H., Kataoka, S. H., Wong, M., Tu, W., Elliott, M. N., & Fink, A. (2003). A mental health intervention for schoolchildren exposed to violence: a randomized controlled trial. *Jama 290*(5), 603–611.

Steinberg, A. M., Brymer, M. J., Kim, S., Briggs, E. C., Ippen, C. G., Ostrowski, S. A., Gully, K. J., & Pynoos, R. S. (2013). Psychometric Properties of the UCLA PTSD Reaction Index: Part I. *Journal of Traumatic Stress 26*(1), 1–9. doi:10.1002/jts.21780

Steiner, H., Garcia, I. G., & Matthews, Z. (1997). Posttraumatic stress disorder in incarcerated juvenile delinquents. *Journal of the American Academy of Child and Adolescent Psychiatry 36*(3), 357–365.

Stolbach, B. C., Minshew, R., Rompala, V., Dominguez, R. Z., Gazibara, T., & Finke, R. (2013). Complex trauma exposure and symptoms in urban traumatized children: A preliminary test of the proposed criteria for developmental Trauma Disorder. *Journal of Traumatic Stress 26*(4), 483–491.

Strand, V. C., Sarmiento, T. L., & Pasquale, L. E. (2005). Assessment and screening tools for trauma in children and adolescents: A Review. *Trauma, Violence, & Abuse 6*(1), 55–78. doi:10.1177/1524838004272559

Taku, K., Kilmer, R. P., Cann, A., Tedeschi, R. G., & Calhoun, L. G. (2012). Exploring posttraumatic growth in Japanese youth. *Psychological Trauma: Theory, Research, Practice, and Policy 4*(4), 411–419. doi:10.1037/a0024363

Tatar, J. R., Cauffman, E., Kimonis, E. R., & Skeem, J. L. (2012). Victimization history and posttraumatic stress: An analysis of psychopathy variants in male juvenile offenders. *Journal of Child & Adolescent Trauma 5*(2), 102–113.

Taylor, L. K., & Weems, C. F. (2009). What do youth report as a traumatic event? Toward a developmentally informed classification of traumatic stressors. *Psychological Trauma: Theory, Research, Practice, and Policy 1*(2), 91–106. doi:10.1037/a0016012

Tedeschi, R. G., Park, C. L., & Calhoun, L. G. (1998). *Posttraumatic growth: Positive changes in the aftermath of crisis.* Mahwah, NJ: Lawrence Erlbaum Associates, Inc.

Terr, L. C. (1991). Childhood traumas: An outline and overview. *American Journal of Psychiatry 148*, 10–20.

Testa, M., Hoffman, J. H., & Livingston, J. A. (2010). Alcohol and sexual risk behaviors as mediators of the sexual victimization–revictimization relationship. *Journal of Consulting and Clinical Psychology 78*(2), 249–259. doi:10.1037/a0018914

Thomson, C., Roberts, K., Curran, A., Ryan, L., & Wright, R. J. (2002). Caretaker-child concordance for children's exposure to violence in a preadolescent inner-city population. *Archives of Pediatrics & Adolescent Medicine, 156*(8), 818–823. doi:10.1001/archpedi.156.8.818

Timmer, S. G., Urquiza, A. J., M Zebell, N., & McGrath, J. M. (2005). Parent-child interaction therapy: Application to maltreating parent-child dyads. *Child Abuse & Neglect 29*(7), 825–842.

Timmer, S. G., Ware, L. M., Urquiza, A. J., & Zebell, N. M. (2010). The effectiveness of Parent-Child Interaction Therapy for victims of interparental violence. *Violence and Victims 25*(4), 486–503. doi:10.1891/0886-6708.25.4.486

Tolin, D. F., & Foa, E. B. (2006). Sex differences in trauma and posttraumatic stress disorder: A quantitative review of 25 years of research. *Psychological Bulletin 132*(6), 959–992. doi:10.1037/0033-2909.132.6.959

Toth, S. L., Maughan, A., Manly, J. T., Spagnola, M., & Cicchetti, D. (2002). The relative efficacy of two interventions in altering maltreated preschool children's representational models: Implications for attachment theory. *Development and Psychopathology 14*(4), 877–908. doi:10.1017/S095457940200411X

Trickett, P. K., Negriff, S., Ji, J., & Peckins, M. (2011). Child maltreatment and adolescent development. *Journal of Research on Adolescence 21*(1), 3–20.

Trickey, D., Siddaway, A. P., Meiser-Stedman, R., Serpell, L., & Field, A. P. (2012). A meta-analysis of risk factors for post-traumatic stress disorder in children and adolescents. *Clinical Psychology Review 32*(2), 122–138. doi:10.1016/j.cpr.2011.12.001

Tupler, L. A., & De Bellis, M. D. (2006). Segmented hippocampal volume in children and adolescents with posttraumatic stress disorder. *Biological Psychiatry 59*(6), 523–529. doi:http://dx.doi.org/10.1016/j.biopsych.2005.08.007

Van der Kolk, B. A. (2007). The history of trauma in psychiatry. In M. J. Friedman, T. M. Keane & P. A. Resick (Eds.), *Handbook of PTSD* (pp. 19–36). New York: Guilford.

van der Kolk, B. A., Roth, S., Pelcovitz, D., Sunday, S., & Spinazzola, J. (2005). Disorders of extreme stress: The empirical foundation of a complex adaptation to trauma. *Journal of Traumatic Stress 18*(5), 389–399.

van der Kolk, B. A., Pynoos, R. S., Cicchetti, D., Cloitre, M., D'Andrea, W., Ford, J. D., Lieberman, A. F., Putnam, F. W., Saxe, G., Spinazzola, J., Stolbach, B. C., & Teicher, M. (2009). Proposal to include a developmental trauma disorder diagnosis for children and adolescents in DSM-V. *Official submission from the National Child Traumatic Stress Network Developmental Trauma Disorder Taskforce to the American Psychiatric Association.*

Van Horn, P. (2011). The impact of trauma on the developing social brain: Development and regulation in relationship. In J. D. Osofsky (Ed.), *Clinical work with traumatized young children* (pp. 11–30). New York: Guldford Press.

Varese, F., Smeets, F., Drukker, M., Lieverse, R., Lataster, T., Viechtbauer, W., Read, J., van Os, J., & Bentall, R. P. (2012). Childhood adversities increase the risk of psychosis: A meta-analysis of patient-control, prospective- and cross-sectional cohort studies. *Schizophrenia Bulletin 38*(4), 661–671. doi:10.1093/schbul/sbs050

Vaughn, M. G., Edens, J. F., Howard, M. O., & Smith, S. T. (2009). An investigation of primary and secondary psychopathy in a statewide sample of incarcerated youth. *Youth Violence and Juvenile Justice 7*(3), 172–188. doi:10.1177/1541204009333792

Verlinden, E., Schippers, M., Van Meijel, E. P., Beer, R., Opmeer, B. C., Olff, M., Boer, F., & Lindauer, R. J. (2013). What makes a life event traumatic for a child? The predictive values of DSM-Criteria A1 and A2. *European journal of psychotraumatology 4.*

Walsh, F. (2016). Traumatic loss and collective trauma: Strengthening family and community resilience. In *Strengthening family resilience* (pp. 232–264). New York: Guilford.

Walsh, F. (2003). Family resilience: A framework for clinical practice. *Family Process 42*(1), 1–18.

Walsh, F. (2006). *Strengthening family resilience.* Guilford Press.

Walsh, K., Danielson, C. K., McCauley, J. L., Saunders, B. E., Kilpatrick, D. G., & Resnick, H. S. (2012). National prevalence of posttraumatic stress disorder among sexually revictimized adolescent, college, and adult household-residing women. *Archives of General Psychiatry 69*(9), 935–942. doi:10.1001/archgenpsychiatry.2012.132

Walsh, K., Latzman, N. E., & Latzman, R. D. (2014). Pathway from child sexual and physical abuse to risky sex among emerging adults: The role of trauma-related intrusions and alcohol problems. *Journal of Adolescent Health 54*(4), 442–448. doi:http://dx.doi.org/10.1016/j.jadohealth.2013.09.020

Walter, K. H., Dickstein, B. D., Barnes, S. M., & Chard, K. M. (2014). Comparing effectiveness of CPI to CPT-C among US. Veterans in an interdisciplinary residential PTSD/TBI treatment program. *Journal of Traumatic Stress 27*(4), 438–445. doi:10.1002/jts.21934

Wamser-Nanney, R., & Vandenberg, B. R. (2013). Empirical support for the definition of a complex trauma event in children and adolescents. *Journal of Traumatic Stress 26*(6), 671–678. doi:10.1002/jts.21857

Wang, L., Zhang, L., Armour, C., Cao, C., Qing, Y., Zhang, J., Liu, P., Zhang, B., Wu, Q., Zhao, Z., & Fan, G. (2015). Assessing the underlying dimensionality of DSM-5 PTSD symptoms in Chinese adolescents surviving the 2008 Wenchuan earthquake. *Journal of Anxiety Disorders 31*(0), 90–97. doi:http://dx.doi.org/10.1016/j.janxdis.2015.02.006

Weathers, F. W., & Keane, T. M. (2007). The Criterion A problem revisited: Controversies and challenges in defining and measuring psychological trauma. *Journal of Traumatic Stress 20*(2), 107–121. doi:10.1002/jts.20210

Weems, C. F., & Graham, R. A. (2014). Resilience and trajectories of posttraumatic stress among youth exposed to disaster. *Journal of Child and Adolescent Psychopharmacology 24*(1), 2–8. doi:10.1089/cap.2013.0042

Weinstein, D., Staffelbach, D., & Biaggio, M. (2000). Attention-deficit hyperactivity disorder and posttraumatic stress disorder: Differential diagnosis in childhood sexual abuse. *Clinical Psychology Review 20*(3), 359–378. doi:http://dx.doi.org/10.1016/S0272-7358(98)00107-X

Wilson, J. P. (2007). The lens of culture. In J. P. Wilson & C. S. Tang (Eds.), *Cross-cultural assessment of psychological trauma and PTSD* (pp. 3–30). New York: Springer.

Witkin, S. J. (2005). Assessing developmental level when representing foster care children. *Human Rights 32*(1), 8.

Woon, F. L., & Hedges, D. W. (2008). Hippocampal and amygdala volumes in children and adults with childhood maltreatment-related posttraumatic stress disorder: A meta-analysis. *Hippocampus 18*(8), 729–736. doi:10.1002/hipo.20437

Yasinski, C., Hayes, A. M., Ready, C. B., Cummings, J. A., Berman, I. S., McCauley, T., Webb, C., & Deblinger, E. (2016). In-session caregiver behavior predicts symptom change in youth receiving Trauma-Focused Cognitive Behavioral Therapy (TF-CBT). *Journal of Consulting and Clinical Psychology 84*(12), 1066–1077. doi:10.1037/ccp0000147

Yehuda, R., Halligan, S. L., & Grossman, R. (2001). Childhood trauma and risk for PTSD: Relationship to intergenerational effects of trauma, parental PTSD, and cortisol excretion. *Development and Psychopathology 13*(3), 733–753.

Yoshinaga, C., Kadomoto, I., Otani, T., Sasaki, T., & Kato, N. (2004). Prevalence of post-traumatic stress disorder in incarcerated delinquents in Japan. *Psychiatry and Clinical Neurosciences 58*(4), 383–388.

Yoshizumi, T., Hamada, S., Kaida, A., Gotow, K., & Murase, S. (2010). Psychometric properties of the Adolescent Dissociative Experiences Scale (A-DES) in Japanese adolescents from a community sample. *Journal of Trauma & Dissociation 11*(3), 322–336. doi:10.1080/15299731003786454

Zhou, X., Wu, X., & Zhen, R. (2016). Understanding the relationship between social support and posttraumatic stress disorder/posttraumatic growth among adolescents after ya'an earthquake: The role of emotion regulation. *Psychological Trauma: Theory, Research, Practice, and Policy.* No Pagination Specified. doi:10.1037/tra0000213

Zoroglu, S. S., Tuzun, U., Sar, V., Tutkun, H., Savaçs, H. A., Ozturk, M., Alyanak, B., & Kora, M. E. (2003). Suicide attempt and self-mutilation among Turkish high school students in relation with abuse, neglect and dissociation. *Psychiatry and Clinical Neurosciences 57*(1), 119–126. doi:10.1046/j.1440-1819.2003.01088.x

Index

OTHER TITLES IN THIS CHILD CLINICAL PSYCHOLOGY "NUTS AND BOLTS" COLLECTION

Samuel T. Gontkovsky, *Editor*

Childhood and Adolescent Obesity
by Lauren Stutts

Intellectual Disabilities
by Charles J. Golden, Lisa K. Lashley, Andrew Grego,
Johanna Messerly, Ronald Okolichany, and Rachel Zachar

Learning Disabilities
by Charles J. Golden, Lisa K. Lashley, Jared S. Link,
Matthew Zusman, Maya Pinjala, Christopher Tirado, and Amber Deckard

Elimination Disorders: Evidence-Based Treatment for Enuresis and Encopresis
by Thomas M. Reimers

Depression in Childhood and Adolescence: A Guide for Practitioners
by Rebecca A. Schwartz-Mette, Hannah R. Lawrence,
Douglas W. Nangle, Cynthia A. Erdley, Laura Andrews,
and Melissa Jankowski

Announcing Digital Content Crafted by Librarians

CPSIA information can be obtained
at www.ICGtesting.com
Printed in the USA
FFOW02n1114050717
37461FF

9 781606 509296